Australasian Language Technology Association Workshop (ALTA 2017)

Brisbane, Australia
6 – 8 December 2017

Editors:

Jojo Sze-Meng Wong
Gholamreza Haffari

ISBN: 978-1-5108-5939-5

Australasian Language Technology Association Workshop 2017

Proceedings of the Workshop

Editors:
Jojo Sze-Meng Wong
Gholamreza Haffari

6–8 December 2017
Queensland University of Technology
Brisbane, Australia

Australasian Language Technology Association Workshop 2017

(ALTA 2017)

`http://alta2017.alta.asn.au`

Online Proceedings:

`http://alta2017.alta.asn.au/proceedings`

Gold Sponsors:

Silver Sponsors:

Bronze Sponsors:

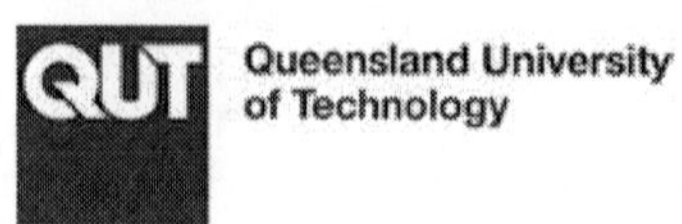

Volume 15, 2017

ISSN: 1834-7037

ALTA 2017 Workshop Committees

Workshop Chairs

- Stephen Wan (Data61)
- Jojo Sze-Meng Wong (Monash University)

Workshop Programme Chairs

- Jojo Sze-Meng Wong (Monash University)
- Gholamreza Haffari (Monash University)

Programme Committee

- Oliver Adams, University of Melbourne
- Timothy Baldwin, University of Melbourne
- Benjamin Borschinger, Google
- Julian Brooke, University of Melbourne
- Lawrence Cavedon, RMIT University
- Trevor Cohn, The University of Melbourne
- Nathalie Colineau, DST Australia
- Mark Dras, Macquarie University
- Dominique Estival, Western Sydney University
- Gabriela Ferraro, CSIRO Data61
- Hamed Hassanzadeh, The Australian e-Health Research Centre
- Nitin Indurkhya, University of New South Wales
- Sarvnaz Karimi, CSIRO Data61
- Mac Kim, CSIRO Data61
- Yitong Li, The University of Melbourne
- Teresa Lynn, Dublin City University
- Andrew MacKinlay, IBM Research
- Diego Mollá-Alliod, Macquarie University
- Anthony Nguyen, The Australian e-Health Research Centre
- Bahadorreza Ofoghi, The University of Melbourne
- Sylvester Orimaye, East Tennessee State University
- Cécile Paris, CSIRO Data61
- Matthias Petri, The University of Melbourne
- Lizhen Qu, CSIRO Data61
- Will Radford, Red Marker
- Abeed Sarker, University of Pennsylvania
- Rolf Schwitter, Macquarie University
- Ehsan Shareghi, Monash University
- Laurianne Sitbon, Queensland University of Technology
- Hanna Suominen, The Australian National University
- Karin Verspoor, The University of Melbourne
- Wei Wang, University of New South Wales
- Ingrid Zukerman, Monash University

Preface

This volume contains the papers accepted for presentation at the Australasian Language Technology Association Workshop (ALTA) 2017, held at Queensland University of Technology in Brisbane, Australia on 6–8 December 2017.

The goals of the workshop are to:

- bring together the Language Technology (LT) community in the Australasian region and encourage interactions and collaboration;
- foster interaction between academic and industrial researchers, to encourage dissemination of research results;
- provide a forum for students and young researchers to present their research;
- facilitate the discussion of new and ongoing research and projects;
- increase visibility of LT research in Australasia and overseas and encourage interactions with the wider international LT community.

This year's ALTA Workshop presents 13 peer-reviewed papers, including 10 long papers and 3 short papers. We received a total of 23 submissions for long and short papers. Each paper was reviewed by three members of the program committee, using a double-blind protocol. Great care was taken to avoid all conflicts of interest.

ALTA 2017 includes a presentations track, following the workshops since 2015 when it was first introduced. This aims to encourage broader participation and facilitate local socialisation of international results, including work in progress and work submitted or published elsewhere. Presentations were lightly reviewed by the ALTA chairs to gauge overall quality of work and whether it would be of interest to the ALTA community. Offering both archival and presentation tracks allows us to grow the standard of work at ALTA, to better showcase the excellent research being done locally.

ALTA 2017 continues the tradition of including a shared task, this year on correcting OCR errors. Participation is summarised in an overview paper by organisers Diego Mollá-Alliod and Steve Cassidy. Participants were invited to submit a system description paper, which are included in this volume without review.

We would like to thank, in no particular order: all of the authors who submitted papers; the programme committee for the time and effort the put into maintaining the high standards of our reviewing process; the co-chair Stephen Wan for coordinating the logistics that go into running the workshop, from arranging the space, catering, budgets, sponsorship and more; the shared task organisers Diego Mollá and Steve Cassidy; our keynote speakers Lewis Mitchell and Robert Dale for agreeing to share their perspectives on the state of the field; and the tutorial presenter Ben Hachey for his efforts towards the three parts of the tutorial. We would like to acknowledge the constant support and advice of the ALTA Executive Committee.

Finally, we gratefully recognise our sponsors: Capital Markets CRC, Sintelix, Google, CSIRO/Data61 and Queensland University of Technology. Importantly, their generous support enabled us to offer travel subsidies to all students presenting at ALTA, and helped to subsidise conference catering costs and student paper awards.

Jojo Sze-Meng Wong
Gholamreza Haffari

ALTA Programme Chairs

ALTA 2017 Programme

Wednesday, 6 December 2017

*Tutorial Session 1 (Monash Caulfield, B214)

13:00–17:00	Tutorial: Ben Hachey *Active Learning ... and Beyond!*
13:00–14:15	*Part 1: From Zero to Hero*
14:15–14:30	Break
14:30–15:45	*Part 2: Live Shared Task*
15:45–16:00	Break
16:00–17:00	*Part 3: Wild Blue Yonder*

Thursday, 7 December 2017

Opening & Keynote (Room P421)	
9:00–9:15	Opening
9:15–10:15	Keynote 1 (from ADCS): Dan Russell *What do you really need to know? Learning and knowing in the age of the Internet*
10:15–10:45	Morning tea
Session 1: Machine Learning and Applications (Room P521)	
10:45–11:05	Paper: Leonardo Dos Santos Pinheiro and Mark Dras *Stock Market Prediction with Deep Learning: A Character-based Neural Language Model for Event-based Trading*
11:05–11:25	Paper: Fei Liu, Trevor Cohn and Timothy Baldwin *Improving End-to-End Memory Networks with Unified Weight Tying*
11:25–11:45	Paper Shivashankar Subramanian, Trevor Cohn, Timothy Baldwin and Julian Brooke *Joint Sentence-Document Model for Manifesto Text Analysis*
11:45–12:05	Paper: Ming Liu, Gholamreza Haffari, Wray Buntine and Michelle Ananda-Rajah *Leveraging Linguistic Resources for Improving Neural Text Classification*
12:05–12:15	Paper: Hamideh Hajiabadi, Diego Molla-Aliod and Reza Monsefi *On Extending Neural Networks with Loss Ensembles for Text Classification*
12:15–13:15	Lunch
Session 2 & Keynote (Room P421)	
13:15–14:15	Keynote 2: Lewis Mitchell *What do you really need to know? Learning and knowing in the age of the Internet*
14:15–14:30	Paper: Shiwei Zhang, Xiuzhen Zhang and Jeffrey Chan (ADCS short paper) *A Word-Character Convolutional Neural Network for Language-Agnostic Twitter Sentiment Analysis*
14:30–14:45	Paper: Lance De Vine, Shlomo Geva and Peter Bruza (ADCS short paper) *Efficient Analogy Completion with Word Embedding Clusters*
14:45–15:05	Paper: Aili Shen, Jianzhong Qi and Timothy Baldwin *A Hybrid Model for Quality Assessment of Wikipedia Articles*
15:05–15:15	Paper: Diego Molla-Aliod *Towards the Use of Deep Reinforcement Learning with Global Policy For Query-based Extractive Summarisation*
Session 3: Translation and Low Resource Languages (Room P521)	
15:45–16:05	Presentation: Inigo Jauregi Unanue, Lierni Garmendia Arratibel, Ehsan Zare Borzeshi and Massimo Piccardi *English-Basque Statistical and Neural Machine Translation*
16:05–16:25	Presentation: Euna Kim *Study on the Role of Machine Translation in Social Network Services in terms of User Centered Orientation: A Case Study of Instagram*
16:25–16:45	Presentation: Yunsil Jo *Study on Documentary Translation for Dubbing*
16:45–17:05	Paper: Oliver Adams, Trevor Cohn, Graham Neubig and Alexis Michaud *Phonemic Transcription of Low-Resource Tonal Languages*
17:05–17:25	Presentation: Hanieh Poostchi, Ehsan Zare Borzeshi and Massimo Piccardi *BiLSTM-CRF for Persian Named-Entity Recognition*
17:25	End of Day 1
19:00	Dinner

Friday, 8 December 2017

9:15–10:15	Keynote 3 (fromADCS): Victor Kovalev, Redbubble (Room P421)
	Solving hard problems at massive scale – applied data science research approach at Redbubble

Session 4: Computational Linguistics and Information Extraction (Room P521)

10:45–10:55	Paper: Dat Quoc Nguyen, Thanh Vu, Dai Quoc Nguyen, Mark Dras and Mark Johnson *From Word Segmentation to POS Tagging for Vietnamese*
10:55–11:15	Paper: Shunichi Ishihara *A Comparative Study of Two Statistical Modelling Approaches for Estimating Multivariate Likelihood Ratios in Forensic Voice Comparison*
11:15–11:35	Paper: Katharine Cheng, Timothy Baldwin and Karin Verspoor *Automatic Negation and Speculation Detection in Veterinary Clinical Text*
11:35–11:55	Paper: Xiang Dai, Sarvnaz Karimi and Cecile Paris *Medication and Adverse Event Extraction from Noisy Text*
11:55–12:15	Paper: Maria Myunghee Kim *Incremental Knowledge Acquisition Approach for Information Extraction on both Semi-structured and Unstructured Text from the Open Domain Web*

12:15	Lunch
13:15–14:15	Keynote 4: Robert Dale, Language Technology Group Pty Ltd (Room P421)
	Commercialised NLP: The state of the art

14:15–15:00	Poster Session (ALTA & ADCS)
15:00–15:30	Afternoon Tea

Shared Task Session (Room P521)

15:30–15:40	Diego Molla-Aliod and Steve Cassidy *Overview of the 2017 ALTA Shared Task: Correcting OCR Errors*
15:40-15:50	Gitansh Khirbat *OCR Post-Processing Text Correction using Simulated Annealing (OPTeCA)*
15:50–16:00	Yufei Wang *SuperOCR for ALTA 2017 Shared Task*

Final Session (Room P521)

16:00–16:15	Best Paper and Poster Presentation Awards
16:15–16:45	Business Meeting
16:45-17:00	Closing
17:00	End of Day 2

Contents

Invited talks

Characterising Information and Happiness in Online Social Activity

Lewis Mitchell (Lecturer in Applied Mathematics, University of Adelaide)

Abstract. Understanding the nature of influence and information propagation in social networks is of clear societal importance, as they form the basis for phenomena like "echo chambers" and "emotional contagion". However, these concepts remain surprisingly ill-defined. In studies of large online social networks, proxies for influence and information are routinely employed, leading to confusion as to whether the phenomena they underlie actually exist. In this talk I will demonstrate how online social media streams can be used as proxies for population-level health characteristics such as obesity and happiness, and introduce information-theoretic tools for constructing social networks from underlying information flows between individuals. I will present results relating individual predictability to popularity and contact volume, and introduce a paradigmatic mathematical model of information flow over social networks.

Bio. Lewis's research focusses on large-scale methods for extracting useful information from online social networks, and on mathematical techniques for inference and prediction using these data. He works on building tools for real-time estimation of social phenomena such as happiness from written text, and prediction of population-level events like disease outbreaks, elections, and civil unrest.

Commercialised NLP: The State of the Art

Robert Dale (Principal Consultant, Language Technology Group Pty Ltd)

Abstract. The last few years have seen a tremendous surge in commercial interest in Artificial Intelligence, and with it, a widespread recognition that technologies based on Natural Language Processing can support valuable commercial applications. In this talk, I'll aim to give a comprehensive picture of the commercial NLP landscape, focussing on what I see as the key categories of activity: [1] virtual assistants, including chatbots; [2] text analytics and text mining technologies; [3] machine translation; [4] natural language generation; and [5] text correction technologies. In each case my goal is to sketch the history of work in the area, to identify the major players, and to give a realistic appraisal of the state of the art.

Bio. Robert Dale runs the Language Technology Group, an independent consultancy providing unbiased advice to corporations and businesses on the selection and deployment of NLP technologies. Until recently, he was Chief Technology Officer of Arria NLG, where he led the development of a cloud-based natural language generation tool; prior to joining Arria in 2012, he held a chair in the Department of Computing at Macquarie University in Sydney, where he was Director of that university's Centre for Language Technology. After receiving his PhD from the University of Edinburgh in 1989, he taught there for several years before moving to Sydney in 1994. He played a foundational role in building up the NLP community in Australia, and was editor in chief of the Computational Linguistics journal from 2003 to 2012. He writes a semi-regular column titled 'Industry Watch' for the Journal of Natural Language Engineering.

Tutorials

Active Learning ... and Beyond!

Ben Hachey (The University of Sydney)

This half-day session will take participants through situations they might face applying Natural Language Processing to real-world problems. We'll choose a canonical task (text classification) and focus on the main issue that faces practitioners in green fields projects — where does the data come from? Our aim is to equip participants with the theoretical background and practical skills to quickly build high-quality text classification models.

Long papers

Stock Market Prediction with Deep Learning:
A Character-based Neural Language Model for Event-based
Trading

Leonardo dos Santos Pinheiro
Macquarie University
Capital Markets CRC
lpinheiro@cmcrc.com

Mark Dras
Macquarie University
mark.dras@mq.edu.au

Abstract

In the last few years, machine learning has become a very popular tool for analyzing financial text data, with many promising results in stock price forecasting from financial news, a development with implications for the Efficient Markets Hypothesis (EMH) that underpins much economic theory. In this work, we explore recurrent neural networks with character-level language model pre-training for both intraday and interday stock market forecasting. In terms of predicting directional changes in the Standard & Poor's 500 index, both for individual companies and the overall index, we show that this technique is competitive with other state-of-the-art approaches.

1 Introduction

Predicting stock market behavior is an area of strong appeal for both academic researchers and industry practitioners alike, as it is both a challenging task and could lead to increased profits. Predicting stock market behavior from the arrival of new information is an even more interesting area, as economists frequently test it to challenge the Efficient Market Hypothesis (EMH) (Malkiel, 2003): a strict form of the EMH holds that any news is incorporated into prices without delay, while other interpretations hold that incorporation takes place over time.

In practice, the analysis of text data such as news announcements and commentary on events is one major source of market information and is widely used and analyzed by investors (Oberlechner and Hocking, 2004).

Financial news conveys novel information to broad market participants and a fast reaction to the release of new information is an important component of trading strategies (Leinweber and Sisk, 2011).

But despite the great interest, attempts to forecast stock prices from unstructured text data have had limited success and there seems to be much room for improvement. This can be in great part attributed to the difficulty involved in extracting the relevant information from the text. So far most approaches to analyzing financial text data are based on bag-of-words, noun phrase and/or named entity feature extraction combined with manual feature selection, but the capacity of these methods to extract meaningful information from the data is limited as much information about the structure of text is lost in the process.

In recent years, the trend for extracting features from text data has shifted away from manual feature engineering and there has been a resurgence of interest in neural networks due to their power for learning useful representations directly from data (Bengio et al., 2013). Even though deep learning has had great success in learning representations from text data (e.g. Mikolov et al. (2013a), Mikolov et al. (2013b) and Kiros et al. (2015)), successful applications of deep learning in textual analysis of financial news have been few, even though it has been demonstrated that its application to event-driven stock prediction is a promising area of research (Ding et al., 2015).

Finding the most informative representation of the data in a text classification problem is still an open area of research. In the last few years a range of different neural networks architectures have been proposed for text classification, each one with strong results on differ-

Leonardo Dos Santos Pinheiro and Mark Dras. 2017. Stock Market Prediction with Deep Learning: A Character-based Neural Language Model for Event-based Trading. In *Proceedings of Australasian Language Technology Association Workshop*, pages 6–15.

ent benchmarks (e.g. Socher et al. (2013), Kim (2014) and Kumar et al. (2016)), and each one proposing different ways to encode the textual information.

One of the most commonly used architectures for modeling text data is the Recurrent Neural Network (RNN). One technique to improve the training of RNNs, proposed by Dai and Le (2015) and widely used, is to pre-train the RNN with a language model. In this work this approach outperformed training the same model from random initialization and achieved state of the art in several benchmarks.

Another strong trend in deep learning for text is the use of a word embedding layer as the main representation of the text. While this approach has notable advantages, word-level language models do not capture sub-word information, may inaccurately estimate embeddings for rare words, and can poorly represent domains with long-tailed frequency distributions. These were motivations for character-level language models, which Kim et al. (2016) and Radford et al. (2017) showed are capable of learning high level representations despite their simplicity. These motivations seem applicable in our domain: character-level representations can for example generalise across numerical data like percentages (e.g. the terms 5% and 9%) and currency (e.g. $1,29), and can handle the large number of infrequently mentioned named entities. Character-level models are also typically much more compact.

In this work we propose an automated trading system that, given the release of news information about a company, predicts changes in stock prices. The system is trained to predict both changes in the stock price of the company mentioned in the news article and in the corresponding stock exchange index (S&P 500). We also test this system for both intraday changes, considering a window of one hour after the release of the news, and for changes between the closing price of the current trading session and the closing price of the next day session. This comparative analysis allow us to infer whether the incorporation of new information is instantaneous or if it occurs gradually over time. Our model consists of a recurrent neural network pre-trained by a character level language model.

The remainder of the paper is structured as follows: In Section 2, we describe event-driven trading and review the relevant literature. In Section 3 we describe our model and the experimental setup used in this work. Section 5 presents and discuss the results. Finally, in Section 6 we summarize our work and suggest directions for future research.

2   Event-based Trading

In recent years, with the advances in computational power and in the ability of computers to process massive amounts of data, algorithmic trading has emerged as a strong trend in investment management (Ruta, 2014). This, combined with the advances in the fields of machine learning and natural language processing (NLP), has been pushing the use of unstructured text data as source of information for investment strategies as well (Fisher et al., 2016).

The area of NLP with the biggest influence in stock market prediction so far has been sentiment analysis, or opinion mining (Pang et al., 2008). Earlier work by Tetlock (2007) used sentiment analysis to analyze the correlation between sentiment in news articles and market prices, concluding that media pessimism may affect both market prices and trading volume. Similarly, Bollen et al. (2011) used a system to measure collective mood through Twitter feeds and showed it to be highly predictive of the Dow Jones Industrial Average closing values. Following these results, other work has also social media information for stock market forecasting (Nguyen et al., 2015; Oliveira et al., 2017, for example).

With respect to direct stock price forecasting, from news articles, many systems based on feature selection have been proposed in the literature. Schumaker et al. (2012) built a system to evaluate the sentiment in financial news articles using a Support Vector Regression learner with features extracted from noun phrases and scored on a positive/negative subjectivity scale, but the results had limited success. Yu et al. (2013) achieved better accuracy with a selection mechanism based on a contextual entropy model which expanded a set of seed words by discovering similar emotion words and their corresponding intensities from online stock market news articles. Hagenau et al. (2013) also achieved good results by applying Chi-square and Bi-normal separation feature selection with n-gram features. As with all sentiment analysis, scope of negation can be an issue: Pröllochs et al. (2016) recently proposed a reinforcement learning method to predict negation scope and showed that it improved the accuracy on a dataset from the financial news domain.

A different approach to incorporate news into stock trading strategies was proposed by Nuij et al. (2014), which used an evolutionary algorithm to combine trading rules using technical indicators and events extracted from news with expert-defined impact scores. While far from using an optimal way to extract information from financial text data their results concluded that the news events were a component of optimal trading strategies.

As elsewhere in NLP, deep learning methods have been used to tackle financial market trading. A key approach that has informed the model and evaluation framework of this paper is that of Ding et al. (2014), which used a two-layer feed forward neural network as well as a linear SVM, treating the question of whether stocks would rise or fall as a classification problem; they found that the deep learning model had a higher accuracy. They also compared bag-of-words as input with structured events extracted from financial news via open information extraction (open IE), with the structured input performing better. They found that prediction accuracy was better for the following day's price movement than for the following week, which was in turn better than the following year, as expected.

In their subsequent work, Ding et al. (2015) used a neural tensor network to learn embeddings of both words and structured events as inputs to their prediction models. They then applied a multichannel deep convolutional network — the channels corresponding to events at different timescales — to predict changes in the Standard & Poor's 500 stock (S&P 500) index and in individual stock prices. This work was followed by Vargas et al. (2017) who combined recurrent and convolution layers with pre-trained word vectors to also pre-dict changes to the S&P 500 index. The architecture here was also multichannel, and incorporated a technical analysis[1] input channel. The results from both pieces of work outperformed the former manual feature engineering approaches.

To the best of our knowledge, character-level sequence modeling has not been applied to stock price forecasting so far; neither has the use of language model pre-training. We note that the event models of Ding et al. (2014) and Ding et al. (2015) make use of generalization and back-off techniques to deal with data sparsity in terms of named entities etc, which as mentioned earlier character-level representations could help address. Also, character-level inputs are potentially complementary to other sorts such as word-level inputs or event representations, in particular with the multichannel architectures used for the work described above: research such as that of Kim (2014) has shown that multiple input representation can be usefully combined, and work using this kind of model such as Ruder et al. (2016) has specifically done this for character-level and word-level or other inputs. In this work, we aim to investigate whether this kind of character-level input may capture useful information for stock price prediction.

3   Model design and Training Details

Following Ding et al. (2014), we have a two-part model. The first builds a representation for the input, which for us is the character-level language model. The second is the recurrent neural network used for the prediction, a classifier that takes the input and predicts whether the price will rise or fall in the chosen timeframe. Both models process text as a sequence of UTF-8 encoded bytes.

3.1   Neural language model

Existing pre-trained embeddings typically come from general domains (Google News,

---

[1]Fundamental analysis looks at fundamental properties of companies (e.g. earnings) to predict stock price movements; the previously described work in this section could be seen as carrying out a kind of fundamental analysis based on information from news reports. Technical analysis looks at past price movements as a guide to future ones.

Table 1: Statistics of Dataset

Data	Training	Validation	Test
Time Interval	02/10/2006 - 18/06/2012	19/06/2012 - 21/02/2013	22/02/2013 - 21/11/2013
Documents	157,033	52,344	51,476
Total bytes	736,427,755	232,440,500	245,771,999
News average per day	126	124	124
News average per company	911	878	897

Wikipedia, etc), but these word embeddings often fail to capture rich domain specific vocabularies. We therefore train our own embeddings on financial domain news text consisting of news articles from Reuters an Bloomberg. The data is further described in Section 4.

For the language model we used a character embedding with 256 units followed by a single layer LSTM (Hochreiter and Schmidhuber, 1997) with 1024 units. The characters are first encoded as bytes to simplify the embedding look-up process. The model looks up the corresponding character embedding and then updates its hidden state and predicts a probability distribution over the next possible byte. Individual text paragraphs are prepended with <s>to simulate a starting token and appended with <\s>to simulate an end token. Figure 1a shows a representation of this network.

The model was trained for 10 epochs on mini-batches of 256 subsequences of length 256. The character embeddings and the LSTM weights are then saved and used to initialize the first two layers of deep neural network for classification. The model is trained with stochastic gradient descent (SGD).

3.2 RNN for Stock Prediction

The second neural network has the same two layers as the language model, but with one additional fully connected layer with 512 units using a Leaky Relu activation (Maas et al., 2013). Only the last output of the LSTM layer is used to connect to the fully connected layer, the rationale being that this final state should encode a full representation the text sentence.

After the embedding look-up and hidden state update, the model goes through the fully connected layer and then predicts the probability of a positive direction price change for the stock price. This model is trained with Adam (Kingma and Ba, 2014) for 50 epochs. Figure 1b displays this architecture.

4 Experiments

Data We evaluated our model on a dataset of financial news collected from Reuters and Bloomberg over the period from October 2006 to November 2013. This dataset was made available by Ding et al. (2014). Stock price data for all S&P 500 companies and for the S&P 500 index were obtained from Thomson Reuters Tick History.[2] Following Radinsky et al. (2012) and Ding et al. (2014) we focus on the news headlines instead of the full content of the news articles for prediction since they found it produced better results. With this data we tested price response to news releases and daily responses, both shortly after ('intraday') and at end of day ('interday') as described below, and both for the stocks mentioned in the news article and for the index. Summary statistics of the data are shown in Table 1.

For intraday prediction, we filtered the news that contained only the name of one company belonging to the S&P 500 index and conducted our experiments on predicting whether the last price after one hour would be higher than the first price after the news release, using the timestamp for the news release. We also tested the S&P 500 index in the same time window.

In the interday prediction we used a setup similar to Ding et al. (2015) and Vargas et al. (2017), in which we concatenated all news articles from the same company on each day and predicted if the closing price in the day $t + 1$ would increase when compared with closing price on day t, and similarly for the S&P 500 index.

Models We compare the model described in Section 3 with several baselines. For the other work using the same dataset (Ding et al., 2015; Vargas et al., 2017), we give the results from

---

[2] https://github.com/philipperemy/financial-news-dataset

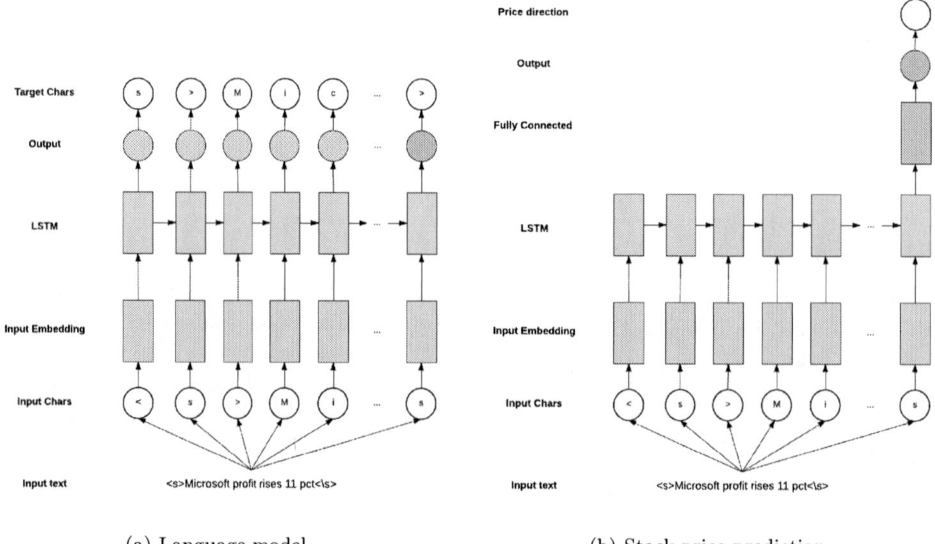

(a) Language model   (b) Stock price prediction

Figure 1: (a) Network architecture for the language model. In each step the output of the LSTM layer predicts the probability distribution of the next character. (b) Networks architecture for the stock prediction network. Only at the final processing of the text the output of the LSTM is used to predict the direction of the stock price.

the respective papers; we use the same experimental setup as they did. These models do not have intraday results, as the authors of those papers did not have stock data at more fine-grained intervals than daily. Only the models presented in Ding et al. (2015) have results for individual stocks, in addition to the S&P 500 Index.

We also reimplemented the model used by Luss and d'Aspremont (2015), which was a competitive baseline for Ding et al. (2015). In this model bags-of-words are used to represent the news documents and Support Vector Machines (SVMs) are used for prediction. We thus have both interday and intraday results for this model.

In the results, the following notation identifies each model:

- CharB-LSTM (ours): character embedding input and LSTM followed by fully connected prediction model.
- WI-RCNN: word embedding and technical indicators input and RCNN prediction model (Vargas et al., 2017).
- SI-RCNN: sentence embedding and technical indicators input and RCNN predic-

tion model (Vargas et al., 2017).

- BW-SVM: bag-of-words and support machines (SVMs) prediction model (Luss and d'Aspremont, 2015).
- E-NN: structured events tuple input and standard neural network prediction model (Ding et al., 2014).
- WB-CNN: sum of each word in a document as input and CNN prediction model (Ding et al., 2015).
- EB-CNN: event embedding prediction model (Ding et al., 2015).

Following Lavrenko et al. (2000) and Ding et al. (2015) we also test the profitability of our proposed model. We follow a slightly different strategy, though. As in Ding et al. (2015) we perform a market simulation considering the behavior of a fictitious trader. This trader will use the predictions of the model to invest $10,000 worth in a stock if the model indicates the price will rise and will hold the position until the end of the current session, selling at the closing price. The same strategy is used for short-selling if the model indicates that an individual stock price will fall. Differently from

Ding et al. (2015) we do not consider profit taking behavior in our simulation. Rather, we plot the behaviour to visualize what happens over time, instead of presenting a single aggregate number. For this simulation we considered only the predictions on a portfolio consisting of the S&P 500 Index constituent companies. We compare the results of this strategy with the S&P 500 Index performance over the same period.

5 Results and Discussion

Language Model   We first look at the quality of the representations learned by the character language model. Considering it was trained exclusively on a dataset of financial news we wondered how well this model would be able to reproduce the information dependencies present in the data such as the time of the events and currency information. The language model seemed capable of reproducing these dependencies. In Table 2 we show some sample text generated by the language model. While semantically incorrect, the representations learned by the model seem able to reproduce to some extent the grammatical structure of the language, as well as understand the entities present in the training dataset and the structure of numerical data.

Model Accuracy   Table 3 shows the experimental results of the model S&P 500 Index prediction on the test dataset, in terms of accuracy of predicting stock price movement, while Table 4 shows the test results of individual company predictions. Similarly to Ding et al. (2015), individual stock prediction performs better than index prediction. Overall, our character-level language model pre-training performs at least as well as all of the other models with the exception of EB-CNN, but with the advantage over EB-CNN of being substantially simpler in implementation in terms of not having a module for modelling events. In general, while the other proposed models use more complex architectures and external features such as technical indicators and structured event detection, our approach leverages only on language model pre-training.

The higher performance of the EB-CNN architecture of Ding et al. (2015) is likely to be due to the neural tensor network component that takes as input word embeddings and returns a representation of events; this provides a boost of 3+% over their comparable CNN model that does not explicitly incorporate events (WB-CNN in our table). This event component is potentially compatible with our approach; they could be combined, for example, by feeding our character-based input to an event component, or as noted earlier via multi-channel inputs, along the lines of Kim (2014).

Market Simulation   In Figure 2 we report the results of the market simulation. Overall, the model is able to outperform the index consistently, despite having greater variance. While the model do not consider trading frictions such as transaction costs and market impact, we believe this these results highlight the viability of the strategy. Exploration of advanced market microstructure implications are beyond the scope of this paper.

Efficient Markets Hypothesis   One interesting aspect of these results is the superior performance of the daily prediction over intraday prediction.

In terms of what this might suggest for the EMH, Malkiel (2003) notes:

> It was generally believed that securities markets were extremely efficient in reflecting information about individual stocks and about the stock market as a whole. The accepted view was that when information arises, the news spreads very quickly and is incorporated into the prices of securities without delay.

In fact, in the original formulation of the EMH, Fama (1970) remarks that "at *any* time prices fully reflect all available information" [italics added], implying instantaneous incorporation of information into prices. Other work such as Grossman and Stiglitz (1980) has argued that there are informational inefficiencies in the market that lead to delays in that information being incorporated into prices. Malkiel (2003) reviews some of the reasons for underreacting to new information, which include judgement biases by traders, such as conservatism (Edwards, 1968), "the

Table 2: Random samples from the character language model

<s>Copper for the region will increase the economy as rising inflation to recover from the property demand proposals for the region's largest economy and a share price of 10 percent of the nation's bonds to contain the company to spend as much as $1.3 billion to $1.2 billion in the same period a year earlier.<\s>

<s>(Reuters) - The Bank of America Corp (NBA.N) said on Wednesday as proposals are seeking to be completed by the end of the year, the biggest shareholder of the stock of a statement to buy the company's casino and the country's biggest economy. "The U.S. is a way that the credit crisis will be a proposal to get a strong results of the budget deficit in the next month," said Toyota Motor Chief Executive Officer Tom Berry said in a telephone interview.<\s>

<s>The U.S. is considering a second straight month in the U.S. and Europe to report the stock of the nation's currency and the previous consecutive month. The company will sell 4.5 billion euros ($3.6 billion) of bonds in the first quarter of 2012, according to the median estimate of analysts surveyed by Bloomberg.<\s>

Figure 2: Equity plot of trading using the proposed event-based strategy.

Table 3: Results of S&P 500 Index prediction

Model	Interday	Intraday
BW-SVM	56.42%	53.22%
CharB-LSTM (ours)	63.34%	59.86%
WI-RCNN	61.29%	*
SI-RCNN	63.09%	*
WB-CNN	61.73%	*
E-NN	58.94%	*
EB-CNN	64.21%	*

Table 4: Results of Individual stock prediction

Model	Interday	Intraday
BW-SVM	58.74%	54.22%
CharB-LSTM (ours)	64.74%	61.68%
WB-CNN	61.47%	*
EB-CNN	65.48%	*

slow updating of models in the face of new evidence".

In terms of looking at the effect of news announcements, there historically haven't been the tools to analyse vast quantities of text to evaluate effects on stock prices. With deep learning, and the online availability of stock prices at fine-grained intervals, it is now possible to look empirically at how long it takes information to be incorporated by assessing how predictable stock prices are as a function of news announcements. Previous work discussed in Section 2 had observed that it was still possible to predict at levels better than chance for up to a year out, although most strongly as time horizons were shorter. However, our preliminary results from our two models with intraday results show that predictability does not decrease monotonically: information is more typically incorporated later than the first hour.

6   Conclusion

This paper presented the use of a simple LSTM neural network with character level embeddings for stock market forecasting using only financial news as predictors. Our results suggest that the use of character level embeddings is promising and competitive with more complex models which use technical indicators and event extraction methods in addition to the news articles.

Character embeddings models are simpler and more memory efficient than word embeddings and are also able to keep sub-word information. With character embeddings the risk of seeing unknown tokens in the test set is diminished, since the data sparsity is much lower than with word embeddings.

In the future we consider testing the use of character embeddings with more complex architectures and possibly the addition of other sources of information to create richer feature sets.

In addition, while previous work has found that including the body text of the news performs worse than just the headline, there may be useful information to extract from the body text, perhaps along the lines of Pang and Lee (2004), which improves sentiment analysis results by snipping out irrelevant text using a graph-theoretic minimum cut approach.

Other directions include looking at predicting price movements at a range of time horizons, in order to gauge empirically how quickly information is absorbed in the market, and relate this to the finance literature on the topic.

Acknowledgements

We thank the Capital Markets CRC for providing financial support for this research.

References

Yoshua Bengio, Aaron Courville, and Pascal Vincent. 2013. Representation learning: A review and new perspectives. *IEEE Transactions on Pattern Analysis and Machine Intelligence* 35(8):1798–1828.

Johan Bollen, Huina Mao, and Xiaojun Zeng. 2011. Twitter mood predicts the stock market. *Journal of Computational Science* 2(1):1–8.

Andrew M Dai and Quoc V Le. 2015. Semi-supervised sequence learning. In C. Cortes, N. D. Lawrence, D. D. Lee, M. Sugiyama, and R. Garnett, editors, *Advances in Neural Information Processing Systems 28*, Curran Associates, Inc., pages 3079–3087. http://papers.nips.cc/paper/5949-semi-supervised-sequence-learning.pdf.

Xiao Ding, Yue Zhang, Ting Liu, and Junwen Duan. 2014. Using structured events to predict stock price movement: An empirical investigation. In *Proceedings of the 2014 Conference on Empirical Methods in Natural Language Processing (EMNLP)*. Association for Computational Linguistics, pages 1415–1425. https://doi.org/10.3115/v1/D14-1148.

Xiao Ding, Yue Zhang, Ting Liu, and Junwen Duan. 2015. Deep learning for event-driven stock prediction. In *Proceedings of the International Joint Conference on Artificial Intelligence (IJCAI)*. pages 2327–2333.

W. Edwards. 1968. Conservatism in human information processing. In B. Kleinmutz, editor, *Formal Representation of Human Judgement*, Wiley, New York.

Eugene Fama. 1970. Efficient Capital Markets: A Review of Theory and Empirical Work. *Journal of Finance* 25:383–417.

Ingrid E Fisher, Margaret R Garnsey, and Mark E Hughes. 2016. Natural language processing in accounting, auditing and finance: a synthesis of the literature with a roadmap for future research. *Intelligent Systems in Accounting, Finance and Management* 23(3):157–214.

Sanford J. Grossman and Joseph E. Stiglitz. 1980. On the Impossibility of Informationally Efficient Markets. *American Economic Review* 70:393–408.

Michael Hagenau, Michael Liebmann, and Dirk Neumann. 2013. Automated news reading: Stock price prediction based on financial news using context-capturing features. *Decision Support Systems* 55(3):685–697.

Sepp Hochreiter and Jürgen Schmidhuber. 1997. Long short-term memory. *Neural Computation* 9(8):1735–1780.

Yoon Kim. 2014. Convolutional neural networks for sentence classification pages 1746–1751. https://doi.org/10.3115/v1/D14-1181.

Yoon Kim, Yacine Jernite, David Sontag, and Alexander M Rush. 2016. Character-aware neural language models. In *Proceedings of the Thirtieth AAAI Conference on Artificial Intelligence*. pages 2741–2749.

Diederik Kingma and Jimmy Ba. 2014. Adam: A method for stochastic optimization. In *Proceedings of the 3rd International Conference on Learning Representations (ICLR)*.

Ryan Kiros, Yukun Zhu, Ruslan R Salakhutdinov, Richard Zemel, Raquel Urtasun, Antonio Torralba, and Sanja Fidler. 2015. Skip-thought vectors. In C. Cortes, N. D. Lawrence, D. D. Lee, M. Sugiyama, and R. Garnett, editors, *Advances in Neural Information Processing Systems 28*. Curran Associates, Inc., pages 3294–3302. http://papers.nips.cc/paper/5950-skip-thought-vectors.pdf.

Ankit Kumar, Ozan Irsoy, Peter Ondruska, Mohit Iyyer, James Bradbury, Ishaan Gulrajani, Victor Zhong, Romain Paulus, and Richard Socher. 2016. Ask me anything: Dynamic memory networks for natural language processing. In Maria Florina Balcan and Kilian Q. Weinberger, editors, *Proceedings of The 33rd International Conference on Machine Learning*. PMLR, New York, New York, USA, volume 48 of *Proceedings of Machine Learning Research*, pages 1378–1387. http://proceedings.mlr.press/v48/kumar16.html.

Victor Lavrenko, Matt Schmill, Dawn Lawrie, Paul Ogilvie, David Jensen, and James Allan. 2000. Language models for financial news recommendation. In *Proceedings of the Ninth International Conference on Information and Knowledge Management*. ACM, pages 389–396.

David Leinweber and Jacob Sisk. 2011. Event-driven trading and the "new news". *The Journal of Portfolio Management* 38(1):110–124.

Ronny Luss and Alexandre d'Aspremont. 2015. Predicting abnormal returns from news using text classification. *Quantitative Finance* 15(6):999–1012.

Andrew L Maas, Awni Y Hannun, and Andrew Y Ng. 2013. Rectifier nonlinearities improve neural network acoustic models. In *Proceedings of the ICML Workshop on Deep Learning for Audio, Speech, and Language Processing*.

Burton G Malkiel. 2003. The efficient market hypothesis and its critics. *The Journal of Economic Perspectives* 17(1):59–82.

Tomas Mikolov, Kai Chen, Greg Corrado, and Jeffrey Dean. 2013a. Efficient estimation of word representations in vector space. *CoRR* abs/1301.3781. http://arxiv.org/abs/1301.3781.

Tomas Mikolov, Ilya Sutskever, Kai Chen, Greg S Corrado, and Jeff Dean. 2013b. Distributed representations of words and phrases and their compositionality. In C. J. C. Burges, L. Bottou, M. Welling, Z. Ghahramani, and K. Q. Weinberger, editors, *Advances in Neural Information Processing Systems 26*. Curran Associates, Inc., pages 3111–3119. http://papers.nips.cc/paper/5021-distributed-representations-of-words-and-phrases-and-their-compositionality.pdf.

Thien Hai Nguyen, Kiyoaki Shirai, and Julien Velcin. 2015. Sentiment analysis on social media for stock movement prediction. *Expert Systems with Applications* 42(24):9603–9611.

Wijnand Nuij, Viorel Milea, Frederik Hogenboom, Flavius Frasincar, and Uzay Kaymak. 2014. An automated framework for incorporating news into stock trading strategies. *IEEE Transactions on Knowledge and Data Engineering* 26(4):823–835.

Thomas Oberlechner and Sam Hocking. 2004. Information sources, news, and rumors in financial markets: Insights into the foreign exchange market. *Journal of Economic Psychology* 25(3):407–424.

Nuno Oliveira, Paulo Cortez, and Nelson Areal. 2017. The impact of microblogging data for stock market prediction: Using twitter to predict returns, volatility, trading volume and survey sentiment indices. *Expert Systems with Applications* 73:125–144.

Bo Pang and Lillian Lee. 2004. A Sentimental Education: Sentiment Analysis Using Subjectivity Summarization Based on Minimum Cuts. In *Proceedings of the 42nd Meeting of the Association for Computational Linguistics (ACL'04), Main Volume*. Barcelona, Spain, pages 271–278. https://doi.org/10.3115/1218955.1218990.

Bo Pang, Lillian Lee, et al. 2008. Opinion mining and sentiment analysis. *Foundations and Trends® in Information Retrieval* 2(1–2):1–135.

Nicolas Pröllochs, Stefan Feuerriegel, and Dirk Neumann. 2016. Negation scope detection in sentiment analysis: Decision support for news-driven trading. *Decision Support Systems* 88:67–75.

Alec Radford, Rafal Józefowicz, and Ilya Sutskever. 2017. Learning to generate reviews and discovering sentiment. *CoRR* abs/1704.01444. http://arxiv.org/abs/1704.01444.

Kira Radinsky, Sagie Davidovich, and Shaul Markovitch. 2012. Learning causality for news events prediction. In *Proceedings of the 21st International Conference on World Wide Web*. ACM, pages 909–918.

Sebastian Ruder, Parsa Ghaffari, and John G. Breslin. 2016. Character-level and Multi-channel Convolutional Neural Networks for Large-scale Authorship Attribution. *CoRR* abs/1609.06686. http://arxiv.org/abs/1609.06686.

Dymitr Ruta. 2014. Automated trading with machine learning on big data. In *IEEE International Congress on Big Data*. IEEE, pages 824–830.

Robert P Schumaker, Yulei Zhang, Chun-Neng Huang, and Hsinchun Chen. 2012. Evaluating sentiment in financial news articles. *Decision Support Systems* 53(3):458–464.

Richard Socher, Alex Perelygin, Jean Wu, Jason Chuang, Christopher D. Manning, Andrew Ng, and Christopher Potts. 2013. Recursive deep models for semantic compositionality over a sentiment treebank. In *Proceedings of the 2013 Conference on Empirical Methods in Natural Language Processing*. Association for Computational Linguistics, pages 1631–1642. https://aclanthology.info/pdf/D/D13/D13-1170.pdf.

Paul C Tetlock. 2007. Giving content to investor sentiment: The role of media in the stock market. *The Journal of Finance* 62(3):1139–1168.

Manuel R Vargas, Beatriz SLP de Lima, and Alexandre G Evsukoff. 2017. Deep learning for stock market prediction from financial news articles. In *IEEE International Conference on Computational Intelligence and Virtual Environments for Measurement Systems and Applications (CIVEMSA)*. IEEE, pages 60–65.

Liang-Chih Yu, Jheng-Long Wu, Pei-Chann Chang, and Hsuan-Shou Chu. 2013. Using a contextual entropy model to expand emotion words and their intensity for the sentiment classification of stock market news. *Knowledge-Based Systems* 41:89–97.

Improving End-to-End Memory Networks with Unified Weight Tying

Fei Liu   **Trevor Cohn**   **Timothy Baldwin**
School of Computing and Information Systems
The University of Melbourne
Victoria, Australia
`fliu3@student.unimelb.edu.au`
`t.cohn@unimelb.edu.au   tb@ldwin.net`

Abstract

Answering questions while reasoning over multiple supporting facts has long been a goal of artificial intelligence. Recently, remarkable advances have been made, focusing on reasoning over natural language-based stories. In particular, end-to-end memory networks (N2N), have achieved state-of-the-art results over such tasks. However, N2Ns are limited by the necessity to choose between two weight tying schemes, neither of which performs consistently well over all tasks. We propose a unified model generalising weight tying and in doing so, make the model more expressive. The proposed model achieves uniformly high performance, improving on the best results for memory network-based models on the `bAbI` dataset, and competitive results on `Dialog bAbI`.

1 Introduction

Deep neural network models have demonstrated strong performance on a number of challenging tasks, such as image classification (He et al., 2016), speech recognition (Graves et al., 2013), and various natural language processing tasks (Bahdanau et al., 2014; Kim, 2014; Xiong et al., 2016). Recently, the augmentation of neural networks with external memory components has been shown to be a powerful means of capturing context of different types (Graves et al., 2014, 2016; Rae et al., 2016). Of particular interest to this work is the work by Sukhbaatar et al. (2015), on end-to-end memory networks (N2Ns), which exhibit remarkable reasoning capabilities, e.g. for reasoning (Weston et al., 2016) and goal-oriented dialogue tasks (Bordes and Weston, 2016). Typically, such

tasks consist of three key components: a sequence of supporting facts (the story), a question, and its answer. An example task is given in Figure 1. Given the first two as input, it is the model's job to reason over the supporting facts and predict the answer to the question.

One drawback of N2Ns is the problem of choosing between two types of weight tying (adjacent and layer-wise; see Section 2 for a technical description). While N2Ns generally work well with either weight tying approach, as reported in Sukhbaatar et al. (2015), the performance is uneven on some difficult tasks. That is, for some tasks, one weight tying approach attains near-perfect accuracy and the other performs poorly, but for other tasks, this trend is reversed.

In this paper, focusing on improving N2N, we propose a unified model, UN2N, capable of dynamically determining the appropriate type of weight tying for a given task. This is realised through the use of a gating vector, inspired by Liu and Perez (2017). Our method achieves the best performance for a memory network-based model on the `bAbI` dataset, superior to both adjacent and layer-wise weight tying, and competitive results on `Dialog bAbI`.

The paper is organised as follows: after we review N2N and related reasoning models in Section 2, we describe our motivation and detail the elements of our proposed model in Section 3. Section 4 and 5 present the experimental results on the `bAbI` and `Dialog bAbI` datasets with analyses in Section 6. Lastly, Section 7 concludes the paper.

2 Related Work

End-to-End Memory Networks: Building on top of memory networks (Weston et al., 2015), Sukhbaatar et al. (2015) introduced N2N, discard-

Fei Liu, Trevor Cohn and Timothy Baldwin. 2017. Improving End-to-End Memory Networks with Unified Weight Tying. In *Proceedings of Australasian Language Technology Association Workshop*, pages 16–24.

> Jeff went to the kitchen. Mary travelled to the hallway. Jeff picked up the milk.
> Jeff travelled to the bedroom. Jeff left the milk. Jeff went to the bathroom.
> Where is the milk now? A: bedroom
> Where is Jeff? A: bathroom
> Where was Jeff before the bedroom? A: kitchen

Figure 1: Example story, question and answer.

ing the memory position supervision and making the model trainable in an end-to-end fashion, through the advent of supporting memories and a memory access controller. Representations of the context sentences $x_1, \ldots, x_n$ in the story are encoded using two sets of embedding matrices A and C (both of size $d \times |V|$ where d is the embedding size and $|V|$ the vocabulary size), and stored in the input and output memory cells $m_1, \ldots, m_n$ and $c_1, \ldots, c_n$, each of which is obtained via $m_i = A\Phi(x_i)$ and $c_i = C\Phi(x_i)$, where $\Phi(\cdot)$ is a function that maps the input into a bag of dimension $|V|$. The input question q is encoded with another embedding matrix $B \in \mathbb{R}^{d \times |V|}$ such that $u = B\Phi(q)$. N2N utilises the question embedding u and the input memory representations m_i to measure the relevance between the question and each supporting context sentence, resulting in a vector of attention weights:

$$p_i = \mathrm{softmax}(u^\top m_i) \qquad (1)$$

where $\mathrm{softmax}(a_i) = \dfrac{e^{a_i}}{\sum_j e^{a_j}}$. Once the attention weights have been computed, the memory access controller receives the response o in the form of a weighted sum over the output memory representations:

$$o = \sum_i p_i c_i \qquad (2)$$

To enhance the model's ability to cope with more challenging tasks requiring multiple supporting facts from the memory, Sukhbaatar et al. (2015) further extended the model by stacking multiple memory layers (also known as "hops"), in which case the output of the kth hop is taken as input to the $(k + 1)^{\text{th}}$ hop:

$$u^{k+1} = o^k + u^k \qquad (3)$$

Lastly, N2N predicts the answer to question q using a softmax function:

$$\hat{y} = \mathrm{softmax}(W(o^K + u^K)) \qquad (4)$$

$$B \dashrightarrow A^1 — A^2 — A^3 \qquad \begin{array}{l} \text{-- ADJ} \\ \text{— LW} \end{array}$$
$$C^1 — C^2 — C^3 \dashrightarrow W^\top$$

Figure 2: Illustration of the two types of weight tying mechanisms based on a N2N model with 3 hops. Lines and dashed lines indicate parameter sharing relationships between embedding matrices.

where $\hat{y}$ is the predicted answer distribution, $W \in \mathbb{R}^{|V| \times d}$ is a parameter matrix for the model to learn (note that in the context of bAbI tasks, answers are single words), and K is the total number of hops.

Current issues and motivation: In Sukhbaatar et al. (2015), two types of weight tying were explored for N2N, namely adjacent ("ADJ") and layer-wise ("LW"). With LW, the input and output embedding matrices are shared across different hops (i.e., $A^1 = A^2 = \ldots = A^K$ and $C^1 = C^2 = \ldots = C^K$), resembling RNNs. With ADJ, on the other hand, not only is the output embedding for a given layer shared with the corresponding input embedding (i.e., $A^{k+1} = C^k$), the answer prediction matrix W and question embedding matrix B are also constrained such that $W^\top = C^K$ and $B = A^1$.

While both ADJ and LW work well, achieving comparable overall performance in terms of mean error over the 20 bAbI tasks, their performance on a subset of the tasks (i.e., tasks 3, 16, 17 and 19, as shown in Table 1) is inconsistent, with one performing very well, and the other performing poorly. Based on this observation, we propose a unified weight tying mechanism exploiting the benefits of both ADJ and LW, and capable of dynamically determining the best weight tying approach for a given task.

Task	N2N	
	ADJ	LW
3: 3 supporting facts	90.7	**97.9**
16: basic induction	**99.6**	48.2
17: positional reasoning	59.3	**81.4**
19: path finding	33.5	**97.7**

Table 1: Accuracy (%) reported in (Sukhbaatar et al., 2015) on a selected subset of the 20 bAbI 10k tasks. Note that performance in the LW column is obtained with a larger embedding size $d = 100$ and ReLU non-linearity applied to the internal state after each hop.

Related reasoning models: Gated End-to-End Memory Networks (GN2Ns) (Liu and Perez, 2017) are a variant of N2N with a simple yet effective gating mechanism on the connections between hops, allowing the model to dynamically regulate the information flow between the controller and the memory. Dynamic Memory Networks (DMNs) and its improved version (DMN+) employ RNNs to sequentially process contextual information stored in the memory. All these models have been shown to have competent reasoning capabilities over the bAbI dataset (Weston et al., 2016).

3 Proposed Model[1]

The key idea in this work is to let the model determine which type of weight tying mechanism it should rely on. Recall that there are two types: ADJ and LW. With ADJ, the input embedding (A^k) of the kth hop is constrained to share the same parameters with the output embedding (C^{k-1}) of the $(k-1)^{\text{th}}$ hop (i.e., $A^k = C^{k-1}$). In contrast, with LW, the same input/output embedding matrices are shared across different hops (i.e., $A^1 = A^2 = \ldots = A^K$ and $C^1 = C^2 = \ldots = C^K$). To this end, we design a dynamic mechanism, allowing the model to decide on the preferred type of weight tying based on the input. Specifically, the key element in UN2N is that embedding matrices are constructed dynamically for each instance. This is in contrast to N2N and GN2N where the same embedding matrices are used for every input. UN2N, utilising a gating vector z (described in Equation (8)), constructs the embedding matrices (i.e., A^k, C^k, B and W) on the fly, influenced

by the information carried by z regarding the input question u^0 as well as the context sentences in the story m_t:

$$A^{k+1} = A^k \odot z + C^k \odot (1 - z) \quad (5)$$

$$C^{k+1} = C^k \odot z + \tilde{C}^{k+1} \odot (1 - z) \quad (6)$$

where $\odot$ is the column element-wise multiplication operation, and $\tilde{C}^{k+1}$ the unconstrained embedding matrix. We further define $A^1 = \tilde{A}^1$ and $C^1 = \tilde{C}^1$, where $\tilde{A}^1$ and $\tilde{C}^1$ are the unconstrained embedding matrices for hop 1. As shown in Equation (5), the input embedding matrix A^{k+1} for the $(k + 1)^{\text{th}}$ hop is composed of a weighted sum of the input and output embedding matrix A^k and C^k for the kth hop, resembling LW and ADJ, respectively. The summation is weighted by the gating vector z. C^{k+1} is constructed in a similar fashion. Ultimately, the larger the values of the elements of z, the more UN2N leans towards LW. Conversely, smaller z values indicate an inclination for ADJ.

Another key to this approach is the gating vector z, which is formulated to incorporate knowledge informative to the choice of the weight tying scheme. Here, we take inspiration from gated end-to-end memory networks ("GN2N": Liu and Perez (2017)), where a gating mechanism is learned in an end-to-end fashion to regulate the information flow between memory hops. In GN2N, the gate value $\text{T}^k(u^k)$ depends only on the input to the kth hop u^k, whereas in this work, we further condition the determination of the weight tying approach on the story (or memory). Concretely, similarly to DMN and DMN+, we encode the story by first reading the memory one step at a time with a GRU:

$$h_{t+1} = \text{GRU}(m_t, h_t) \quad (7)$$

where t is the current time step and m_t is the context sentence in the story at time t. Then, the last hidden state h_T of the GRU is taken to be the representation of the story.[2] Next, z is defined to be a vector of dimension d:

$$z = \sigma\left(W_z \begin{bmatrix} u^0 \\ h_T \end{bmatrix} + b_z\right) \quad (8)$$

where W_z is a weight matrix, b_z a bias term ,σ the sigmoid function and $\begin{bmatrix} u^0 \\ h_T \end{bmatrix}$ the concatenation

---

[1]For better readability, a summary table of notations used in this paper is in Table 2.

[2]We also performed additional experiments with a bi-directional GRU over the memory as in Xiong et al. (2016), but did not observe any performance gain.

Var.	Description	Dim.
d	Dimensionality of embeddings	$\mathbb{R}$
$|V|$	Vocabulary size	$\mathbb{R}$
$\boldsymbol{m}_i^k$	Input memory embedding of the ith context sentence at the kth hop	$\mathbb{R}^d$
$\boldsymbol{c}_i^k$	Output memory embedding of the ith context sentence at the kth hop	$\mathbb{R}^d$
$\boldsymbol{u}^k$	Question embedding at the kth hop	$\mathbb{R}^d$
$\boldsymbol{o}^k$	Weighted output embedding at the kth hop	$\mathbb{R}^d$
$\boldsymbol{z}$	Gating vector to dynamically determine the type of weight tying	$\mathbb{R}^d$
$\boldsymbol{h}_t$	Hidden GRU representation of processed memory at step t	$\mathbb{R}^d$
$\boldsymbol{b}_z$	Bias term for computing $\boldsymbol{z}$	$\mathbb{R}^d$
$\boldsymbol{A}^k$	Embedding matrix for input memory cell at the kth hop	$\mathbb{R}^{d \times |V|}$
$\boldsymbol{C}^k$	Embedding matrix for output memory cell at the kth hop	$\mathbb{R}^{d \times |V|}$
$\tilde{\boldsymbol{A}}^k$	Unconstrained embedding matrix for input memory cell at the kth hop	$\mathbb{R}^{d \times |V|}$
$\tilde{\boldsymbol{C}}^k$	Unconstrained embedding matrix for output memory cell at the kth hop	$\mathbb{R}^{d \times |V|}$
$\boldsymbol{B}$	Embedding for question at the 1st hop	$\mathbb{R}^{d \times |V|}$
$\boldsymbol{W}$	Weight matrix for the classifier at the last (K^{th}) hop	$\mathbb{R}^{|V| \times d}$
$\boldsymbol{W}_z$	Weight matrix for computing $\boldsymbol{z}$	$\mathbb{R}^{d \times 2d}$
$\boldsymbol{H}$	Weight matrix for linear transformation between hops	$\mathbb{R}^{d \times d}$

Table 2: Notation summary.

of $\boldsymbol{u}^0$ and $\boldsymbol{h}_T$. Essentially, the gating vector $\boldsymbol{z}$ is now dependent on not only the question $\boldsymbol{u}^0$, but also the context sentences in the memory encoded in $\boldsymbol{h}_T$. Note that the gating vector $\boldsymbol{z}$ can be replaced by a gating scalar z, but we choose to use a vector for more fine-grained control as in LSTMs (Hochreiter and Schmidhuber, 1997) and GRUs (Cho et al., 2014).

To simplify the model, we constrain $\boldsymbol{B}$ and $\boldsymbol{W}^\top$ to share the same parameters as $\boldsymbol{A}^1$ and $\boldsymbol{C}^K$. Moreover, following Sukhbaatar et al. (2015), we add a linear mapping $\boldsymbol{H} \in \mathbb{R}^{d \times d}$ to the update connection between memory hops, but in our case, down-weight it by $1 - \boldsymbol{z}$, resulting in:

$$\boldsymbol{u}^{k+1} = \boldsymbol{o}^k + (\boldsymbol{H} \odot (1 - \boldsymbol{z}))\boldsymbol{u}^k \qquad (9)$$

Regularisation: In order to prevent the input and output embedding matrices $\boldsymbol{A}^k$ and $\boldsymbol{C}^k$ from being dominated by the unconstrained embedding matrices, it is necessary to restrain the magnitude of the values in $\tilde{\boldsymbol{A}}^1$ and $\tilde{\boldsymbol{C}}^k$. Therefore, in addition to the cross entropy loss over N training instances:

$$\mathcal{L} = \sum_N \text{CrossEntropy}(\boldsymbol{y}, \hat{\boldsymbol{y}}) \qquad (10)$$

where $\boldsymbol{y}$ and $\hat{\boldsymbol{y}}$ are the true and predicted answer, we enforce a regularisation penalty and formulate

the new objective function as:

$$\mathcal{L}' = \mathcal{L} + \lambda \cdot (||\tilde{\boldsymbol{A}}^1||_2^2 + \sum_k ||\tilde{\boldsymbol{C}}^k||_2^2) \qquad (11)$$

Model implementation: we implement UN2N with TensorFlow (Abadi et al., 2015) and the code is available at `https://github.com/liufly/umemn2n`.

4 QA `bAbI` Experiments

In this section, the experimental setup is detailed, followed by the results.

4.1 Experimental Setup

Dataset: We evaluate the proposed model over the `bAbI` dataset (Weston et al., 2016) (v1.2), featuring 20 different natural-language-based reasoning tasks in the form of: (1) a list of supporting statements $(x_1, \ldots, x_n)$; (2) a question (q); and (3) the answer (y, typically a single word or short phrase). Each task in `bAbI` is synthetically generated with a distinct emphasis on a specific type of reasoning. In order to predict the desired answer, the model is required to locate (or focus on) the relevant context sentences among irrelevant distractors in the memory. As with `N2N`, our model can be trained in a fully end-to-end fashion and requires only the answers themselves as the supervision signal. The dataset comes in two sizes, with

Task	N2N		DMN	DMN+	GN2N	UN2N
	ADJ	LW				
1: 1 supporting fact	**100.0**	**100.0**	**100.0**	**100.0**	**100.0**	**100.0**
2: 2 supporting facts	99.7	99.7	98.2	99.7	**100.0**	99.2
3: 3 supporting facts	90.7	97.9	95.2	**98.9**	95.5	95.5
4: 2 argument relations	**100.0**	**100.0**	**100.0**	**100.0**	**100.0**	**100.0**
5: 3 argument relations	99.4	99.2	99.3	99.5	**99.8**	99.3
6: yes/no questions	**100.0**	99.9	**100.0**	**100.0**	**100.0**	**100.0**
7: counting	96.3	98.0	96.9	97.6	98.2	**98.9**
8: lists/sets	99.2	99.1	96.5	**100.0**	99.7	99.5
9: simple negation	99.2	99.7	**100.0**	**100.0**	**100.0**	**100.0**
10: indefinite knowledge	97.6	**100.0**	97.5	**100.0**	99.8	**100.0**
11: basic coreference	**100.0**	99.9	99.9	**100.0**	**100.0**	**100.0**
12: conjunction	**100.0**	**100.0**	**100.0**	**100.0**	**100.0**	**100.0**
13: compound coreference	**100.0**	**100.0**	99.8	**100.0**	**100.0**	**100.0**
14: time reasoning	**100.0**	99.9	**100.0**	**100.0**	**100.0**	**100.0**
15: basic deduction	**100.0**	**100.0**	**100.0**	**100.0**	**100.0**	**100.0**
16: basic induction	99.6	48.2	99.4	54.7	**100.0**	99.9
17: positional reasoning	59.3	81.4	59.6	**95.8**	72.2	90.7
18: size reasoning	93.3	94.7	95.3	97.9	91.5	**99.4**
19: path finding	33.5	97.7	34.5	**100.0**	69.0	84.0
20: agent's motivation	**100.0**	**100.0**	**100.0**	**100.0**	**100.0**	**100.0**
Average	93.4	95.8	93.6	97.2	96.3	**98.3**

Table 3: Accuracy (%) on the 20 bAbI 10k tasks for our proposed method (UN2N) and various benchmark methods. **Bold** indicates the best result for a given task.

either 1k or 10k training instances per task. In this work, we focus exclusively on the 10k version.[3]

Training Details: Following Sukhbaatar et al. (2015), we hold out 10% of the bAbI training set to form a development set. Position encoding and temporal encoding (with 10% random noise) are also incorporated into the model. Training is performed over 100 epochs with a batch size of 32 using the Adam optimiser (Kingma and Ba, 2015) with a learning rate of 0.005. Following Sukhbaatar et al. (2015), linear start is employed in all our experiments for the first 20 epochs. All weight parameters are initialised based on a Gaussian distribution with zero mean and $\sigma = 0.1$. Gradients with an ℓ_2 norm of 40 are divided by a scalar to have norm 40. Also following Sukhbaatar et al. (2015), we use only the most recent 50 sentences as the memory and set the number of memory hops to 3, the embedding size to 20, and λ to

0.001.

Consistent with other published results over bAbI (Sukhbaatar et al., 2015; Graves et al., 2016; Seo et al., 2017), we repeat training 30 times for each task, and select the model which performs best on the development set.

4.2 Results

The results on the 20 bAbI QA tasks are presented in Table 3. We benchmark against other memory network based models: (1) N2N with ADJ and LW (Sukhbaatar et al., 2015); (2) DMN (Kumar et al., 2016) and its improved version DMN+ (Xiong et al., 2016); and (3) GN2N (Liu and Perez, 2017).

Major improvements on the difficult tasks. The most noticeable performance gains are over tasks 16, 17 and 19 where, compared with the vanilla N2N, UN2N achieves much better results than the worst of ADJ and LW, surpassing both ADJ and LW in the case of tasks 17 and 18. This confirms the validity of the model.

---

[3]We also conducted experiments on the 1k dataset but observed weak performance. We suspect that this is largely due to overfitting given the added complexity of UN2N compared with N2N.

UN2N maintains equally competitive performance on the other tasks. Our unified weight tying scheme does not degrade performance on the less challenging tasks.

Best performing memory network on bAbI 10k. UN2N achieves the best combined results over bAbI 10k, superior to the previous top model DMN+ where two GRUs are employed to process the memory at sentence and hop level; there is a particularly big improvement on task 16 (UN2N = 99.9 vs. DMN+ = 54.7). It is worth noting that UN2N achieves this with a much smaller embedding size $d = 20$ compared to 80 in DMN+.

Comparison with the state-of-the-art. Seo et al. (2017) report a higher overall score (99.3) for a deep learning model which is unrelated to memory networks and thus not immediately comparable with this work. It should also be noted that their model is based on embeddings of size $d = 200$, much larger than UN2N's 20, and that when their model is restricted to an embedding size of $d = 50$, the reported result is 96.8, lower than ours with $d = 20$.

5 Dialog bAbI Experiments

In addition to the experiments on the natural language-based QA bAbI dataset in Section 4, we conduct further experiments on a goal-oriented, dialog-based dataset: Dialog bAbI (Bordes and Weston, 2016).

5.1 Experimental Setup

Dataset: In this work, we employ a collection of goal-oriented dialog tasks, Dialog bAbI, all in a restaurant reservation scenario, developed by Bordes and Weston (2016), consisting of 6 categories each with a specific focus on tasking on aspect of an end-to-end dialog system: 1. issuing API calls, 2. updating API calls, 3. displaying options, 4. providing extra-information, 5. conducting full dialogs (the aggregation of the first 4 tasks), 6. Dialog State Tracking Challenge 2 corpus (DSTC-2). Task 1-5 are generated synthetically in the form of conversation between a user and a bot with entities drawn from a knowledge base with facts defining restaurants and their associated properties (e.g., location and price range, 7 properties in total). Starting with a request from the user, a dialog proceeds with subsequent and alternating user-bot utterances. The bot (or system)

needs to figure out the user intention and answer (or react) accordingly. A separate collection of test sets, with entities not occurring in the training set, have also been developed to evaluate the ability of the bot to deal with out-of-vocabulary (OOV) items. Task 6 is based on and derived from the second Dialog State Tracking Challenge (Henderson et al., 2014) with real human-bot conversations.

Training Details: Following the works of (Bordes and Weston, 2016) and (Liu and Perez, 2017), we frame the task in the same fashion: at the t-th time step, the preceding sequence of utterances, $c_1^u, c_1^r, c_2^u, c_2^r, \ldots, c_{t-1}^u, c_{t-1}^r$ (alternating between the user request, denoted c_i^u and the system response, denoted c_i^r), is stored in the memory as m_i and c_i. Taking the memory as contextual evidence, the goal of the model is to offers an answer c_t^r (the bot utterance at time t) to the question c_t^u (the user utterance at time t).

It is important to notice that the answers in this dataset may no longer be a single but can be comprised of multiple ones. Following (Bordes and Weston, 2016), we replace the final prediction step in Equation (4) with:

$$\hat{a} = \mathrm{softmax}(u^\top W' \Phi(y_1), \ldots, u^\top W' \Phi(y_{|C|}))$$

where $W' \in \mathbb{R}^{d \times |V|}$ is the weight parameter matrix for the model to learn, $u = o^K + u^K$ (K is the total number of hops), y_i is the ith response in the candidate set C such that $y_i \in C$, $|C|$ the size of the candidate set, and $\Phi(\cdot)$ a function which maps the input text into a bag of dimension $|V|$.

Additionally, we also append several key features to Φ, following (Bordes and Weston, 2016) and (Liu and Perez, 2017). First, we mark the identity of the speaker of a given utterance (either user or bot). Second, we extend Φ by 7 additional features, one for each of the 7 properties associated with a restaurant. Each of these 7 features indicates whether there are any exact matches between words in the candidate and those in the question or memory. We refer to these 7 features as the *match* features.

In terms of the training procedure, experiments are carried out with the same configuration as described in Section 4.1. As a large variance can be observed due to how sensitive memory-based models are to parameter initialisation, following (Sukhbaatar et al., 2015) and (Liu and Perez, 2017), we repeat each training 10 times using the

Task	−match			+match		
	N2N	GN2N	UN2N	N2N	GN2N	UN2N
1. Issuing API calls	99.9	**100.0**	**100.0**	**100.0**	**100.0**	**100.0**
2. Updating API calls	**100.0**	**100.0**	**100.0**	98.3	**100.0**	**100.0**
3. Displaying options	**74.9**	**74.9**	**74.9**	**74.9**	**74.9**	**74.9**
4. Providing information	**59.5**	57.2	57.2	**100.0**	**100.0**	**100.0**
5. Full dialogs	96.1	96.3	**99.2**	93.4	98.0	**99.4**
Average	86.1	85.7	**86.3**	93.3	94.6	**94.9**
1. (OOV) Issuing API calls	72.3	82.4	**83.0**	96.5	**100.0**	**100.0**
2. (OOV) Updating API calls	**78.9**	**78.9**	**78.9**	**94.5**	94.2	94.4
3. (OOV) Displaying options	74.4	**75.3**	75.2	75.2	75.1	**75.3**
4. (OOV) Providing information	**57.6**	57.0	57.0	**100.0**	**100.0**	**100.0**
5. (OOV) Full dialogs	65.5	66.7	**67.8**	77.7	79.4	**79.5**
Average	69.7	72.1	**72.4**	88.8	89.7	**89.8**
6. Dialog state tracking 2	41.1	**47.4**	42.4	41.0	**48.7**	42.9

Table 4: Per-response accuracy on the `Dialog bAbI` tasks. N2N: (Bordes and Weston, 2016). GN2N: (Liu and Perez, 2017). +match suggests the use of the *match* features in Section 5.1. **Bold** indicates the best result in each group (with or without the *match* features) for a given task.

same hyper-parameters and choose the best system based on validation performance.

5.2 Results

The results on the `Dialog bAbI` tasks are shown in Table 4. In terms of baselines, we benchmark against other memory network-based models:[4] (1) N2N (Sukhbaatar et al., 2015); and (2) GN2N (Sukhbaatar et al., 2015). While the results of GN2N is achieved with ADJ, the type of weight tying for N2N is not reported in (Bordes and Weston, 2016).

Improvements on task 5. It can be observed that UN2N offers consistent performance boost on task 5 across all experiments settings, especially in the non-OOV group. Given that task 5 is the aggregation of the first 4 tasks, the performance increase suggests that the hybrid weight-tying mechanism in UN2N is better capable of coping with tasks of various nature.

Equally competitive performance on task 1-4. UN2N achieves comparable, if not slightly better in some cases, performance on task 1-4.

Performance on task 6. Compared to N2N, UN2N improves the performance consistently with or without the match features. In contrast to GN2N, however, this is not the case. The cause for this performance gap requires further investigation and we leave this exercise for future work.

6 Analysis

To gain a better understanding of what the model has learned, we visualise the gating vectors z trained on the difficult bAbI tasks (i.e., 3, 16, 17 and 19), in the form of a 2-d PCA scatter plot in Figure 3. Four distinct clusters, representing the 4 different tasks, are easily identifiable. Moreover, it can be observed that tasks 3, 17 and 19 are rather close, reflecting the fact that LW performs better than ADJ over these three tasks. That is, Figure 3 is further evidence that our model dynamically learns the best weight tying method for a given task.

7 Conclusion

In this paper, we have presented UN2N, a model based on N2N with a unified weight tying scheme and demonstrated the effectiveness of the proposed method on a set of natural-language-based reasoning and dialog tasks.

---

[4]Seo et al. (2017) report a higher accuracy on `Dialog bAbI`. However, their model, based on RNNs, is rather different from memory networks and therefore deemed not immediately comparable and unrelated to the goal of this work: improving memory network-based models.

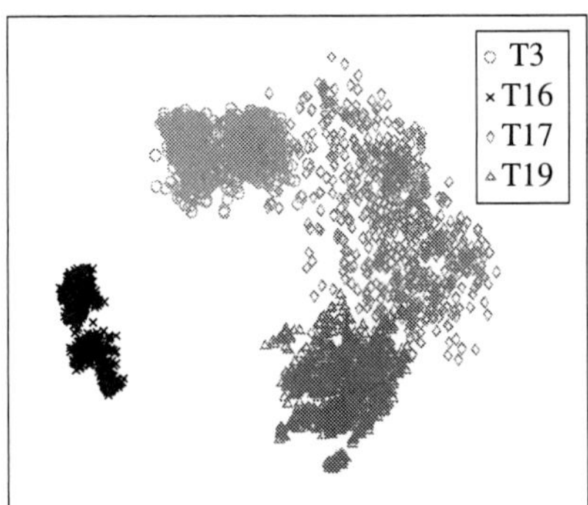

Figure 3: PCA scatter plot of the gating vectors z over tasks 3, 16, 17 and 19.

Acknowledgments

We thank the anonymous reviewers for their valuable feedback, and gratefully acknowledge the support of Australian Government Research Training Program Scholarship. This work was also supported in part by the Australian Research Council.

References

Martín Abadi, Ashish Agarwal, Paul Barham, Eugene Brevdo, Zhifeng Chen, Craig Citro, Greg S. Corrado, Andy Davis, Jeffrey Dean, Matthieu Devin, Sanjay Ghemawat, Ian Goodfellow, Andrew Harp, Geoffrey Irving, Michael Isard, Yangqing Jia, Rafal Jozefowicz, Lukasz Kaiser, Manjunath Kudlur, Josh Levenberg, Dan Mané, Rajat Monga, Sherry Moore, Derek Murray, Chris Olah, Mike Schuster, Jonathon Shlens, Benoit Steiner, Ilya Sutskever, Kunal Talwar, Paul Tucker, Vincent Vanhoucke, Vijay Vasudevan, Fernanda Viégas, Oriol Vinyals, Pete Warden, Martin Wattenberg, Martin Wicke, Yuan Yu, and Xiaoqiang Zheng. 2015. TensorFlow: Large-scale machine learning on heterogeneous systems. Software available from tensorflow.org. https://www.tensorflow.org/.

Dzmitry Bahdanau, Kyunghyun Cho, and Yoshua Bengio. 2014. Neural machine translation by jointly learning to align and translate. In *Proceedings of the 3rd International Conference on Learning Representations (ICLR 2015)*. San Diego, USA.

Antoine Bordes and Jason Weston. 2016. Learning end-to-end goal-oriented dialog. *arXiv preprint arXiv:1605.07683* .

Kyunghyun Cho, Bart Van Merriënboer, Dzmitry Bahdanau, and Yoshua Bengio. 2014. On the properties of neural machine translation: Encoder-decoder approaches. In *Proceedings of SSST-8, Eighth Workshop on Syntax, Semantics and Structure in Statistical Translation*. Doha, Qatar, pages 103–111.

Alex Graves, Abdel-rahman Mohamed, and Geoffrey Hinton. 2013. Speech recognition with deep recurrent neural networks. In *2013 IEEE International Conference on Acoustics, Speech and Signal Processing (ICASSP 2013)*. Vancouver, Canada, pages 6645–6649.

Alex Graves, Greg Wayne, and Ivo Danihelka. 2014. Neural Turing machines. *arXiv preprint arXiv:1410.5401* .

Alex Graves, Greg Wayne, Malcolm Reynolds, Tim Harley, Ivo Danihelka, Agnieszka Grabska-Barwińska, Sergio Gómez Colmenarejo, Edward Grefenstette, Tiago Ramalho, John Agapiou, et al. 2016. Hybrid computing using a neural network with dynamic external memory. *Nature* 538(7626):471–476.

Kaiming He, Xiangyu Zhang, Shaoqing Ren, and Jian Sun. 2016. Deep residual learning for image recognition. In *the 29th IEEE Conference on Computer Vision and Pattern Recognition (CVPR 2016)*. Las Vegas, USA.

Matthew Henderson, Blaise Thomson, and Jason D. Williams. 2014. The second dialog state tracking challenge. In *Proceedings of the 15th Annual Meeting of the Special Interest Group on Discourse and Dialogue (SIGDIAL 2014)*. Philadelphia, USA, pages 263–272.

Sepp Hochreiter and Jürgen Schmidhuber. 1997. Long short-term memory. *Neural computation* 9(8):1735–1780.

Yoon Kim. 2014. Convolutional neural networks for sentence classification. In *Proceedings of the 2014 Conference on Empirical Methods in Natural Language Processing (EMNLP 2014)*. Doha, Qatar.

Diederik Kingma and Jimmy Ba. 2015. Adam: A method for stochastic optimization. In *Proceedings of the 3th International Conference on Learning Representations (ICLR 2015)*. San Diego, USA.

Ankit Kumar, Ozan Irsoy, Jonathan Su, James Bradbury, Robert English, Brian Pierce, Peter Ondruska, Ishaan Gulrajani, and Richard Socher. 2016. Ask me anything: Dynamic memory networks for natural language processing. In *Proceedings of the 33rd International Conference on Machine Learning (ICML 2016)*. New York, USA.

Fei Liu and Julien Perez. 2017. Gated end-to-end memory networks. In *Proceedings of the 15th Conference of the European Chapter of the Association for Computational Linguistics (EACL 2017)*. Valencia, Spain, pages 1–10.

Jack Rae, Jonathan J Hunt, Ivo Danihelka, Timothy Harley, Andrew W Senior, Gregory Wayne, Alex Graves, and Tim Lillicrap. 2016. Scaling memory-augmented neural networks with sparse reads and writes. In *Proceedings of Advances in Neural Information Processing Systems (NIPS 2016)*. Barcelona, Spain, pages 3621–3629.

Minjoon Seo, Sewon Min, Ali Farhadi, and Hannaneh Hajishirzi. 2017. Query-reduction networks for question answering. In *Proceedings of the 5th International Conference on Learning Representations (ICLR 2017)*.

Sainbayar Sukhbaatar, Arthur Szlam, Jason Weston, and Rob Fergus. 2015. End-to-end memory networks. In *Proceedings of Advances in Neural Information Processing Systems (NIPS 2015)*. Montréal, Canada, pages 2440–2448.

Jason Weston, Antoine Bordes, Sumit Chopra, Alexander M Rush, Bart van Merriënboer, Armand Joulin, and Tomas Mikolov. 2016. Towards AI-complete question answering: A set of prerequisite toy tasks. In *Proceedings of the 4th International Conference on Learning Representations (ICLR 2016)*. San Juan, Puerto Rico.

Jason Weston, Sumit Chopra, and Antoine Bordes. 2015. Memory networks. In *Proceedings of the 3rd International Conference on Learning Representations (ICLR 2015)*. San Diego, USA.

Caiming Xiong, Stephen Merity, and Richard Socher. 2016. Dynamic memory networks for visual and textual question answering. In *Proceedings of the 33rd International Conference on Machine Learning (ICML 2016)*. New York, USA, pages 2397–2406.

Joint Sentence–Document Model for Manifesto Text Analysis

Shivashankar Subramanian   Trevor Cohn   Timothy Baldwin   Julian Brooke
School of Computing and Information Systems
University of Melbourne
shivashankar@student.unimelb.edu.au, {t.cohn, tbaldwin, julian.brooke}@unimelb.edu.au

Abstract

Election manifestos document the intentions, motives, and views of political parties. They are often used for analysing party policies and positions on various issues, as well as for quantifying a party's position on the left–right spectrum. In this paper we propose a model for automatically predicting both types of analysis from manifestos, based on a joint sentence–document approach which performs both sentence-level thematic classification and document-level position quantification. Our method handles text in multiple languages, via the use of multilingual vector-space embeddings. We empirically show that the proposed joint model performs better than state-of-art approaches for the document-level task and provides comparable performance for the sentence level task, using manifestos from thirteen countries, written in six different languages.

1   Introduction

Election manifestos are a core artifact in political text analysis. One of the widely used datasets by political scientists is the Comparative Manifesto Project (CMP) dataset, initiated by Volkens et al. (2011), that collects party manifestos from elections in many countries around the world. The goal of the project is to provide a large data collection to support political studies on electoral processes. A sub-part of the manifestos has been manually annotated at the sentence-level with one of over fifty fine-grained political themes, divided into 7 coarse-grained topics (see Table 5). These are important because it can be seen as party positions on fine-grained policy themes and also the

coded text can be used for various downstream tasks (Lowe et al., 2011). While manual annotations are very useful for political analyses, they come with two major drawbacks. First, it is very time-consuming and labor-intensive to manually annotate each sentence with the correct category from a complex annotation scheme. Secondly, coder preferences towards particular categories might lead to annotation inconsistencies and affect comparability between manifestos annotated by different coders (Mikhaylov et al., 2012). In order to overcome these challenges, fine and coarse-level manifesto sentence classification was addressed using supervised machine learning techniques (Verberne et al., 2014; Zirn et al., 2016). Nonetheless, manually-coded manifestos remain the crucial data source for studies in computational political science (Lowe et al., 2011; Nanni et al., 2016).

Other than the sentence-level labels, the manifesto text also has document-level signals, which quantify its position on the left–right spectrum (Slapin and Proksch, 2008). Though sentence-level classification and document-level quantification tasks are inter-dependent, existing work handles them separately. We instead propose a joint approach to model the two tasks together. Overall, the contributions of this work are as follows:

- we empirically study the utility of multilingual embeddings for cross-lingual manifesto text analysis — at the sentence (for 57-class classification) and document-levels (for RILE score regression)

- we evaluate the effectiveness of modelling the sentence- and document-level tasks together

- we study the value of *country* information used in conjunction with text for the

Shivashankar Subramanian, Trevor Cohn, Timothy Baldwin and Julian Brooke. 2017. Joint Sentence-Document Model for Manifesto Text Analysis. In *Proceedings of Australasian Language Technology Association Workshop*, pages 25–33.

document-level regression task.

2 Related Work

The recent adoption of NLP methods has led to significant advances in the field of Computational Social Science (Lazer et al., 2009), including political science (Grimmer and Stewart, 2013). Some popular tasks addressed with political text include: party position analysis (Biessmann, 2016); political leaning categorization (Akoglu, 2014; Zhou et al., 2011); stance classification (Sridhar et al., 2014); identifying keywords, themes & topics (Karan et al., 2016; Ding et al., 2011); emotion analysis (Rheault, 2016); and sentiment analysis (Bakliwal et al., 2013). The source data includes manifestos, political speeches, news articles, floor debates and social media posts.

With the increasing availability of large-scale datasets and computational resources, large-scale comparative political text analysis has gained the attention of political scientists (Lucas et al., 2015). For example, rather than analyzing the political manifestos of a particular party during an election, mining different manifestos across countries over time can provide deeper comparative insights into political change.

Existing classification models, except (Glavaš et al., 2017), utilize discrete representation of text (i.e., bag of words). Also, most of the work analyzes manifesto text at the country level. Recent work has demonstrated the utility of neural embeddings for multi-lingual coarse-level topic classification (7 major categories) over manifesto text (Glavaš et al., 2017). The authors show that multi-lingual embeddings are more effective in the cross-lingual setting, where labeled data is used from multiple languages. In this work, we focus on cross-lingual fine-grained thematic classification (57 categories in total), where we have labeled data for all the languages.

For the document-level quantification task, much work has used label count aggregation of manually-annotated sentences as features (Lowe et al., 2011; Benoit and Däubler, 2014), while other work has used dictionary- based supervised methods, or unsupervised factor analysis based techniques (Hjorth et al., 2015; Bruinsma and Gemenis, 2017). The latter method uses discrete word representations and deals with mono-lingual text only. In Glavas et al. (2017), the authors lever-age neural embeddings for cross-lingual EU parliament speech text quantification with two pivot texts for extreme left and right positions. They represent the documents using word embeddings averaged with TF-IDF scores as weights. All these approaches model the sentence and document-level tasks separately.

3 Manifesto Text Analysis

In the CMP, trained annotators manually label manifesto sentences according to the 57 fine-grained political categories (shown in Table 5), which are grouped into seven policy areas: External Relations, Freedom and Democracy, Political System, Economy, Welfare and Quality of Life, Fabric of Society, and Social Groups. Political parties either write their promises as a bulleted list of individual sentences, or structured as paragraphs (an example is given in Figure 4), providing more information on topic coherence. Also the length of documents, measured as the number of sentences, varies greatly between manifestos. The typical length (in sentences) over manifestos (948 in total) from 13 countries — Austria, Australia, Denmark, Finland, France, Germany, Italy, Ireland, New Zealand, South Africa, Switzerland, United Kingdom and United States — is 516.7±667. Variance in the number of sentences across documents in conjunction with class imbalance makes automated thematic classification a challenging task.

While annotating, a sentence is split into multiple segments if it discusses unrelated topics or different aspects of a larger policy, e.g. (as indicated by the different colors, and associated integer labels):

> We need to address our close ties with our neighbours (107) as well as the unique challenges facing small business owners in this time of economic hardship. (402)

Such examples are not common, however.[1] Also the segmentation was shown to be inconsistent and to have no effect on quantifying the proportion of sentences discussing various topics and document-level regression tasks (Däubler et al., 2012). Hence, consistent with previous work

---

[1] In Däubler et al. (2012), based on a sample of 15 manifestos, the authors noted that around 7.7% of sentences encode multiple topics.

(Biessmann, 2016; Glavaš et al., 2017), we consider the sentence-level classification to be a multi-class single-label problem. We use the segmented text when available (especially for evaluation), and complete sentences otherwise.

A manifesto as a whole can be positioned on the left–right spectrum based on the proportion of topics discussed. We use the RILE score, which is defined as the difference between the count of sentences discussing left- and right-leaning topics (Budge and Laver, 1992):

$$\text{RILE} = \sum_{r \in R} \text{per}_r - \sum_{l \in L} \text{per}_l \qquad (1)$$

where R and L denote right and left political themes (see Figure 5), and per_t denotes the share of each topic t as given in Table 5, per document. Note that the RILE score is provided for almost all the manifestos in the CMP dataset, but the sentence-level annotations are provided only for a subset of manifestos. That is, in some cases, the underlying annotations that the RILE score calculation was based on is often not available for a given manifesto.

4   Proposed Approach

We propose a joint sentence–document model to classify manifesto sentences into one out of 57 categories and also quantify the document-level RILE score. The joint formulation is employed not only to capture the task inter-dependencies, but also to use annotations at different levels of granularity (sentence and document) effectively — a RILE score is available for 948 manifestos from 13 countries, whereas sentence-level annotations are available only for 235 manifestos. We use a hierarchical neural network to model the sentence-level classification and document-level regression tasks. The proposed architecture is given in Figure 1. Since the text across countries is multi-lingual in nature, we use multi-lingual embeddings to represent words (e_w) (Ammar et al., 2016). We refer to the total set of manifestos available for training as D, and the subset which is annotated with sentence-level labels as D_s. We denote each manifesto as d, which has l_d sentences $s_1, s_2, ..., s_{l_d}$. We also use i to index documents ($i{=}d$) wherever necessary to avoid ambiguity in differentiating from sentence-level variables.

4.1   Sentence-level Model

We represent each sentence using the average embedding of its constituent words, $s_j = \frac{1}{|s_j|} \sum_{w \in s_j} e_w$. The average embedding representation is given as input to a hidden layer with rectified linear activation units (ReLU) to get the hidden representation. Finally, the predictions are obtained using a softmax layer, which takes the hidden representation as input and gives the probability of 57 classes as output, denoted $\hat{\mathbf{y}}_{ij}$. We use the cross-entropy loss function for the sentence-level model. For sentences in D_s, with ground truth labels $\mathbf{y}_{ij}$ (using a one-hot encoding), the loss function is given as follows:

$$\mathcal{L}_S = -\frac{1}{|D_s|} \sum_{i=1}^{|D_s|} \sum_{j=1}^{l_d} \sum_{k=1}^{K} y_{ijk} \log \hat{y}_{ijk} \qquad (2)$$

4.2   Joint Sentence–Document Model

Using the hierarchical neural network, we model the sentence-level classification and document-level regression tasks together. In the joint model, we use an unrolled (time-distributed) neural network model for the sentences in a manifesto (d). Here, the model minimizes cross-entropy loss for sentences over each temporal layer ($j = 1 \ldots l_d$). We use average-pooling with the concatenated hidden representations ($\mathbf{h}_{ij}$) and predicted output distributions ($\hat{\mathbf{y}}_{ij}$) of individual sentences, to represent a document,[2] i.e., $\mathbf{r}_d = \frac{1}{|l_d|} \sum_{j \in d} \begin{bmatrix} \hat{\mathbf{y}}_{ij} \\ \mathbf{h}_{ij} \end{bmatrix}$.

The range of RILE is $[-100, 100]$, which we scale to the range $[-1, 1]$. Hence we use a final tanh layer, with $\hat{z}_i = \mathbf{w}_r^\top \mathbf{h}_d + b$, where $\mathbf{h}_d = \text{ReLU}(W_d^\top \mathbf{r}_d)$. Since it is a regression task, we minimize the mean-squared error loss function between the predicted $\hat{z}_i$ and actual RILE score z_i,

$$\mathcal{L}_D = \frac{1}{|D|} \sum_{i=1}^{|D|} ||\hat{z}_i - z_i||_2^2 \qquad (3)$$

Overall, the loss function for the joint model, combining Equations 2 and 3, is:

$$\alpha \mathcal{L}_S + (1 - \alpha)\mathcal{L}_D \qquad (4)$$

where $0 \leq \alpha \leq 1$ is a hyperparameter which is tuned on a development set.

We evaluate both cascaded and joint training for this objective function:

---

[2]We observed that the concatenated representation performed better than using either hidden representation or output distribution.

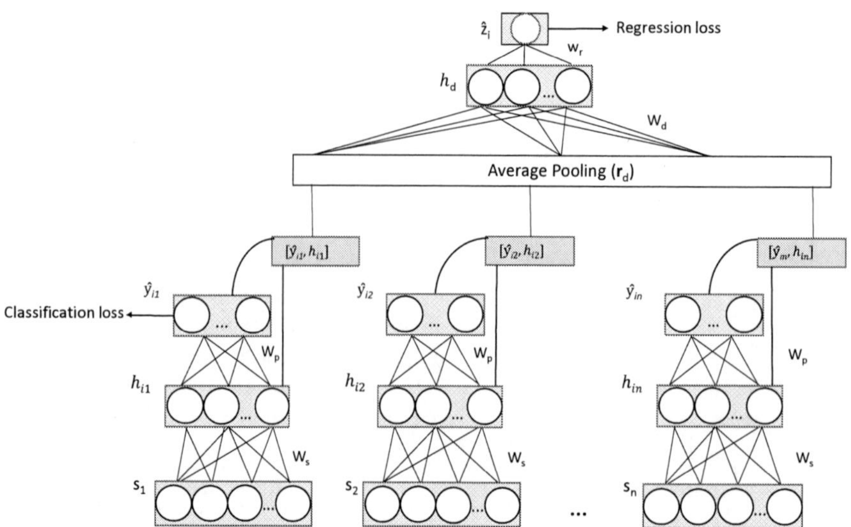

Figure 1: Hierarchical Neural Network for Joint Sentence–Document Analysis. s_1, s_2,...s_n are input sentences ($n=l_d$), W_s and W_p are shared across unrolled sentences. $\hat{\mathbf{y}}_{ij}$ denotes 57 classes and $\hat{z}_i$ denotes the estimated RILE score

Cascaded Training: The sentence-level model is trained using D_s, to minimize $\mathcal{L}_S$ in Equation 2, and the pre-trained sentence-level model is used to obtain document-level representation $\mathbf{r_d}$ for all the manifestos in the training set D. Then the document-level regression task is trained to minimize $\mathcal{L}_D$ from Equation 3. Here, the sentence-level model parameters are fixed when the document-level regression model is trained using $\mathbf{r_d}$.

Joint Training: The entire network is updated by minimizing the joint loss function from Equation 4. As in cascaded training, the sentence-level model is pre-trained using labeled sentences. Here the sentence-level model uses both labeled and unlabeled data.

We use the Adam optimizer (Kingma and Ba, 2014) for parameter estimation. The proposed architecture evaluates the effectiveness of posing sentence-level topic classification as a precursor to perform document-level RILE prediction, rather than learning a model directly. We also study the effect of the quantity of annotated text at both the sentence- and document-level for the RILE prediction task.

5 Experiments

5.1 Setting

As mentioned earlier, we use manifestos collected and annotated by political scientists as part of CMP. In this work, we used 948 manifestos from 13 countries, which are written in 6 different languages — Danish (Denmark), English (Australia, Ireland, New Zealand, South Africa, United Kingdom, United States), Finnish (Finland), French (France), German (Austria, Germany, Switzerland), and Italian (Italy). Out of the 948 manifestos, 235 are annotated with sentence level labels (from Table 5). We have RILE scores for all the 948 manifestos. Statistics about number of annotated documents and sentences across languages are given in Table 1. Class distribution based on average percentage of sentences coded under each class is given in Figure 2. Top-3 frequent set of classes include 000 (above 8%) , 504 (6-8%) and 305 & 503 (4-6%); and 26 classes occur 0-1%.

We use off-the-shelf pre-trained multi-lingual word embeddings[3] to represent words. We empirically chose embeddings trained using translation invariance approach (Ammar et al., 2016), with size 512 for our work. The neural network model has a single hidden layer for all the sentence and document-level approaches.

---

[3] http://128.2.220.95/multilingual

Lang.	# Docs (Ann.)	# Sents (Ann.)
Danish	175 (36)	32161 (8762)
English	312 (94)	227769 (73682)
Finnish	97 (16)	18717 (8503)
French	53 (10)	24596 (5559)
German	216 (65)	146605 (79507)
Italian	95 (14)	40010 (4918)
Total	948 (235)	489858 (180931)

Table 1: Statistics of dataset, 'Ann.' refers to annotated at sentence level.

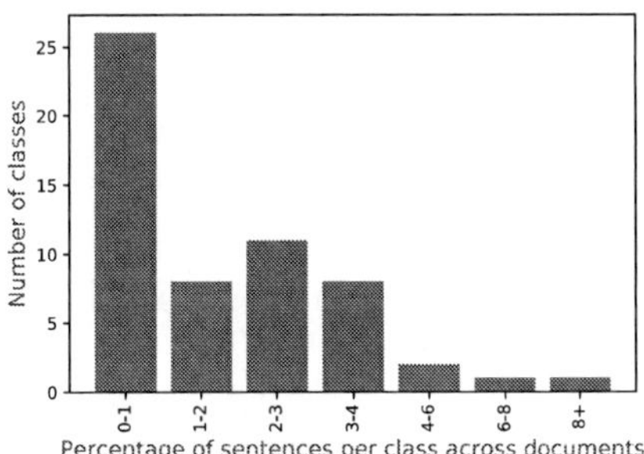

Figure 2: Class distribution based on average percentage of sentences coded under each class

5.2 Sentence-Level Classification

We first compare traditional bag-of-words discrete representation with distributed neural representation for words for fine-grained thematic classification, under mono-lingual training setting (*Mono-lingual*). Hence we compare the following approaches.

Bag-of-words (*BoW-LR*, BoW-NN): We use TF-IDF representation for sentences and build a model for each language separately. We use Logistic Regression classifier (Biessmann, 2016), which is referred as *BoW-LR*. We also use Neural Network classifier, which we refer to as *BoW-NN*.

Language-wise average embedding (*AE-NN$_m$*): We build a neural network classifier per language, with average multi-lingual neural embedding as sentence representation.

Since distributed representation allows to leverage text across languages, we evaluate the following approaches with combined training sentences across languages (*Cross-lingual*).

Convolutional Neural Network (*CNN*): CNN was shown to be effective for cross-lingual manifesto text coarse-level topic classification (Glavaš et al., 2017). So, we evaluate CNN with a similar architecture — single convolution layer (32 filters with window size 3), followed by single max pooling layer and finally a softmax layer. We use multi-lingual neural embeddings to represent words.

Combined average embedding (*AE-NN$_c$*): We build a neural network classifier with training instances combined across languages, with average neural embedding as sentence representation. This is our proposed approach for sentence-level model.

Commonly for all empirical evaluations, we compute micro-averaged performance with 80-20% train-test ratio across 10 runs with random split (at document level), where the 80% split also contains sentence level annotated documents proportionally. Optimal model parameters we found for the proposed model (Figure 1) are $|\mathbf{h}_{ij}| = 300$ (for sentences), $|\mathbf{h}_d| = 10$. We compute F-score[4] to evaluate sentence classification performance. Sentence classification performance is given in Table 2. Under mono-lingual setting (Table 2), using word embeddings did not provide better performance compared to bag-of-words.

Under cross-lingual setting, *AE-NN$_c$* is the sentence-level neural network model. We use *AE-NN$_c$* in the *cascaded training* for obtaining document-level RILE prediction. Note that in *cascaded training*, sentence and document-level models are trained separately in a cascaded fashion. Joint-training results where the sentence model is trained in a semi-supervised way together with document-level regression task is referred to as *JT$_s$*. We set α=0.4 (in equation 4) empirically which gave the best score for both sentence and document-level tasks. We observed a trade-off in performance with different α, with lesser α (0.1), document-level correlation increases (to 0.52) while sentence-level F-score decreases (to 0.33). Higher value of α (0.9) gives performance closer to cascaded training. *JT$_s$* has a comparable performance with *AE-NN$_c$*. The proposed approach (joint-training) does not provide any improvement for the sentence classification task.

---

[4]Harmonic mean of precision and recall, `https://en.wikipedia.org/wiki/F1_score`

| | Mono-lingual | | | Cross-lingual | | |
Lang.	*BoW-LR*	*BoW-NN*	*AE-NN$_m$*	*CNN*	*AE-NN$_c$*	*JT$_s$*
da	0.29	**0.35**	0.24	0.30	0.28	0.30
en	0.36	0.38	**0.42**	0.40	**0.42**	0.41
fi	0.21	0.29	0.26	**0.30**	0.27	0.26
fr	0.28	0.36	0.24	0.36	0.37	**0.38**
de	0.30	0.31	0.31	0.31	0.31	**0.33**
it	0.32	**0.33**	0.25	0.30	0.32	0.26
Avg.	0.32	0.34	0.35	0.34	**0.36**	0.35

Table 2: Micro-Averaged F-measure for sentence classification. Best scores are given in bold.

5.3 Document-Level Regression

For the document-level regression task, the following are baseline approaches. Note that we use tanh output for all the models, since the range of re-scaled RILE is from -1 to +1.

Bag-of-words (*BoW-NN$_d$*): We use TF-IDF representation for documents and build a neural network model for each language.

Average embedding (*AE-NN$_d$*): We use average embedding of words as document representation to build a neural network model.

Bag-of-Centroids (*BoC*): Here the word embeddings are clustered into K different clusters using K-Means clustering algorithm, and words (1-gram) in each document are assigned to clusters based on its euclidean-distance (dist) to cluster-centroids (C) (Lebret and Collobert, 2014),

$$\text{cluster}(w) = \underset{k}{\text{argmin}}\,\text{dist}(C_k, w).$$

Finally, each document is represented by the distribution of words mapped to different clusters ($1 \times K$ vector). We use a neural network regression model with bag-of-centroids representation. Results with K=1000, which performed best is given in Table 3.

Sentence-level model and RILE formulation (*AE-NN$_c^{rile}$*): Here the predictions of sentence-level model (*AE-NN$_c$*) are used directly with RILE formulation (equation (1)) to derive RILE score for manifestos.

Cross-lingual scaling (*CLS*): This is a recent unsupervised approach for cross-lingual political speech text positioning task (Glavas

Approach	MSE($\downarrow$)	$r(\uparrow)$
BoW-NN$_d$	0.054	0.23
AE-NN$_d$	0.057	0.14
BoC	0.052	0.33
AE-NN$_c^{rile}$	0.060	0.35
CLS	–	0.24
Cas$_d$	0.050	0.41
JT$_d$	**0.044**	**0.47**

Table 3: RILE score prediction performance. Best scores are given in bold (higher is better for r, and lower is better for MSE).

et al., 2017). Authors use average word-embeddings weighed by TF-IDF score to represent documents.[5] Then a graph is constructed using pair-wise distance of documents. Given two pivots texts for extreme left and right positions [-1, +1], label propagation approach is used to quantify other documents in the graph.

RILE score regression performance results are given in Table 3. Other than *BoW-NN$_d$* all other approaches are cross-lingual. We evaluate document-level performance using mean-squared-error (MSE) and Pearson correlation (r). Since *CLS* solves it as a classification problem, MSE is not applicable. The proposed approach's performance, using cascaded training is referred to as *Cas$_d$* and jointly trained model is referred to as *JT$_d$*. Overall the jointly trained model performs best for document-level task, with a comparable performance at sentence-level task.

---

[5]We use this aggregate representation since it was shown to be better than word alignment and scoring approach (Glavas et al., 2017)

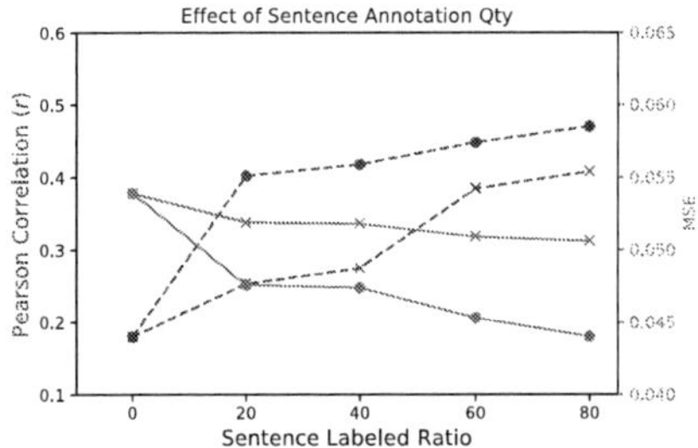

(a) Fixing 80% training documents with RILE score, ratio of documents with sentence-level annotations is varied.

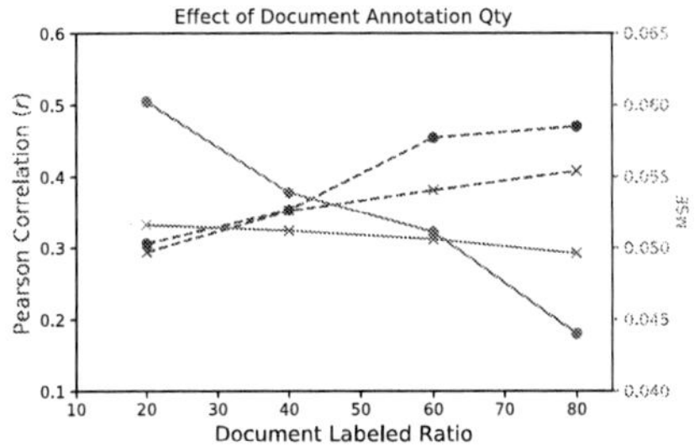

(b) Fixing 80% training documents with sentence-level annotations, ratio of documents with RILE score is varied.

Figure 3: Study with Quantity of Annotation. In 3(a) and 3(b) cross(×) denotes Cas_d and circle(○) denotes JT_d

Approach	MSE	r
stack	0.045 (0.001 ↓)	0.49 (0.02 ↑)
non-linear stack	0.048 (0.004 ↓)	0.48 (0.01 ↑)

Table 4: RILE score prediction performance with *country* information. Difference compared to JT_d is given within paranthesis. ↑ – improvement, ↓ – decrease in performance

5.5 Use of Country Information

Since the definition of left–right varies between countries, we study the influence of *country* information in the proposed model with *joint-training*. We use two ways to incorporate country information (Hoang et al., 2016): (a) *stack* — one-hot encoding (13 countries, 1×13 vector) of each manifesto's *country* is concatenated with hidden representation of the document ($\mathbf{r}_d$ in Figure 1) (b) *non-linear stack* — one-hot-encoded country vector is passed through a hidden layer with tanh non-linear activation and concatenated with $\mathbf{r}_d$. With both the models we observed mild improvement in correlation (given in Table 4).

5.4 Quantity of Annotation

We measure the importance of annotated text at sentence and document-level for RILE score regression task. We vary the percentage of labeled data, while keeping the test sample size at 20% as before. In the first setting, we keep the training ratio of documents at 80%, within that 80% we increase the proportion of documents with sentence-level annotations — from 0 (document average embedding setting, AE-NN_d) to 80%. Results are given in Figure 3a. Similarly, in the other setting, we keep the training set with 80% sentence-level annotated documents (which is ∼20% of the total data), and add documents (with only RILE score), increasing the training set from 20 to 80%. Results of this study are given in Figure 3b. We observed that, jointly-trained model uses sentence-level annotations more effectively than cascaded approach (Figure 3a) — even with less sentence-level annotations. Also, with less document-level signal (up to 40%) for training, both the approaches perform similarly (r). As the training ratio increases, joint-training leverages both sentence and document-level signals effectively.

6   Conclusion and Future Work

In this work we evaluated the utility of a joint sentence–document model for sentence-level thematic classification and document-level RILE score regression tasks. Our observations are as follows: (a) joint model performs better than state-of-art approaches for document-level regression task (b) joint-training leverages sentence-level annotations more effectively than cascaded approach for RILE score regression task, with no gains for sentence classification task. There are many extensions possible to the current work. First is to handle class imbalance in the dataset with a cost-sensitive objective function. Secondly, CNN gave a comparable performance with Neural Network, which motivates the need to evaluate an end-end sequential architecture to obtain sentence and document embeddings. Off-the-shelf embeddings leads to out-of-vocabulary scenarios. It could be beneficial to adapt word-embeddings with manifesto corpus. Finally, background information such as country can be leveraged more effectively.

During our nation's darkest hours, Americans have strived mightily and succeeded in meeting the challenges of their times∫ The question before us is whether we will do the same during this bright moment;∫whether we will seize this moment to bring more prosperity and progress to more Americans than ever before;∫whether, having finally conquered our financial deficits, we will have the courage to conquer the other deficits – in health care, in education, in the environment – that challenge us today.∫

601
606
410
305

Figure 4: Manifesto snippet for Democratic Party of USA, 2000 — ∫ denotes sentence segment. See Table 5 for code description.

CMP Coding Scheme

- Domain 1. External Relations
101 Foreign Special Relationships: Positive
102 Foreign Special Relationships: Negative
103 Anti-Imperialism
104 Military: Positive
105 Military: Negative
106 Peace
107 Internationalism: Positive
108 European Community/Union: Positive
109 Internationalism: Negative
110 European Community/Union: Negative

- Domain 2: Freedom and Democracy
201 Freedom and Human Rights
202 Democracy
203 Constitutionalism: Positive
204 Constitutionalism: Negative

- Domain 3: Political System
301 Decentralisation
302 Centralisation
303 Governmental and Administrative Efficiency
304 Political Corruption
305 Political Authority

- Domain 4: Economy
401 Free Market Economy
402 Incentives: Positive
403 Market Regulation
404 Economic Planning
405 Corporatism/Mixed Economy
406 Protectionism: Positive
407 Protectionism: Negative
408 Economic Goals
409 Keynesian Demand Management
410 Economic Growth: Positive

411 Technology and Infrastructure: Positive
412 Controlled Economy
413 Nationalisation
414 Economic Orthodoxy
415 Marxist Analysis
416 Anti-Growth Economy: Positive

- Domain 5: Welfare and Quality of Life
501 Environmental Protection
502 Culture: Positive
503 Equality: Positive
504 Welfare State Expansion
505 Welfare State Limitation
506 Education Expansion
507 Education Limitation

- Domain 6: Fabric of Society
601 National Way of Life: Positive
602 National Way of Life: Negative
603 Traditional Morality: Positive
604 Traditional Morality: Negative
605 Law and Order: Positive
606 Civic Mindedness: Positive
607 Multiculturalism: Positive
608 Multiculturalism: Negative

- Domain 7: Social Groups
701 Labour Groups: Positive
702 Labour Groups: Negative
703 Agriculture and Farmers: Positive
704 Middle Class and Professional Groups
705 Underprivileged Minority Groups
706 Non-economic Demographic Groups

000 No meaningful category applies

Table 5: Comparative Manifesto Project — 57 policy themes. *Left* topics are given in *red* and *right* topics are given in *blue* and the *rest* are considered neutral

References

Leman Akoglu. 2014. Quantifying political polarity based on bipartite opinion networks. In *AAAI*.

Waleed Ammar, George Mulcaire, Yulia Tsvetkov, Guillaume Lample, Chris Dyer, and Noah A Smith. 2016. Massively multilingual word embeddings. *arXiv preprint arXiv:1602.01925* .

Akshat Bakliwal, Jennifer Foster, Jennifer van der Puil, Ron O'Brien, Lamia Tounsi, and Mark Hughes. 2013. Sentiment analysis of political tweets: Towards an accurate classifier. In *ACL*.

Kenneth Benoit and Thomas Däubler. 2014. Putting text in context: How to estimate better left-right positions by scaling party manifesto data using item response theory. In *Mapping Policy Preferences from Texts Conference*.

Felix Biessmann. 2016. Automating political bias prediction. In *arXiv:1608.02195*.

B. Bruinsma and K. Gemenis. 2017. Validating Wordscores. *ArXiv e-prints* .

Ian Budge and Michael Laver. 1992. *Party policy and government coalitions*. St. Martin's Press New York.

Thomas Däubler, Kenneth Benoit, Slava Mikhaylov, and Michael Laver. 2012. Natural sentences as valid units for coded political texts. *British Journal of Political Science* .

Zhuoye Ding, Qi Zhang, and Xuanjing Huang. 2011. Keyphrase extraction from online news using binary integer programming. In *IJCNLP*.

Goran Glavaš, Federico Nanni, and Simone Paolo Ponzetto. 2017. Cross-lingual classification of topics in political texts. In *ACL WS*.

Goran Glavas, Federico Nanni, and Simone Paolo Ponzetto. 2017. Unsupervised cross-lingual scaling of political texts. In *EACL*.

Justin Grimmer and Brandon M Stewart. 2013. Text as data: The promise and pitfalls of automatic content analysis methods for political texts. *Political analysis* .

Frederik Hjorth, Robert Klemmensen, Sara Hobolt, Martin Ejnar Hansen, and Peter Kurrild-Klitgaard. 2015. Computers, coders, and voters: Comparing automated methods for estimating party positions. *Research & Politics* .

Cong Duy Vu Hoang, Gholamreza Haffari, and Trevor Cohn. 2016. Incorporating side information into recurrent neural network language models. In *NAACL-HLT*.

Mladen Karan, Jan Šnajder, Daniela Širinic, and Goran Glavaš. 2016. Analysis of policy agendas: Lessons learned from automatic topic classification of croatian political texts. In *LaTeCH*.

Diederik P. Kingma and Jimmy Ba. 2014. Adam: A method for stochastic optimization. *CoRR* abs/1412.6980.

David Lazer, Alex Sandy Pentland, Lada Adamic, Sinan Aral, Albert Laszlo Barabasi, Devon Brewer, Nicholas Christakis, Noshir Contractor, James Fowler, Myron Gutmann, et al. 2009. Life in the network: the coming age of computational social science. *Science (New York, NY)* 323(5915):721.

Rémi Lebret and Ronan Collobert. 2014. N-gram-based low-dimensional representation for document classification. *arXiv preprint arXiv:1412.6277* .

Will Lowe, Kenneth Benoit, Slava Mikhaylov, and Michael Laver. 2011. Scaling policy preferences from coded political texts. In *Legislative studies quarterly*. Wiley Online Library.

Christopher Lucas, Richard A Nielsen, Margaret E Roberts, Brandon M Stewart, Alex Storer, and Dustin Tingley. 2015. Computer-assisted text analysis for comparative politics. *Political Analysis* 23(2):254–277.

Slava Mikhaylov, Michael Laver, and Kenneth R Benoit. 2012. Coder reliability and misclassification in the human coding of party manifestos. In *Political Analysis*.

Federico Nanni, Cäcilia Zirn, Goran Glavaš, Jason Eichorst, and Simone Paolo Ponzetto. 2016. Topfish: topic-based analysis of political position in us electoral campaigns. In *PolText*.

Ludovic Rheault. 2016. Expressions of anxiety in political texts. In *NLP+ CSS 2016*. page 92.

Jonathan B Slapin and Sven-Oliver Proksch. 2008. A scaling model for estimating time-series party positions from texts. Wiley Online Library, volume 52, pages 705–722.

Dhanya Sridhar, Lise Getoor, and Marilyn Walker. 2014. Collective stance classification of posts in online debate forums. In *ACL*.

Suzan Verberne, Eva D'hondt, Antal van den Bosch, and Maarten Marx. 2014. Automatic thematic classification of election manifestos. In *Information Processing & Management*.

Andrea Volkens, Onawa Lacewell, and Sven Regel Henrike Schultzeand Annika Werner. Pola Lehmann. 2011. The manifesto data collection. manifesto project (mrg/cmp/marpor). In *Wissenschaftszentrum Berlin fur Sozialforschung (WZB)*.

Daniel Xiaodan Zhou, Paul Resnick, and Qiaozhu Mei. 2011. Classifying the political leaning of news articles and users from user votes. In *ICWSM*.

Cäcilia Zirn, Goran Glavaš, Federico Nanni, Jason Eichorts, and Heiner Stuckenschmidt. 2016. Classifying topics and detecting topic shifts in political manifestos. In *PolText*.

Leveraging linguistic resources for improving neural text classification

Ming Liu
FIT, Monash University
ming.m.liu@monash.edu

Gholamreza Haffari
FIT, Monash University
gholamreza.haffari@monash.edu

Wray Buntine
FIT, Monash University
wray.buntine@monash.edu

Michelle R. Ananda-Rajah
Alfred Health and Monash University
michelle.ananda-rajah@monash.edu

Abstract

This paper presents a deep linguistic attentional framework which incorporates word level concept information into neural classification models. While learning neural classification models often requires a large amount of labelled data, linguistic concept information can be obtained from external knowledge, such as pre-trained word embeddings, WordNet for common text and MetaMap for biomedical text. We explore two different ways of incorporating word level concept annotations, and show that leveraging concept annotations can boost the model performance and reduce the need for large amounts of labelled data. Experiments on various data sets validate the effectiveness of the proposed method.

1 Introduction

Text classification is an important task in natural language processing, such as sentiment analysis, information retrieval, web page ranking and document classification (Pang et al., 2008). Recently, deep neural models have been widely used in this area due to their abstract framework and good performance. While these models are being used frequently, they require a large amount of labelled data and training time.

The core idea of text neural classification models is that text signals are fed into composition and activation functions via deep neural networks, and then a softmax classifier generates the final label as a probability distribution. Unlike standard n-gram models, word representation (Mikolov et al., 2013) is distributed and manual features are not usually necessary in deep neural models.

Though promising, most current text neural classification models still lack the ability of mod-eling linguistic information of the language, especially in domains where annotations are time-consuming and expensive such as biomedical text. In this work, we use some prior knowledge from pre-trained word embeddings or knowledge bases, and explore different ways of incorporating this prior knowledge into existing deep neural classification models. Our model is an integration of a simple neural bag of words model, which works in 2 steps:

1. create mappings from a sequence of word tokens into concept tokens (based on the given pre-trained word embeddings or knowledge bases),

2. combine the embeddings of both word and concept tokens and pass the resulting embedding through a deep feed-forward classification model to make the final prediction.

The motivation of our work is to incorporate extra knowledge from pre-trained word embeddings or knowledge bases such as WordNet for common text, MetaMap for biomedical text. Our main contributions are: (1) creating linguistically-related concepts of words from external knowledge bases; (2) incorporating the concept information either through what we call direct or gated mappings. We show that leveraging concept annotations can boost the model performance and reduce the need for large amounts of labelled data, and the concept information can be incorporated more effectively in a gated mapping manner.

The remainder of this paper is organized as follows. Section 2 reviews the related work. Section 3 introduces the architecture of incorporating concept information. Data sets and implementation details are described in section 4. Section 5 demonstrates the effectiveness of our method with experiments. Finally, section 6 offers concluding remarks.

Ming Liu, Gholamreza Haffari, Wray Buntine and Michelle Ananda-Rajah. 2017. Leveraging linguistic resources for improving neural text classification. In *Proceedings of Australasian Language Technology Association Workshop*, pages 34–42.

2 Related Work

This section describes some related work on deep neural models for text classification and several common knowledge bases.

2.1 Text classification with deep neural models

Composition functions play a key role in many deep neural models. Generally, composition functions fall into two categories: unordered and syntactic. Unordered functions regard input text as bags of word embeddings (Iyyer et al., 2015), while syntactic models take word order and sentence structure into account (Mikolov et al., 2010; Socher et al., 2013b). Previously published results have shown that syntactic models have outperformed unordered ones on many tasks. RecNN-based approaches (Socher et al., 2011, 2013a,b) rely on parsing trees to construct the semantic function, in which each leaf node in the tree corresponds to a word. Recursive neural models then compute parent vectors in a bottom up fashion using different types of compositionality functions. While parsing is the first step, RecNNs are restricted to modelling short text like sentences rather than documents. Recurrent neural networks (RNNs) (Mikolov et al., 2010) are another natural choice to model text due to their capability of processing arbitrary-length sequences. Unfortunately, a problem with RNNs is that the transition function inside can cause the gradient vector to grow or decay exponentially over long sequences. The LSTM architecture (Hochreiter and Schmidhuber, 1997) addresses this problem by introducing a memory cell that is able to preserve state over a long period of time. Tree-LSTM (Tai et al., 2015) is an extension of standard LSTM in that Tree-LSTM computes its hidden state from the current input and the hidden states of arbitrarily many child units. Convolutional networks (Kalchbrenner et al., 2014) also model word order in local windows and have achieved performance comparable or better than that of RecNNs or RNNs on many tasks.

While models that use syntactic functions need large training time and data, unordered functions allow a tradeoff between training time and model complexity. Unlike some of the previous syntactic approaches, paragraph vector (Le and Mikolov, 2014) is capable of constructing representations of input sequences of variable length. It does not require task-specific tuning of the word weighting function nor does it rely on the parse trees. A compatible unordered method is also used in DANs (Iyyer et al., 2015), which averages the embeddings for all of a document's tokens and feeds that average through multiple layers. They show non-linearly transforming the input is more important than tailoring a network to incorporate word order and syntax.

2.2 Exploiting linguistic resources

Besides distributed word representation, there exist many large-scale knowledge bases (KBs) in general or specific domains that can be used as prior information for text classification models. WordNet (Miller, 1995) is the most widely used lexical reference system which organizes nouns, verbs, adjectives and adverbs into synonym sets (synsets). Synsets are interlinked by a number of conceptual-semantic and lexical relations such as hypernym, synonym and meronym, etc. WordNet has already been used in reducing vector dimensionality for many text clustering tasks and showed that the lexical categories within it is quite useful. It includes a core ontology and a lexicon. The latest version is WordNet 3.0 which consists of 155,287 lexical entries and 117,659 synsets.

In the medical domain, some domain knowledge that may be useful to classifiers is also available in the form of existing knowledge sources (Baud et al., 1996). The UMLS (Bodenreider, 2004) knowledge sources provide huge amounts of linguistic information readily available to the medical community. SNOMED (Spackman et al., 1997) is today the largest source of medical vocabulary (132,643 entries) organised in a systematic way. The GALEN (Rector, 1995) consortium is working together since 1992 and has produced, using the GRAIL representation language, a general model of medicine with nearly 6,000 concepts. The MED (Medical Entities Dictionary) (Cimino, 2000) is a large repository of medical concepts that are drawn from a variety of sources either developed or used at the New York Presbyterian Hospital, including the UMLS, ICD9-CM and LOINC. Currently numbering over 100,000, these concepts correspond to coded terms used in systems and applications throughout both medical centers (Columbia-Presbyterian and New York-Cornell). MetaMap (Aronson, 2001) was developed to map biomedical free text to biomedical knowledge representation in which concepts were classified by semantic type and both hierarchical and non-hierarchical relationships among the concepts. In spite of the fact that KBs play an important role for biomedical NLP tasks, to the best of our knowledge, there is little work on integrating KBs with word embedding models for biomedical NLP tasks.

In this paper, we propose models which incorporate concept information from such external knowledge as word clusters in pre-trained word embeddings or different knowledge bases. This prior concept knowledge is leveraged and fed into a neural bag of words model through a weighted composition. We explore two different ways of incorporation and show that our model can achieve near state of art performance on different text classification tasks.

3 The Model

In this paper, we investigate the feasibility of incorporating prior knowledge from pre-trained word embeddings and various knowledge bases into a traditional neural classification model. As an initial task, we aim to find out what kind of knowledge bases can be used for different domains and how the model can benefit from the additional common and specific concept information.

Assume that we have L training examples $\{X^d, y^d\}_{d=1}^{|L|}$, X^d is composed of a word sequence $\{x_i^d\}_{i=1}^{|X^d|}$. Suppose we have M knowledge bases $\mathcal{C}^{(j)}$, $j \in \{1, 2, 3, ..., M\}$ and define a mapping: $\mathcal{V} \rightarrow \mathcal{C}^{(j)}$ from a word into a specific concept or topic, i.e. $\mathcal{C}^{(j)} = \{c_1^j, ..., c_K^j\}$, where $x \in \mathcal{V}$ and $c_k^j \in \mathcal{C}^{(j)}$. With each knowledge base $\mathcal{C}^{(j)}$, similar words are to be gathered in the same group with the same topic or concept. For instance, given the sentence *Since the previous examination much of the ground-glass opacity identified has resolved.* We could have such concept annotations based on different lexical resources:

- **WordNet** *Previous[adj.pertainyms] examination[noun.quantity] opacity[noun.state] identify[verb.peception] resolve[verb.change]*

- **MetaMap** *Previous[Temporal Concept] examination[Therapeutic or Preventive Procedure] opacity[Finding]*

identified[Qualitative Concept] resolved[Conceptual Entity]

The question is how to incorporate the word level concept information into existing neural classification models. In the following, we first describe a simple and effective neural bag-of-words model, and explore two different ways of incorporating linguistic concept information into the model. We also find the sources which can provide different concept annotations.

3.1 Neural bag of words model

The Neural bag-of-words model (NBOW) differs from traditional bag-of-words model in that each word in a sequence is represented by a distributed rather than one-hot representation. With the above assumption, the model maps an input document $\{x_i\}_{i=1}^{|X^d|}$ into y with m labels. We first apply a composition function to average the sequence of word embeddings $e(x_i)$ for $x_i \in X$. The output of this composition function is fed into a logistic regression function.

To be specific, in an initial setting of NBOW, we can get an averaged word embedding z for any set of words $\{x_i\}_{i=1}^{|X|}$:

$$z = \frac{1}{|\boldsymbol{X}|} \sum_{i=1}^{|\boldsymbol{X}|} e(x_i).$$

Feeding z to a softmax layer gives probability for each output label:

$$\hat{y} = \text{softmax}(\boldsymbol{W}_s \cdot \boldsymbol{z} + \boldsymbol{b}).$$

Alternatively, more layers can be created on top of z to generate more abstract representations. The objective function is to minimize the cross entropy error, which for a single training example with true label y is:

$$\ell\,(\hat{y}) = -\sum_{p=1}^{m} y_p \log(\hat{y}_p).$$

The following section will describe how we extend this NBOW model by integrating linguistic concept information into z.

3.2 Incorporating Linguistic Concept Information

Direct mapping: Given a document $\{x_i\}_{i=1}^{|X|}$, we can get the corresponding annotations $\{c_i^j\}_{i=1}^{|X|}$ based on $\mathcal{C}^{(j)}, j = \{1, ..., M\}$, which means additional input is available for the classifier. The question is how we can effectively make use of these annotations based on various $\mathcal{C}^{(j)}, j = \{1, ..., M\}$. In order to represent these concept information, we design two model variants, the first

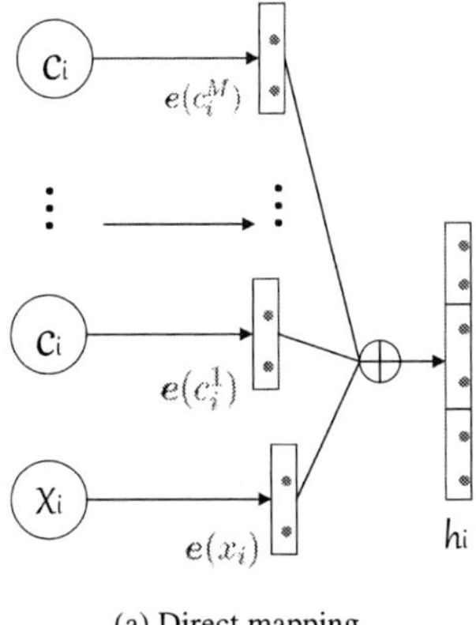

(a) Direct mapping.

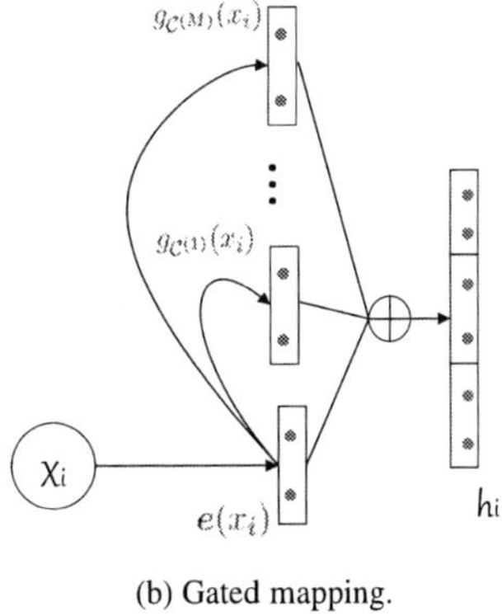

(b) Gated mapping.

Figure 1: Direct and gated mapping.

one is conducted by direct mapping, and the second one is done through gated mapping.

With direct mapping, the embeddings for a specific token x_i and its concept annotation c_i are initialized separately. Therefore, the input for the following composition function is the concatenation of $e(x_i)$ and $e(c_i^j), j = \{1, ..., M\}$. In this case, the new hidden representation for x_i is h_i:

$$h_i = e(x_i) \oplus e(c_i^1) \oplus ... \oplus e(c_i^M).$$

Gated mapping: Gated mapping leads to a concept representation by sharing weight with the word representation, the mapping is conducted through a non-linear transformation $g(x)$ instead of direct initialization.:

$$g_{\mathcal{C}(j)}(x_i) = \tanh(W_{\mathcal{C}(j)} \cdot e(x_i) + b_{\mathcal{C}(j)}),$$

where $W_{\mathcal{C}(j)}$ is a three dimensional weight indexing matrix which corresponds to different knowledge bases, $b_{\mathcal{C}(j)}$ is the bias vector. Hence, the new hidden representation is h_i:

$$h_i = e(x_i) \oplus g_{\mathcal{C}(1)}(x_i) \oplus ... \oplus g_{\mathcal{C}(M)}(x_i).$$

The resulted gated representation thus computes concept embedding by transforming the original word embeddings from a word semantic space into a concept semantic space based on the given concept annotations.

Figure 1 shows the difference between these two methods. The steps for feeding the newly concatenated word-concept vector h_i into the following layers is the same. But not all words contribute equally to the representation of the document meaning, we further introduce an attention mechanism to extract such words that are important to the meaning of the document and aggre-

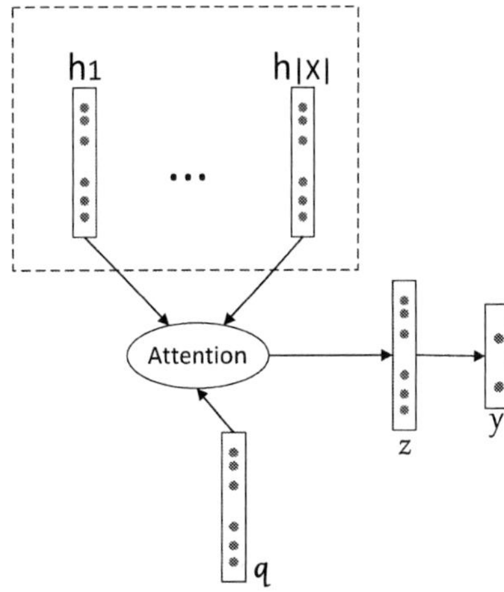

Figure 2: Framework of our model

gate the representation of those informative words to form a single hidden vector. Specifically, we introduce a context vector q,

$$u_i = \tanh(W_q \cdot h_i + b_q),$$
$$\alpha_i = \frac{\exp(u_i^T q)}{\sum_{i=1}^{|X|} \exp(u_i^T q)},$$
$$z = \sum_{i=1}^{|X|} \alpha_i h_i.$$

With z, the final prediction is made with a softmax layer:

$$\hat{y} = \text{softmax}(W_s \cdot z + b).$$

Figure 2 gives the framework of our model. The two variants of the model are neural bag of words with either direct or gated mapping.

3.3 Sources of concept information

We collect concept annotation from three sources: the word clusters returned by GloVe word embeddings, lexical categories from WordNet, and biomedical concepts from MetaMap.

Word clusters from GloVe word embeddings Global K-means clustering algorithm (Likas et al., 2003) is used to create K word clusters from pre-trained GloVe word embeddings (Pennington et al., 2014). The algorithm is conducted in an incremental approach: To create K word clusters, all intermediate problems with $1, 2, ..., K - 1$ clusters are sequentially solved. The core idea of this method is that an optimal solution for a clustering problem with K clusters can be obtained by using a series of local optimal searches. We tested different K which varies from 50 to 200.

WordNet lexical categories By using WordNet lexical categories we have mapped each word remained after the preprocessing to lexical categories. WordNet 3.0 (Miller, 1995) offers categorization of 155,287 words into 44 WordNet lexical categories. Since many words may have different categories, a word sense disambiguation technique is required in order to not add noise to the later concept mapping. We use disambiguation by context (Hotho et al., 2003). This technique returns the concept which maximizes a function depending on the conceptual vicinity.

MetaMap concepts MetaMap (Aronson, 2001) provides 133 specific concepts for biomedical words.

4 Datasets and implementation details

In this section, we introduce our experimental datasets and some implementation details.

4.1 Datasets

We select 3 datasets of different sizes, corresponding to varying classification tasks. Some statistics about these datasets is summarized in Table 1.

20 Newsgroups This is a news categorization dataset (Lang, 1995). It has a collection of approximately 20,000 newsgroup documents, partitioned (nearly) evenly across 20 different newsgroups. Some of the newsgroups are very closely related to each other, while others are highly unrelated. Each news belongs to one out of 20 labels.

IMDB This core dataset (Maas et al., 2011) contains 50,000 reviews which are divided evenly into 25k train and 25k test sets. The overall distribution of labels is balanced (25k positive and 25k negative).

CT reports Additionally, we use 1000 CT scan reports (Martinez et al., 2015) with either positive or negative labels for fungal disease. These reports have technical medical content and highly specialized conventions, which are arguably the most distant genre from the above three datasets.

4.2 Implementation details

Preprocessing The same preprocessing steps were used for all the datasets. We lower-cased all the tokens, removed stop words and replaced those low-frequency tokens with a UNK representation. All the numbers were replaced with a NUM symbol. Specifically, since all the CT reports were obtained from local hospitals, any potentially identifying information such as name, address, age, birthday and gender were removed. For each CT report, we used the free-text section, which contains the radiologist's interpretation of the scan and the reason for the requested scan as written by clinicians.

Word embeddings For the first 2 datasets, we initialized word embeddings with the GloVe word vectors with 400 thousand vocabulary and 6 billion tokens. For the out-of-vocabulary words, we initialized their word embeddings randomly. For pathology reports, we have another 6000 CT documents which are unannotated by doctors. Therefore, a specific biomedical word embedding was randomly initialized with both unlabelled and labelled training data alongside other model parameters. The embedding dimension is set to be 100 for biomedical text and 300 for news and review text.

Learning and hyperparameters To avoid overfitting, a dropout rate 0.3 is used on the word embedding layer (Srivastava et al., 2014). Mini-batch size is 32, the update method is AdaGrad (Duchi et al., 2011), the initial learning rate is 0.01. During training, we conduct experiments in the following to see if word embedding update during training can have an effect on the model performance. For all experiments, we iterate over the training set for 10 times, and pick the model which has the least training loss as the final model, all the

Dataset		Number of docs.				
	Classes	Total	Training	Development	Test	Vocab. size
20News	20	18.8k	10.3k	1k	7.5k	218k
IMDB	2	50k	23k	2k	25k	116K
CT reports	2	1.0k	-	-	-	4.4k

Table 1: Statistics about the four datasets used in our experiments.

results on the test sets are performed from the final models.

5 Experiments

We evaluate the two variants of our model with 5 types of concept information incorporation: word clusters returned by applying K-means to GloVe word vectors, lexical categories returned from WordNet, biomedical concepts from MetaMap, both clusters returned from GloVe clusters and WordNet, and all the concepts from the three knowledge sources. We first do concept annotation from GloVe word clusters and manage to find out the best K for clustering GloVe words, then see whether concept information from different knowledge bases help and compare in each case to several strong baselines.

5.1 Choosing the number of GloVe embedding clusters

We assumed the number of concept clusters (K) would have an impact on the model performance, therefore we have to test K for different datasets accordingly. For 20News and IMDB, we used 10% of the training set as development data. For CT reports, we used 10-fold cross validation. In the following, we use NBOW-DM and NBOW-GM to represent our two model variants, the direct mapping and gated mapping variants, respectively. Figure 3 and 4 show the test accuracy of our two model variants with various K from 50 to 200, we find that the best results can be got when K is 120,150 for 20News and IMDB respectively. This scenario is in our expectation that for larger datasets, there tend to be more groups of concepts. For CT reports, we notice there is a large fluctuation, partly because the GloVe embeddings we used are trained on top of Wikipedia text which are not specific for the biomedical terms in CT reports. In the following comparison experiment, the most appropriate K (120, 150, 90) is set accordingly for these 3 datasets.

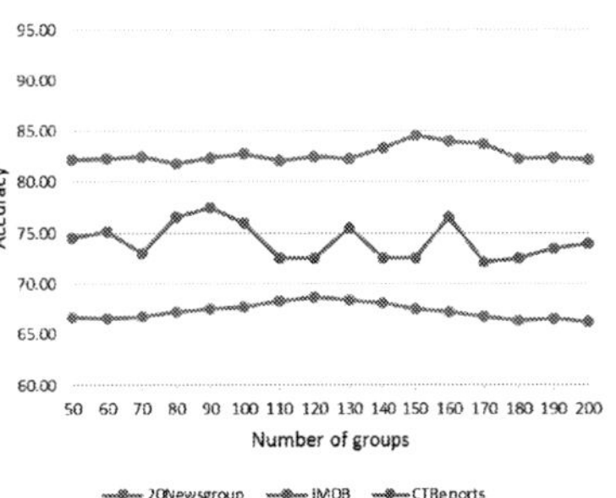

Figure 3: Accuracy of NBOW-DM-GloVe clusters

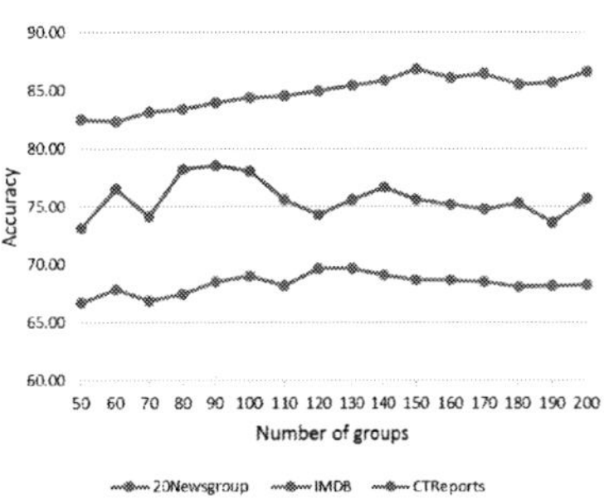

Figure 4: Accuracy of NBOW-GM-GloVe clusters

5.2 Model effectiveness with fixed word embeddings

First, we conduct several experiments in which the pre-trained word embeddings is fixed during training. We hope to answer two questions via these experiments: 1) whether the concept incorporation from different lexical resources provide additional information; 2) which incorporation method is better, direct or gated mapping. As shown in Table 2, concept information from GloVe clusters, WordNet and MetaMap helps propagate the general topic expression to classifiers. Also, gated mapping brings more benefits than direct mapping.

Model	Datasets		
	20News	IMDB	CTReports
NBOW-fixed	66.50	84.01	74.53
NBOW-DM-fixed-noAttention			
-GloVe	66.83	84.25	74.10
-WordNet	66.43	84.33	74.25
-GloVe+WordNet	66.60	84.35	74.40
-MetaMap	-	-	75.02
-All	-	-	75.25
NBOW-GM-fixed-noAttention			
-GloVe	67.10	84.35	74.18
-WordNet	67.53	84.53	74.35
-GloVe+WordNet	67.42	84.76	74.58
-MetaMap	-	-	75.53
-All	-	-	76.15
NBOW-DM-fixed-Attention			
-GloVe	66.43	84.75	74.37
-WordNet	**67.54**	84.85	74.35
-GloVe+WordNet	66.12	**85.02**	74.80
-MetaMap	-	-	75.50
-All	-	-	**76.24**
NBOW-GM-fixed-Attention			
-GloVe	68.13	86.15	75.20
-WordNet	68.20	86.26	75.30
-GloVe+WordNet	**68.55***	**86.85***	75.37
-MetaMap	-	-	76.82
-All	-	-	**77.10***

Table 2: Evaluation with fixed word embeddings during training.

5.3 Comparison with the state-of-art with updated word embeddings

As we had wondered if update word embeddings during training would enhance the model performance, we re-ran the experiments with all the same settings except that the original word vectors could be updated. Most current neural models for text classification are variants of either recurrent or convolutional networks. Besides NBOW, we use another two strong baselines: the first one is DCNN (Kalchbrenner et al., 2014) which extends traditional CNN with dynamic k-max pooling, the second one is SVM with unigram features as well as additional concept annotations from the same five different sources. We also test our two model variants without the attention layer, in which the attention computation is replaced by an averaged summation.

As shown in Table 3, on 20 Newsgroup, our first model variant NBOW-DM-Attention achieves slightly better result on 20 Newsgroup with the incorporation of GloVe clusters. It is also noticed that the incorporation of WordNet categories hurt the model in some degree, we analyze that it is caused by the limited vocabulary size compared to that of GloVe, as well as the interme-

Model	Datasets		
	20News	IMDB	CTReports
NBOW	67.62	84.32	76.20
DCNN	68.13	85.90	76.95
SVM			
-unigram	63.00	75.43	63.46
-unigram+Glove	64.20	75.53	63.81
-unigram+WordNet	64.13	75.62	63.58
-unigram+GloVe+WordNet	64.35	76.03	63.81
-unigram+MetaMap	-	-	64.52
-unigram+All	-	-	64.82
NBOW-DM-noAttention			
-GloVe	67.83	84.40	76.25
-WordNet	67.43	84.58	76.39
-GloVe+WordNet	67.60	84.83	76.45
-MetaMap	-	-	77.92
-All	-	-	78.14
NBOW-GM-noAttention			
-GloVe	68.15	85.12	77.13
-WordNet	68.65	85.65	77.15
-GloVe+WordNet	68.92	86.10	77.50
-MetaMap	-	-	78.20
-All	-	-	79.05
NBOW-DM-Attention			
-GloVe	**68.69**	84.62	77.50
-WordNet	67.53	84.80	76.30
-GloVe+WordNet	67.60	**85.16**	79.21
-MetaMap	-	-	78.02
-All	-	-	**80.43**
NBOW-GM-Attention			
-GloVe	69.62	86.85	78.52
-WordNet	68.50	89.43	77.43
-GloVe+WordNet	**69.82***	**90.10***	79.80
-MetaMap	-	-	80.26
-All	-	-	**82.56***

Table 3: Evaluation with updated word embeddings during training.

diate disambiguation step during concept annotation. Our second model variant NBOW-GM-Attention with GloVe amd WordNet concept embeddings achieves best results on 20 Newsgroup, compared with the baselines and the first model variant NBOW-DM-Attention. While on IMDB, NBOW-GM-Attention with concept incorporation from GloVe and WordNet achieves the best, even if NBOW-DM-Attention with the same setting does not beat DCNN. On CT Reports, both our two model variants achieve better accuracy with all the group information from GloVe, WordNet and MetaMap. Besides, it is noticed that the variants with attentions generally perform better than those with no attentions. Overall, the results show that NBOW-GM-Attention generally performs better than NBOW-DM-Attention, which indicates that the concept incorporation by gated mapping is more reliable than that of a direct concept embedding, and the incorporation of appropriate concept information with our second model variant makes a contribution to the classification tasks.

5.4 Error analysis and improvement

CT reports, which have technical content and highly specialized conventions, are arguably the most distant genre from news and movie reviews among those we consider. Therefore, we manually check the false predictions returned by our best model above. It turns out the classifier cannot capture two kinds of patterns: In the first, there is some context information provided in the report which contains comparison with a previous patient record, e.g. in the sentence "hypodense liver lesion in segment has significantly decreased in size from 12mm to 7mm", the diagnosis of whether the patient is infected or not relies on the magnitude of "decrease", which is highly professional. Second, human label noise occurs in some cases when doctors will not make immediate decisions, for instance "suspicious for infection" and "likely to be infected" happen in both positive and negative reports.

In order to see whether modeling context information can help or not, we conduct two transformation for h_i to get a new $\tilde{h}_i$, one is convolution-based (CNN-GM): $\tilde{h}_i = \tanh(W_c \cdot (h_{i-1} \oplus h_i \oplus h_{i+1}) + b_r)$, the other is recurrence-based (RNN-GM): $\tilde{h}_i = \tanh(W_h \cdot h_i + W_r \cdot \tilde{h}_{i-1} + b_r)$. Thus, in the above NBOW-GM settings, $\tilde{h}_i = h_i$. We use the three corresponding gated mapping variant with the best settings, and compare the number of parameters and the average running time per epoch. Table 4 shows that RNN-GM generally performs best at the cost of more parameters and training time per epoch. In contrast, CNN-GM is a trade-off between model complexity and performance. All timing experiments are specific for CT reports and performed on a single core of an Intel I5 processor with 8GB of RAM.

Model	20News	IMDB	CTReports	Parameters	Time(s)
NBOW-GM	69.82	90.10	82.56	3480.40k	15s
CNN-GM	71.58	**91.23**	86.13	3488.05k	21s
RNN-GM	**72.00**	91.05	**86.96**	3500.50k	30s

Table 4: Evaluation of gated mapping with convolution or recurrence transformation.

6 Conclusions and future work

In this paper, we propose two different methods for incorporating concept information from external knowledge bases into a neural bag of words model: the neural bag of words with either direct mapping (NBOW-DM) or gated mapping (NBOW-GM), which leverages both the word and concept representation through multiple hidden layers before classification. The model with gated mapping does better than direct mapping, and performs competitively with more complicated neural models as well as a traditional statistic model on different text classification tasks, and achieves good results on a practical biomedical text classification task. Moreover, our two model variants are also time efficient. They generally require less training time than their counterparts, which allow them to be used for datasets where few annotation is available or manual annotation is expensive.

For future work, we will consider using some global semantic information such as Rhetorical Structure Theory (RST), which is a theory of discourse that has enjoyed popularity in NLP. RST posits that a document can be represented by a tree whose leaves are elementary discourse units. We seek to develop approaches to combine local linguistic and global semantic knowledge into our model.

On the other hand, our proposed method takes the information from outsourced knowledge bases into account and ignores the information of unlabelled data. We will considering using deep reinforcement learning to learn how to select the query unlabelled data points in a sequential manner, formulated as a Markov decision process. With more labels as well as information from some prior knowledge bases, our model can be developed for large scale text processing and analysis.

References

Alan R Aronson. 2001. Effective mapping of biomedical text to the UMLS metathesaurus: the MetaMap program. In *Proceedings of the AMIA Symposium*. American Medical Informatics Association, page 17.

Robert H Baud, Anne-Marie Rassinoux, Christian Lovis, Judith Wagner, Vincent Griesser, Pierre-Andre Michel, and Jean-Raoul Scherrer. 1996. Knowledge sources for natural language processing. In *Proceedings of the AMIA Annual Fall Symposium*. American Medical Informatics Association, page 70.

Olivier Bodenreider. 2004. The unified medical language system (UMLS): integrating biomedical terminology. *Nucleic acids research* 32(suppl_1):D267–D270.

James J Cimino. 2000. From data to knowledge through concept-oriented terminologies: experience with the medical entities dictionary. *Journal of the American Medical Informatics Association* 7(3):288–297.

John Duchi, Elad Hazan, and Yoram Singer. 2011. Adaptive subgradient methods for online learning and stochastic optimization. *Journal of Machine Learning Research* 12(Jul):2121–2159.

Sepp Hochreiter and Jürgen Schmidhuber. 1997. Long short-term memory. *Neural computation* 9(8):1735–1780.

Andreas Hotho, Steffen Staab, and Gerd Stumme. 2003. Ontologies improve text document clustering. In *Data Mining, 2003. ICDM 2003. Third IEEE International Conference on*. IEEE, pages 541–544.

Mohit Iyyer, Varun Manjunatha, Jordan L Boyd-Graber, and Hal Daumé III. 2015. Deep unordered composition rivals syntactic methods for text classification. In *ACL (1)*. pages 1681–1691.

Nal Kalchbrenner, Edward Grefenstette, and Phil Blunsom. 2014. A convolutional neural network for modelling sentences. *arXiv preprint arXiv:1404.2188* .

Ken Lang. 1995. Newsweeder: Learning to filter netnews. In *Proceedings of the 12th international conference on machine learning*. volume 10, pages 331–339.

Quoc Le and Tomas Mikolov. 2014. Distributed representations of sentences and documents. In *Proceedings of the 31st International Conference on Machine Learning (ICML-14)*. pages 1188–1196.

Aristidis Likas, Nikos Vlassis, and Jakob J Verbeek. 2003. The global k-means clustering algorithm. *Pattern Recognition* 36(2):451–461.

Andrew L. Maas, Raymond E. Daly, Peter T. Pham, Dan Huang, Andrew Y. Ng, and Christopher Potts. 2011. Learning word vectors for sentiment analysis. In *Proceedings of the 49th Annual Meeting of the Association for Computational Linguistics: Human Language Technologies*. Association for Computational Linguistics, Portland, Oregon, USA, pages 142–150. http://www.aclweb.org/anthology/P11-1015.

David Martinez, Michelle R Ananda-Rajah, Hanna Suominen, Monica A Slavin, Karin A Thursky, and Lawrence Cavedon. 2015. Automatic detection of patients with invasive fungal disease from free-text computed tomography (CT) scans. *Journal of biomedical informatics* 53:251–260.

Tomas Mikolov, Martin Karafiát, Lukas Burget, Jan Cernockỳ, and Sanjeev Khudanpur. 2010. Recurrent neural network based language model. In *Interspeech*. volume 2, page 3.

Tomas Mikolov, Ilya Sutskever, Kai Chen, Greg S Corrado, and Jeff Dean. 2013. Distributed representations of words and phrases and their compositionality. In *Advances in neural information processing systems*. pages 3111–3119.

George A Miller. 1995. WordNet: a lexical database for English. *Communications of the ACM* 38(11):39–41.

Bo Pang, Lillian Lee, et al. 2008. Opinion mining and sentiment analysis. *Foundations and Trends® in Information Retrieval* 2(1–2):1–135.

Jeffrey Pennington, Richard Socher, and Christopher D Manning. 2014. Glove: Global vectors for word representation. In *Proceedings of the conference on empirical methods in natural language processing(EMNLP)*. volume 14, pages 1532–1543.

Alan L Rector. 1995. Coordinating taxonomies: Key to re-usable concept representations. In *Conference on Artificial Intelligence in Medicine in Europe*. Springer, pages 15–28.

Richard Socher, John Bauer, Christopher D Manning, and Andrew Y Ng. 2013a. Parsing with compositional vector grammars. In *ACL (1)*. pages 455–465.

Richard Socher, Jeffrey Pennington, Eric H Huang, Andrew Y Ng, and Christopher D Manning. 2011. Semi-supervised recursive autoencoders for predicting sentiment distributions. In *Proceedings of the conference on empirical methods in natural language processing*. Association for Computational Linguistics, pages 151–161.

Richard Socher, Alex Perelygin, Jean Y Wu, Jason Chuang, Christopher D Manning, Andrew Y Ng, Christopher Potts, et al. 2013b. Recursive deep models for semantic compositionality over a sentiment treebank. In *Proceedings of the conference on empirical methods in natural language processing (EMNLP)*. volume 1631, page 1642.

Kent A Spackman, Keith E Campbell, and Roger A Côté. 1997. SNOMED RT: a reference terminology for health care. In *Proceedings of the AMIA annual fall symposium*. American Medical Informatics Association, page 640.

Nitish Srivastava, Geoffrey E Hinton, Alex Krizhevsky, Ilya Sutskever, and Ruslan Salakhutdinov. 2014. Dropout: a simple way to prevent neural networks from overfitting. *Journal of Machine Learning Research* 15(1):1929–1958.

Kai Sheng Tai, Richard Socher, and Christopher D Manning. 2015. Improved semantic representations from tree-structured long short-term memory networks. *arXiv preprint arXiv:1503.00075* .

A Hybrid Model for Quality Assessment of Wikipedia Articles

Aili Shen   **Jianzhong Qi**   **Timothy Baldwin**
School of Computing and Information Systems
The University of Melbourne
Victoria, Australia
`ailis@student.unimelb.edu.au`
`jianzhong.qi@unimelb.edu.au`   `tb@ldwin.net`

Abstract

The task of document quality assessment is a highly complex one, which draws on analysis of aspects including linguistic content, document structure, fact correctness, and community norms. We explore the task in the context of a Wikipedia article assessment task, and propose a hybrid approach combining deep learning with features proposed in the literature. Our method achieves 6.5% higher accuracy than the state of the art in predicting the quality classes of English Wikipedia articles over a novel dataset of around 60k Wikipedia articles. We also discuss limitations with this task setup, and possible directions for establishing more robust document quality assessment evaluations.

1 Introduction

With the advent of Web 2.0, it has become much easier to collaboratively write and distribute documents, such as Wikipedia articles, or questions and answers in StackOverflow. The quality of such documents, however, varies greatly, ranging from well-written documents to poorly written documents with little if any content.

Automatic quality assessment is needed for the following reasons. First, the number of digital documents being generated is huge and continues to grow. It is infeasible to assess the quality of all documents manually and in a timely manner. Second, even given the same grading scheme, people assess quality of documents in a subjective way, which makes it difficult to reach consensus among raters and assign a proper quality class to a document. An automatic labeling approach, however, can enable immediate feedback to both contributors and readers, ideally with a justification for why a given label has been assigned. A high quality class assignment can give users greater trust in the document, while a low-quality class assignment can direct the efforts of contributors to improve certain articles.

In the absence of a general-purpose document quality assessment dataset, we use and expand on a document quality dataset sourced from English Wikipedia. The quality of Wikipedia articles is inconsistent, for reasons including: (1) not all contributors (i.e., users who edit a Wikipedia article) are experts in the area of the articles they edit, and different contributors have different writing styles; (2) some articles receive more attention than others, resulting in imbalances in the level of peer; (3) there is article vandalism (Wikipedia Vandalism) that lowers quality of Wikipedia articles.

Officially, there are six quality classes of Wikipedia articles, which are (in descending order of quality): *Featured Article* (FA), *Good Article* (GA), *B-class Article* (B), *C-class Article* (C), *Start Article* (Start), and *Stub Article* (Stub). The quality class of an article is determined by Wikipedia reviewers, and any registered user can become a reviewer. A general description of the criteria of different quality classes can be found in the Wikipedia grading scheme page.[1] The difference between different quality classes is subjective and ambiguous, especially for adjacent classes. This presents significant challenges in assigning quality classes consistently. Furthermore, there maybe some qualitative differences between different datasets. If there are more articles whose quality is at the boundary of adjacent classes, these articles are more likely to be misclassified into their adjacent classes. Lastly, the quality labels assigned to Wikipedia articles are not always trustworthy. For example, there are some noisy data

---

[1] `https://en.wikipedia.org/wiki/Template:Grading_scheme`

Aili Shen, Jianzhong Qi and Timothy Baldwin. 2017. A Hybrid Model for Quality Assessment of Wikipedia Articles. In *Proceedings of Australasian Language Technology Association Workshop*, pages 43–52.

points (e.g., an empty article is labeled as an FA article in the 30K dataset — see Section 5.1).

In this paper, we formulate the assessment of Wikipedia article quality as a classification problem and propose a hybrid model combining deep learning and hand-engineered features. We show that *long short-term memories* (LSTMs) (Hochreiter and Schmidhuber, 1997) generate effective document representations for article quality classification. We also show that there is benefit to supplementing the document embedding with hand-engineered features, to better capture the subtleties of the task.

This paper makes the following contributions:

(i) We formulate the quality assessment of Wikipedia articles as a classification problem, and propose a novel approach which combines LSTMs with hand-engineered features.

(ii) We construct a large-scale Wikipedia article dataset with quality class labels, by combining an existing dataset with newly-crawled data; this will be released for public use on acceptance of this paper.[2]

(iii) We report empirical results of the proposed model on three datasets, and show that the proposed model achieves state-of-the-art results in quality classification accuracy.

2 Related Work

A number of approaches for quality assessment of Wikipedia articles have been proposed, which can be classified into three categories: (i) metadata based approaches; (ii) article internal feature-based approaches; and (iii) meta-data and article internal feature-based approaches. In addition to quality assessment of Wikipedia articles, there is some work measuring essays written by (second) language learners and content quality in community question answering (cQA). As our main focus is on assessing quality of Wikipedia articles, this will be the focus of the literature review, with a brief mention of work on automatic essay scoring and cQA content quality assessment at the end of the section.

Meta-data based approaches use the meta-data of Wikipedia articles, e.g., contributors of the articles, to perform quality classification. For example, Stein and Hess (2007) and Adler et al. (2008) use the authority of the contributors to measure the quality of Wikipedia articles. Suzuki (2015) uses *h*-index and *p*-ratio to measure editor quality and uses editor quality to assess the quality of Wikipedia articles. Li et al. (2015) use article–editor networks and PageRank to assess Wikipedia article quality. These approaches require collecting large amounts of meta-data about the articles such as their edit history, and article quality prediction is indirect, i.e., based on external evidence such as article contributors instead of the article content itself.

Article internal features refer to features derived from the articles themselves. Various such features have been used for Wikipedia article quality assessment. Blumenstock (2008) uses article length as a metric to assess the quality of Wikipedia articles. A high accuracy is achieved in separating featured articles from non-featured articles despite the simplicity of this approach. Lipka and Stein (2010) use writing style, which is represented by exploiting binarized character trigram features, to identify featured articles. Warncke-Wang et al. (2013) propose a model to assess article quality, which includes five features extracted from article text: completeness, informativeness, number of headings, and ratio of number of references to article length. Later, Warncke-Wang et al. (2015) propose a model including 11 structural features (such as number of references) and use a random forest ("RF") to classify Wikipedia articles by quality. Dang and Ignat (2016a) further add nine readability metrics (such as Flesch reading-ease score) to the structural features, and use a RF to classify Wikipedia articles based on their quality. Based on these last two studies, an online Objective Revision Evaluation Service (ORES) has been built to measure the quality of Wikipedia articles (Halfaker and Taraborelli, 2015). ORES requires the revision ID of a Wikipedia article as its input parameter. Our experimental datasets do not contain such information. Thus, we compare with the model proposed by Dang and Ignat (2016a) instead of ORES in the experiments.

Recently, Dang and Ignat (2016b) use a distributed memory version of *Paragraph Vector* (Le and Mikolov, 2014) to learn document embeddings, which they fed into a four-layer neural network to classify articles for quality. This study does not consider the order of sentences, which

---

may affect article quality: if the sentences in an article are not ordered in a logical way, it is more difficult for reviewers and readers to understand the article, and the quality will be lower. Our approach differs from that of Dang and Ignat (2016b) in that we use an LSTM, which captures the order between sentences, to learn a high-level representation of Wikipedia articles. Furthermore, although neural networks can learn features from the article content, they require a large training dataset. Due to the limited availability of labeled Wikipedia articles, we supplement the document embedding with hand-engineered features, which can lead to better quality prediction even with a relatively small volume of training data. Cheng et al. (2016) adopt a similar idea in an app recommendation scenario.

There are also hybrid approaches that use both meta-data and article internal features for quality assessment. Stvilia et al. (2005) present seven Information Quality metrics based on article features and edit history of 834 articles. Dalip et al. (2009) analyze the effect of different feature sets on Wikipedia article quality assessment. The feature sets considered include article text, revision history, and citation network (where nodes are articles and edges are citations between them). A regression model is proposed for quality class prediction. Dalip et al. (2009) find that textual features extracted from articles are the best indicators to distinguish articles of different quality classes.

For the related task of automatic essay scoring, the following dimensions are often captured: topic relevance, organization and coherence, word usage and sentence complexity, and grammar and mechanics. To measure whether an essay is relevant to its "prompt" (i.e., the description of the essay topic), lexical overlap and semantic overlap between an essay and its corresponding prompt can be used (Phandi et al., 2015; Persing and Ng, 2014). Lexical overlap and semantic similarity features are exploited to measure coherence between different discourse elements, sentences, and paragraphs (Higgins et al., 2004; McNamara et al., 2015). Attali and Burstein (2004) explore word features, such as the number of verb formation errors, average word frequency, and average word length, to measure word usage and lexical complexity. Intelli-Metric (Rudner et al., 2006) uses sentence structure features, such as syntactic variety and readability, to measure sentence variety

and complexity. The effects of grammatical and mechanics errors on the quality of an essay are measured via word and POS n-gram features and "mechanics" features (e.g., spelling, capitalization, and punctuation), respectively (Persing and Ng, 2013; Higgins et al., 2004).

To measure content quality in cQA, researchers exploit various features from different sources, such as the content itself, the user's profile, asking and answering interaction among users, and usage of the content. The most common feature used is the content length (Jeon et al., 2006; Suryanto et al., 2009). Agichtein et al. (2008) explore syntactic and semantic complexity features, such as the entropy of word lengths and various readability scores. Le et al. (2016) exploit user's characteristic features (e.g., the grade level or the rank of the user in cQA) and the user's historical features (e.g., the number of questions asked by the user, and the number of answers given by the user). Suryanto et al. (2009) and Jurczyk and Agichtein (2007) exploit asking and answering expertise features, which can be computed through the HITS algorithm (Kleinberg, 1999). Asking expertise (hub values) of a user is derived from the answering expertise of other users answering questions posted by this user. A user's answering expertise (authority score) is derived from the asking expertise of other users posting questions answered. Usage features, such as the number of clicks (views), are also beneficial in measuring content quality in cQA (Burel et al., 2012).

3 Problem Definition

We formulate quality assessment of Wikipedia articles as a multi-class classification problem.

The input of the problem is a set of Wikipedia articles denoted by $\mathbb{D}$. Each article is denoted as a tuple $\langle a, c \rangle$, where a represents the article content, and c is a latent true quality class of the article. The value of c belongs to a set $\mathbb{C}$ of quality classes: $\mathbb{C} = \{\mathsf{FA}, \mathsf{GA}, \mathsf{B}, \mathsf{C}, \mathsf{Start}, \mathsf{Stub}\}$.

We aim to predict a quality class $\hat{c}$ for each article, such that $\hat{c}$ is as close as possible to the true latent quality class c of the article. Our classification model to achieve this purpose is essentially a mapping function: $f : \mathbb{D} \rightarrow \mathbb{C}$. Here, the optimization goal of the mapping function is to minimize the difference between the predicted quality class $\hat{c}$ and the true latent quality class c of an article.

4 The Proposed Hybrid Model

The proposed classification model is a hybrid model that integrates neural network document embeddings and hand-engineered features. In this section, we first describe the LSTM-based model to document embeddings of Wikipedia articles, then we present the hand-engineered features, and finally we describe how we combine the two.

4.1 Document Embedding Learning

We adopt a bidirectional LSTM model to generate document embeddings of Wikipedia articles; we will refer to this model as Bi-LSTM. The input of Bi-LSTM is the text of an article, and the output is a document embedding, which we later integrate with hand-engineered features.

We explain our model in detail as illustrated in Fig. 1. First, an average-pooling layer is applied to word embeddings within a sentence to obtain a sentence embedding. Each word is represented as a word embedding (Bengio et al., 2003), which is a continuous, real-valued vector.

Second, we use a bidirectional LSTM to generate a document embedding over the sentence embeddings. Suppose that an article contains n sentences: $s_1, \ldots, s_n$, the bidirectional LSTM contains a forward LSTM which reads an article from sentence s_1 to s_n and a backward LSTM which reads an article from sentence s_n to s_1. Given a sentence s_j, we can obtain its hidden state h_j of s_j by concatenating the forward output $\overrightarrow{h}_j$ and the backward output $\overleftarrow{h}_j$, i.e., $h_j = [\overrightarrow{h}_j, \overleftarrow{h}_j]$.

Last, a max-pooling layer is applied to select the most salient features among the component sentences. Then the output of the max-pooling layer is fed into a feedforward neural network with ReLU as the activation function, which produces our neural network learned high-level representation f_l.

4.2 Hand-Engineered Features

Following Dang and Ignat (2016a), we use structural features and readability scores as the hand-engineered features for quality class prediction. The structural features can capture the structure information of articles and the readability scores can reflect writing styles. These features are listed in Table 1.

The structural features reflect article quality in different ways. For example, *article length* captures how much content an article contains (with

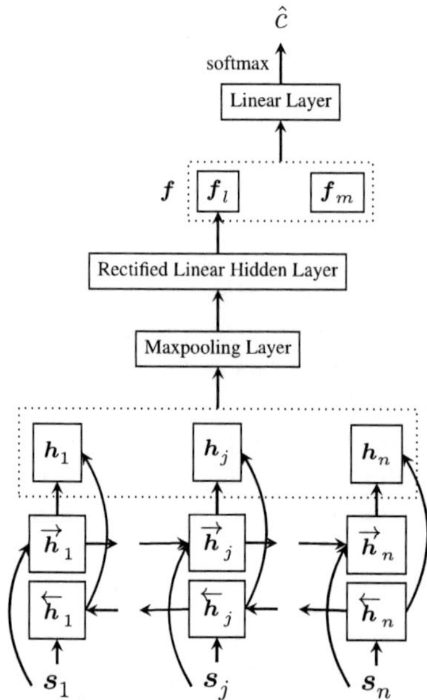

Figure 1: Overview of the proposed model.

the expectation that articles that do not contain much content are usually of low quality). The *number of references, number of links to other Wikipedia pages*, and *number of citation templates* show how the article editors support their content by using information from different sources, which makes the article more reliable and of higher quality. The *number of level 2 and level 3+ headings* reflect how the content is organized. Usually, Wikipedia articles of high quality have appropriate *number of level 2 and level 3+ headings*.

Readability scores reflect the use of language and how easy to read an article is. *Flesch reading score, Flesch-Kincaid grade level, Smog index*, and *Linsear write formula* use the average syllable per word or the number of polysyllables with different weight values to measure how difficult a text is to understand. Both *Coleman-Liau index* and *Automated readability index* use the average word length with different weight values to measure the readability of texts. *Difficult words, Dale-Chall score*, and *Gunning-Fog index* use the number of difficult words or percentage of difficult words to measure the comprehension difficulty of a text. Here, a word is considered difficult if it is not in a list of 3000 common English words that fourth-grade American students can reliably un-

Structural Features	Readability Scores
Article length in bytes	Flesch reading score (Kincaid et al., 1975)
Number of references	Flesch-Kincaid grade level (Kincaid et al., 1975)
Number of links to other Wikipedia pages	Smog index (Mc Laughlin, 1969)
Number of citation templates	Coleman-Liau index (Coleman and Liau, 1975)
Number of non-citation templates	Automated readability index (Senter and Smith, 1967)
Number of categories linked in the text	Difficult words (Chall and Dale, 1995)
Number of images / length of the article	Dale-Chall score (Dale and Chall, 1948)
Information noise score (Zhu and Gauch, 2000)	Linsear write formula (Chen, 2012)
Article having an infobox or not	Gunning-Fog index (Gunning, 1969)
Number of level 2 headings	
Number of level 3+ headings	

Table 1: Hand-engineered features.

derstand.

Hand-engineered features are extracted using the open-source packages *wikiclass*[3] and *textstat*:[4] *wikiclass* is used to extract structural features and *textstat* is used to compute readability scores.

4.3 The Proposed Hybrid Model Bi-LSTM⁺

The proposed hybrid model, denoted as Bi-LSTM⁺, concatenates the neural network learned high-level representation f_l with hand-engineered features f_m, which results in the combined feature vector f. The combined features f are used to classify Wikipedia articles according to their quality. This is done by feeding the combined feature vector f into a linear layer and softmax layer to predict the probability distribution over quality classes. We use the cross-entropy between ground truth distribution and predicted distribution as the loss function to train our model.

5 Experiments

We report the results of an empirical study on the proposed hybrid model in this section.

5.1 Datasets

In our experiments, we use three different datasets with different numbers of Wikipedia articles: 20K dataset,[5] 30K dataset,[6] and 60K dataset. The Wikipedia articles in these datasets contain manually labeled quality classes, which are used as the

	20K	30K	60K
FA	2414	4920	9908
GA	3160	4891	9898
B	3201	4913	9913
C	3318	4907	9907
Start	4096	4910	9910
Stub	4243	4915	9915
Total	20432	29456	59451

Table 2: Datasets used in our experiments.

ground truth in our experiments. The 20K dataset is provided by Warncke-Wang et al. (2015). The 30K dataset is provided by the Wikimedia Foundation. The 60K dataset is obtained by combining the 30K dataset with newly crawled articles of different quality classes. We wrote a Python script to crawl articles from each quality class, and eliminate talk pages from the crawled data, resulting in about 5K articles from each quality class. We crawl about 5K articles from each quality class because there are only about 5K FA articles from the featured article category and we want the dataset to be evenly distributed (among the labeled Wikipedia articles, 71% is labeled as Stub and 0.096% is labeled as FA). Table 2 summarizes the quality class distributions of the three datasets.

5.2 Experimental Setting

We divide a Wikipedia article into sentences and tokenize them using *NLTK* (Bird, 2006; Bird et al., 2010). Words appearing more than 20 times are retained in building the vocabulary. All low frequency words are replaced by the special UNK token. We use the pre-trained *GloVe* (Pennington et al., 2014) 50-dimensional word embeddings to

---

[3] https://github.com/wiki-ai/wikiclass
[4] https://pypi.python.org/pypi/textstat/0.3.1
[5] http://figshare.com/articles/English_Wikipedia_Quality_Assessment_Dataset/1375406
[6] https://datasets.wikimedia.org/public-datasets/enwiki/

represent words found in the GloVe dataset. For words that cannot be found in GloVe, word embeddings are randomly initialized based on sampling from a uniform distribution $U(-1, 1)$. All word embeddings are updated in the training process.

For evaluation, we perform 10-fold cross-validation over the three datasets, using 90% as training data (10% of which is in turn used as the development set for early stopping), and the rest test data. We report the *average classification accuracy* (combined across the cross validation folds).

Hyper-parameters of the proposed model are tuned on the development set for a given iteration of cross validation. We set the word embedding dimension to 50 and the hidden size of Bi-LSTM⁺ to 256. Then the concatenation of the forward and backward LSTMs gives us 512 dimensions for the document embedding. The feedforward neural network produces the output f_l, which is a real-valued vector with 40 dimensions. Concatenating with hand-engineered features f_m, which is a real-valued normalized vector with 20 dimensions, we obtain the combined features of f with 60 dimensions for each article, which are used as the features for Wikipedia article quality classification. A linear layer and softmax layer are applied on the combined features f, which produces the predicted distribution $\hat{c}$. To save training time, articles with more than 350 sentences are clipped and only the first 350 sentences are used. During training, we use a mini-batch size of 128. We use the Adam optimizer (Kingma and Ba, 2014) to train the model with a learning rate of 0.001. Dropout layers are applied to the input of Bi-LSTM⁺ and the neural network learned high-level representation f_l with a dropout probability of 0.5.

5.3 Experimental Results

We compare the proposed model Bi-LSTM⁺ with two state-of-the-art approaches RF (Dang and Ignat, 2016a) and Doc2Vec (Dang and Ignat, 2016b). RF only uses the structural features and readability scores as features to build a random forest. Doc2Vec uses Paragraph Vectors to learn document embeddings, and builds a classification model on top of this. The hyper-parameters of RF and Doc2Vec are set as described in the corresponding papers. We also compare with a model using only Bi-LSTM learned document embed-

	20K	30K	60K
RF	**63.70%**	58.63%	61.71%
Doc2Vec	59.84%	54.98%	61.46%
Bi-LSTM	56.04%	54.36%	65.16%
Bi-LSTM⁺	63.59%	**58.98%**	**68.17%**†

Table 3: Results.

dings, denoted as Bi-LSTM.

Table 3 shows the experimental results. We see that on the 20K and 30K datasets, Bi-LSTM⁺ and RF have very close performance: RF has a 0.11% higher accuracy on the 20K dataset while Bi-LSTM⁺ has a 0.35% higher accuracy on the 30K dataset. Wilcoxon signed-rank test demonstrates that the performance difference of RF and Bi-LSTM⁺ is not significant over the 20K and 30K datasets. However, on the larger 60K dataset, Bi-LSTM⁺ gains a 6.5% higher accuracy than that of RF. The performance gain of Bi-LSTM⁺ is statistically significant ($p < 0.01$) on the 60K dataset, which is emphasized using a † symbol. Doc2Vec and Bi-LSTM have a lower accuracy than that of Bi-LSTM⁺ on all three datasets.

6 Analysis and Discussion

In this section, the performance of the hybrid model Bi-LSTM⁺ is analyzed, and we discuss the task of of quality assessment of Wikipedia articles.

6.1 Analysis

Impact of hand-engineered features on dataset of different sizes. Bi-LSTM⁺ and RF have very close performance on the 20K and 30K datasets, which shows the effectiveness of hand-engineered features in article quality classification over smaller datasets. Meanwhile, the better performance of Bi-LSTM⁺ on the 60K dataset highlights the advantage of a neural network based model when there is more training data. Further, by comparing Bi-LSTM with Bi-LSTM⁺, we find that the improvement gained by adding hand-engineered features decreases as the dataset size gets larger: the hand-engineered features produce an accuracy improvement of 7.55% on the 20K dataset, 4.62% on the 30K dataset, and 3.01% on the 60K dataset. This suggests that as the dataset size increases, the neural network can learn more robust features directly from the document content, and hence the performance improvement of Bi-LSTM⁺ from the hand-engineered features decreases.

Quality	FA	GA	B	C	Start	Stub	Class Total	Accuracy
FA	880	55	44	6	0	6	991	88.80%
GA	111	701	137	34	7	0	990	70.81%
B	45	67	619	197	48	16	992	62.40%
C	13	50	205	598	96	29	991	60.34%
Start	4	1	71	191	513	211	991	51.77%
Stub	1	0	9	24	144	814	992	82.06%
Predicted Total	1054	874	1085	1050	808	1076	5947	69.36%

Table 4: Confusion matrix of Bi-LSTM[+] on a test set of the 60K dataset. The last column is the accuracy for each class. Diagonal elements (gray cells) of the matrix are correct predictions. Rows are actual quality classes, and columns are the predicted quality classes.

Different classification accuracy of different quality classes. To further analyze the performance of our model Bi-LSTM[+], we dive into the classification results of each quality class. We show the confusion matrix of the experiment on one fold test set of the 60K dataset in Table 4. A total of 5947 articles are used for testing in this experiment. In the matrix, the diagonal elements show the number of correct predictions for each class. For example, 880 FA articles have been predicted as FA correctly. Each row in the matrix shows the prediction result for the articles of a certain class. For example, the first row shows that among the 991 FA articles, 880, 55, 44, 6, 0, and 6 articles are predicted to be FA, GA, B, C, Start, and Stub, respectively. Each column shows the numbers of articles of different classes that have been predicted to be a certain class. For example, the first column shows that there are 880, 111, 45, 13, 4, and 1 articles of different classes predicted to be FA.

It is more difficult to classify articles at adjacent quality classes. In Table 4, for example, there are 191 and 211 Start articles that have been misclassified as C and Stub articles, respectively, which are adjacent classes of Start articles. The low accuracy of B, C, and Start articles demonstrates that they are more difficult to classify correctly. The proposed model Bi-LSTM[+] achieves a higher accuracy on both FA and GA, which can be explained by that both FA and GA pass an official review and that the difference between them is clearer. In fact, it is difficult to classify articles in adjacent classes even for a human reader, e.g., B article *Wave Hill Station*[7] and C article *Ivanhoe*,[8] are difficult for humans to assign the correct label

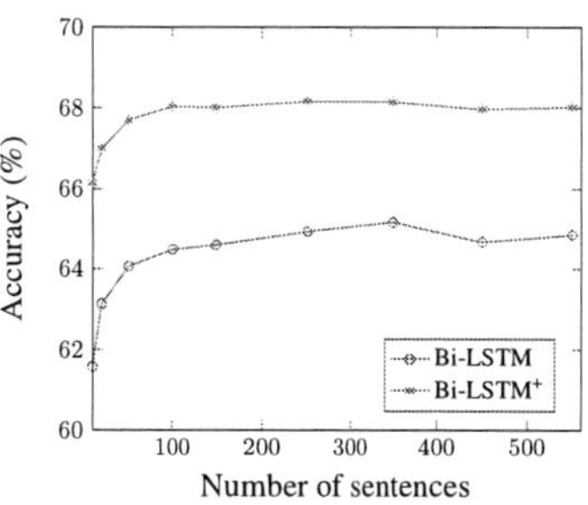

Figure 2: Performance of Bi-LSTM and Bi-LSTM[+] on the 60K dataset varying number of sentences.

to. If we allow an article to be classified into adjacent classes (e.g., it is regarded as a correct classification if a GA article is classified into its adjacent classes FA or B.), then the overall accuracy of the proposed model Bi-LSTM[+] will increase to 93.14% from 69.36%.[9]

Impact of hand-engineered features on models using different number of sentences in each article. To further justify the use of hand-engineered features, we vary the number of sentences fed into Bi-LSTM[+] and Bi-LSTM, and compare the accuracy of the two models on the 60K dataset. We feed from the first 10 to the first 550 sentences of each article into Bi-LSTM and Bi-LSTM[+], respectively. From Fig. 2, we can see that the performance gain of Bi-LSTM[+] over Bi-LSTM is most significant (up to 4.57%) when the number of sentences is below 100. As the number of sentences continues to increase, the performance gain becomes smaller. This suggests that when the number of sentences per article is small, there are less features that can be learned by the neural network. The performance of Bi-LSTM[+]

[7]https://en.wikipedia.org/w/index.php?title=Wave_Hill_Station&oldid=767773441

[8]https://en.wikipedia.org/w/index.php?title=Ivanhoe&oldid=802355224

[9]This number is higher than 68.17% shown in Table 3 because this is the result of one fold of 10-fold cross-validation.

can be better compensated by the hand-engineered features. As we train on more sentences, more features are learned by the neural network, and the contributions of hand-engineered features become less. We also see that, beyond 350 sentences, the performance of Bi-LSTM⁺ does not increase any more. This is because the neural network may forget the afore-learned features, which are more important, if there is too much content to learn from. Thus, we have used 350 sentences per article as our default setting in the experiments.

6.2 Discussion

We also ran an experiment where we formulated the quality assessment task as a regression problem. The dependent variable is the quality class, and the independent variables are the combined features f. We convert the quality class to integers: Stub to 0, Start to 1, C to 2, B to 3, GA to 4, and FA to 5. After we get the predicted quality value of the test data using the regression model, we convert back to the quality class by rounding (and truncating at either end of the scale).

When we regard the quality assessment of Wikipedia articles as a regression problem, the classification accuracy is poor, and we thus do not report the results here. This may be because it is difficult to learn when the quality assessment of Wikipedia articles is regarded as a regression problem. In the future, we will formulate the quality assessment of Wikipedia articles as an ordinal regression problem where only the relative ordering between different quality classes is important.

It is inappropriate to compare performance across different datasets, even with ones of the same size. We perform an experiment on the newly crawled 30K dataset. The accuracy of RF, Doc2Vec, Bi-LSTM, and Bi-LSTM⁺ is 65.53%, 67.46%, 75.34%, and 76.33%, respectively. The accuracy of all approaches on the newly crawled 30K dataset is higher (ranging from 6.9% to 20.98%) than that on the 30K dataset provided by Wikimedia Foundations. One reason for the performance difference is that there are noisy data points in the 30K dataset provided by Wikimedia Foundations, even after removing articles with obvious problems (e.g., an empty article is labeled as an FA article). Another reason is that there may be some qualitative differences between the 30K dataset provided by Wikimedia Foundations and our newly crawled 30K dataset. For example, there may be more articles whose quality is at the boundary of adjacent classes in the 30K dataset provided by the Wikimedia Foundation than those in our newly crawled 30K dataset and more articles being misclassified into their adjacent classes, which results in poor performance of all approaches over the 30K dataset provided by the Wikimedia Foundation.

Returning to our original objective of general-purpose document quality assessment, the most commonly used quality factors across different domains include: grammaticality, readability, stylistics, structure, correctness, and technical depth. These quality factors, however, have different impact on document quality across different domains. For example, people emphasize grammaticality more in Wikipedia articles and essays written by (second) language learners than in the case of cQA posts. Features used in automated essay scoring and quality assessment in cQA, which are applicable to assessing the quality of Wikipedia articles, will be exploited in the future. We also expressed misgivings about the quality of the labels in the Wikipedia dataset. We did not perform inter-annotator agreement analysis since each article only has a single quality class label assigned by the Wikipedia community. In the future, we want to validate our proposed approach on datasets with quality ratings from different annotators on each of the aforementioned six dimensions, for a more robust evaluation.

7 Conclusions

We propose a hybrid model to classify Wikipedia articles based on their quality, which integrates Bi-LSTM learned document embeddings with hand-engineered features for article quality classification. As part of this, we construct a novel dataset. Experimental results show that the proposed model achieves a 6.5% higher accuracy than state-of-the-art approaches over a set of 60K Wikipedia articles. The results also show that hand-engineered features play an important role in obtaining the correct classification, which justifies the use of such features, especially when the size of the training data is limited. Further, the quality of documents should be assessed from different dimensions and different annotators should be employed to alleviate subjectivity of assessing document quality.

References

B. Thomas Adler, Krishnendu Chatterjee, Luca De Alfaro, Marco Faella, Ian Pye, and Vishwanath Raman. 2008. Assigning trust to wikipedia content. In *Proceedings of the 4th International Symposium on Wikis*. pages 26:1–26:14.

Eugene Agichtein, Carlos Castillo, Debora Donato, Aristides Gionis, and Gilad Mishne. 2008. Finding high-quality content in social media. In *Proceedings of the International Conference on Web Search and Web Data Mining*. pages 183–194.

Yigal Attali and Jill Burstein. 2004. Automated essay scoring with e-rater® v. 2.0. *ETS Research Report Series* 2004(2).

Yoshua Bengio, Réjean Ducharme, Pascal Vincent, and Christian Jauvin. 2003. A neural probabilistic language model. *Journal of Machine Learning Research* 3(Feb):1137–1155.

Steven Bird. 2006. NLTK: the natural language toolkit. In *Proceedings of the 21st International Conference on Computational Linguistics and 44th Annual Meeting of the Association for Computational Linguistics*. pages 69–72.

Steven Bird, Ewan Klein, and Edward Loper. 2010. Natural language processing with python: analyzing text with the natural language toolkit. *Language Resources and Evaluation* 44(4):421–424.

Joshua E. Blumenstock. 2008. Size matters: word count as a measure of quality on wikipedia. In *Proceedings of the 17th International Conference on World Wide Web*. pages 1095–1096.

Grégoire Burel, Yulan He, and Harith Alani. 2012. Automatic identification of best answers in online enquiry communities. In *The Semantic Web: Research and Applications - 9th Extended Semantic Web Conference*. pages 514–529.

Jeanne Sternlicht Chall and Edgar Dale. 1995. *Readability revisited: The new Dale-Chall readability formula*. Brookline Books.

Hai-Hon Chen. 2012. How to use readability formulas to access and select english reading materials. *Journal of Educational Media & Library Sciences* 50(2):229–254.

Heng-Tze Cheng, Levent Koc, Jeremiah Harmsen, Tal Shaked, Tushar Chandra, Hrishi Aradhye, Glen Anderson, Greg Corrado, Wei Chai, Mustafa Ispir, et al. 2016. Wide & deep learning for recommender systems. In *Proceedings of the 1st Workshop on Deep Learning for Recommender Systems*. pages 7–10.

Meri Coleman and T. L. Liau. 1975. A computer readability formula designed for machine scoring. *Journal of Applied Psychology* 60(2):283.

Edgar Dale and Jeanne S. Chall. 1948. A formula for predicting readability: Instructions. *Educational Research Bulletin* pages 37–54.

Daniel H. Dalip, Marcos A. Gonçalves, Marco Cristo, and Pável Calado. 2009. Automatic quality assessment of content created collaboratively by web communities: a case study of wikipedia. In *Proceedings of the 9th ACM/IEEE-CS Joint Conference on Digital libraries*. pages 295–304.

Quang-Vinh Dang and Claudia-Lavinia Ignat. 2016a. Measuring quality of collaboratively edited documents: the case of wikipedia. In *The 2nd IEEE International Conference on Collaboration and Internet Computing*. pages 266–275.

Quang-Vinh Dang and Claudia-Lavinia Ignat. 2016b. Quality assessment of wikipedia articles without feature engineering. In *Proceedings of the 16th ACM/IEEE-CS Joint Conference on Digital Libraries*. pages 27–30.

Robert Gunning. 1969. The fog index after twenty years. *International Journal of Business Communication* 6(2):3–13.

Aaron Halfaker and Dario Taraborelli. 2015. Artificial intelligence service ores gives wikipedians x-ray specs to see through bad edits. *[online] Available: https://blog.wikimedia.org/2015/11/30/artificial-intelligence-x-ray-specs* .

Derrick Higgins, Jill Burstein, Daniel Marcu, and Claudia Gentile. 2004. Evaluating multiple aspects of coherence in student essays. In *Human Language Technology Conference of the North American Chapter of the Association for Computational Linguistics*. pages 185–192.

Sepp Hochreiter and Jürgen Schmidhuber. 1997. Long short-term memory. *Neural Computation* 9(8):1735–1780.

Jiwoon Jeon, W. Bruce Croft, Joon Ho Lee, and Soyeon Park. 2006. A framework to predict the quality of answers with non-textual features. In *Proceedings of the 29th Annual International ACM SIGIR Conference on Research and Development in Information Retrieval*. pages 228–235.

Pawel Jurczyk and Eugene Agichtein. 2007. Discovering authorities in question answer communities by using link analysis. In *Proceedings of the Sixteenth ACM Conference on Information and Knowledge Management*. pages 919–922.

J. Peter Kincaid, Robert P. Fishburne Jr., Richard L. Rogers, and Brad S. Chissom. 1975. Derivation of new readability formulas (automated readability index, fog count and flesch reading ease formula) for navy enlisted personnel. Technical report, DTIC Document.

Diederik P. Kingma and Jimmy Ba. 2014. Adam: A method for stochastic optimization. *CoRR* abs/1412.6980. http://arxiv.org/abs/1412.6980.

Jon M. Kleinberg. 1999. Authoritative sources in a hyperlinked environment. *J. ACM* 46(5):604–632.

Long T. Le, Chirag Shah, and Erik Choi. 2016. Evaluating the quality of educational answers in community question-answering. In *Proceedings of the 16th ACM/IEEE-CS on Joint Conference on Digital Libraries*. pages 129–138.

Quoc Le and Tomas Mikolov. 2014. Distributed representations of sentences and documents. In *Proceedings of the 31st International Conference on Machine Learning*. volume 14, pages 1188–1196.

Xinyi Li, Jintao Tang, Ting Wang, Zhunchen Luo, and Maarten De Rijke. 2015. Automatically assessing wikipedia article quality by exploiting article–editor networks. In *37th European Conference on Information Retrieval*. pages 574–580.

Nedim Lipka and Benno Stein. 2010. Identifying featured articles in wikipedia: writing style matters. In *Proceedings of the 19th International Conference on World Wide Web*. pages 1147–1148.

G. Harry Mc Laughlin. 1969. Smog grading-a new readability formula. *Journal of Reading* 12(8):639–646.

Danielle S McNamara, Scott A Crossley, Rod D Roscoe, Laura K Allen, and Jianmin Dai. 2015. A hierarchical classification approach to automated essay scoring. *Assessing Writing* 23:35–59.

Jeffrey Pennington, Richard Socher, and Christopher D. Manning. 2014. Glove: Global vectors for word representation. In *Proceedings of the 2014 Conference on Empirical Methods in Natural Language Processing*. volume 14, pages 1532–1543.

Isaac Persing and Vincent Ng. 2013. Modeling thesis clarity in student essays. In *Proceedings of the 51st Annual Meeting of the Association for Computational Linguistics*. pages 260–269.

Isaac Persing and Vincent Ng. 2014. Modeling prompt adherence in student essays. In *Proceedings of the 52nd Annual Meeting of the Association for Computational Linguistics*. pages 1534–1543.

Peter Phandi, Kian Ming Adam Chai, and Hwee Tou Ng. 2015. Flexible domain adaptation for automated essay scoring using correlated linear regression. In *Proceedings of the 2015 Conference on Empirical Methods in Natural Language Processing*. pages 431–439.

Lawrence M Rudner, Veronica Garcia, and Catherine Welch. 2006. An evaluation of intellimetric essay scoring system. *The Journal of Technology, Learning and Assessment* 4(4).

R. J. Senter and E. A. Smith. 1967. Automated readability index. Technical report, DTIC Document.

Klaus Stein and Claudia Hess. 2007. Does it matter who contributes: a study on featured articles in the german wikipedia. In *Proceedings of the 18th Conference on Hypertext and Hypermedia*. pages 171–174.

Besiki Stvilia, Michael B. Twidale, Linda C. Smith, and Les Gasser. 2005. Assessing information quality of a community-based encyclopedia. In *Proceedings of the 2005 International Conference on Information Quality*. pages 442–454.

Maggy Anastasia Suryanto, Ee-Peng Lim, Aixin Sun, and Roger H. L. Chiang. 2009. Quality-aware collaborative question answering: methods and evaluation. In *Proceedings of the Second International Conference on Web Search and Web Data Mining*. pages 142–151.

Yu Suzuki. 2015. Quality assessment of wikipedia articles using h-index. *Journal of Information Processing* 23(1):22–30.

Morten Warncke-Wang, Vladislav R. Ayukaev, Brent Hecht, and Loren Terveen. 2015. The success and failure of quality improvement projects in peer production communities. In *Proceedings of the 18th ACM Conference on Computer Supported Cooperative Work & Social Computing*. pages 743–756.

Morten Warncke-Wang, Dan Cosley, and John Riedl. 2013. Tell me more: an actionable quality model for wikipedia. In *Proceedings of the 9th International Symposium on Open Collaboration*. pages 8:1–8:10.

Wikipedia Vandalism. Accessed Jun., 2017. Wikipedia vandalism. `https://en.wikipedia.org/wiki/Wikipedia:Vandalism`.

Xiaolan Zhu and Susan Gauch. 2000. Incorporating quality metrics in centralized/distributed information retrieval on the world wide web. In *Proceedings of the 23rd Annual International ACM SIGIR Conference on Research and Development in Information Retrieval*. pages 288–295.

Phonemic Transcription of Low-Resource Tonal Languages

Oliver Adams,♠ Trevor Cohn,♠ Graham Neubig,♡ Alexis Michaud♣
♠Computing and Information Systems, The University of Melbourne, Australia
♡Language Technologies Institute, Carnegie Mellon University, USA
♣CNRS-LACITO, National Center for Scientific Research, France
oadams@student.unimelb.edu.au, tcohn@unimelb.edu.au,
gneubig@cs.cmu.edu, alexis.michaud@cnrs.fr

Abstract

Transcription of speech is an important part of language documentation, and yet speech recognition technology has not been widely harnessed to aid linguists. We explore the use of a neural network architecture with the connectionist temporal classification loss function for phonemic and tonal transcription in a language documentation setting. In this framework, we explore jointly modelling phonemes and tones versus modelling them separately, and assess the importance of pitch information versus phonemic context for tonal prediction. Experiments on two tonal languages, Yongning Na and Eastern Chatino, show the changes in recognition performance as training data is scaled from 10 minutes to 150 minutes. We discuss the findings from incorporating this technology into the linguistic workflow for documenting Yongning Na, which show the method's promise in improving efficiency, minimizing typographical errors, and maintaining the transcription's faithfulness to the acoustic signal, while highlighting phonetic and phonemic facts for linguistic consideration.

1 Introduction

Language documentation involves eliciting speech from native speakers, and transcription of these rich cultural and linguistic resources is an integral part of the language documentation process. However, transcription is very slow: it often takes a linguist between 30 minutes to 2 hours to transcribe and translate 1 minute of speech, depending on the transcriber's familiarity with the language and the difficulty of the content. This is a bottleneck in the standard documentary linguistics workflow: linguists accumulate considerable amounts of speech, but do not transcribe and translate it all, and there is a risk that untranscribed recordings could end up as "data graveyards" (Himmelmann, 2006, 4,12-13). There is clearly a need for "devising better ways for linguists to do their work" (Thieberger, 2016, 92).

There has been work on low-resource speech recognition (Besacier et al., 2014), with approaches using cross-lingual information for better acoustic modelling (Burget et al., 2010; Vu et al., 2014; Xu et al., 2016; Müller et al., 2017) and language modelling (Xu and Fung, 2013). However, speech recognition technology has largely been ineffective for endangered languages since architectures based on hidden Markov models (HMMs), which generate orthographic transcriptions, require a large pronunciation lexicon and a language model trained on text. These speech recognition systems are usually trained on a variety of speakers and hundreds of hours of data (Hinton et al., 2012, 92), with the goal of generalisation to new speakers. Since large amounts of text are used for language model training, such systems often do not incorporate pitch information for speech recognition of tonal languages (Metze et al., 2013), as they can instead rely on contextual information for tonal disambiguation via the language model (Le and Besacier, 2009; Feng et al., 2012).

In contrast, language documentation contexts often have just a few speakers for model training, and little text for language model training. However, there may be benefit even in a system that overfits to these speakers. If a *phonemic* recognition tool can provide a canvas transcription for manual correction and linguistic analysis, it may be possible to improve the leverage of linguists. The data collected in this semi-automated workflow can then be used as training data for further re-

Oliver Adams, Trevor Cohn, Graham Neubig and Alexis Michaud. 2017. Phonemic Transcription of Low-Resource Tonal Languages. In *Proceedings of Australasian Language Technology Association Workshop*, pages 53–60.

finement of the acoustic model, leading to a snow-ball effect of better and faster transcription.

In this paper we investigate the application of neural speech recognition models to the task of phonemic and tonal transcription in a resource-scarce language documentation setting. We use the connectionist temporal classification (CTC) formulation (Graves et al., 2006) for the purposes of direct prediction of phonemes and tones given an acoustic signal, thus bypassing the need for a pronunciation lexicon, language model, and time alignments of phonemes in the training data. By drastically reducing the data requirements in this way, we make the use of automatic transcription technology more feasible in a language documentation setting.

We evaluate this approach on two tonal languages, Yongning Na and Eastern Chatino (Cruz and Woodbury, 2006; Michaud, 2017). Na is a Sino-Tibetan language spoken in Southwest China with three tonal levels, High (H), Mid (M) and Low (L) and a total of seven tone labels. Eastern Chatino, spoken in Oaxaca, Mexico, has a richer tone set but both languages have extensive morphotonology. Overall estimates of numbers of speakers for Chatino and Na are similar, standing at about 40,000 for both (Simons and Fennig, 2017), but there is a high degree of dialect differentiation within the languages. The data used in the present study are from the Alawa dialect of Yongning Na, and the San Juan Quiahije dialect of Eastern Chatino; as a rule-of-thumb estimate, it is likely that these materials would be intelligible to a population of less than 10,000 (for details on the situation for Eastern Chatino, see Cruz (2011, 18-23)).

Though a significant amount of Chatino speech has been transcribed (Chatino Language Documentation Project, 2017), its rich tone system and opposing location on the globe make it a useful point of comparison for our explorations of Na, the language for which automatic transcription is our primary practical concern. Though Na has previously had speech recognition applied in a pilot study (Do et al., 2014), phoneme error rates were not quantified and tone recognition was left as future work.

We perform experiments scaling the training data, comparing joint prediction of phonemes and tones with separate prediction, and assessing the influence of pitch information versus phonemic context on phonemic and tonal prediction in the CTC-based framework. Importantly, we qualitatively evaluate use of this automation in the transcription of Na. The effectiveness of the approach has resulted in its incorporation into the linguist's workflow. Our open-source implementation is available online.[1]

2 Model

The underlying model used is a long short-term memory (LSTM) recurrent neural network (Hochreiter and Schmidhuber, 1997) in a bidirectional configuration (Schuster and Paliwal, 1997). The network is trained with the connectionist temporal classification (CTC) loss function (Graves et al., 2006). Critically, this alleviates the need for alignments between speech features and labels in the transcription which we do not have. This is achieved through the use of a dynamic programming algorithm that efficiently sums over the probability of neural network output label that correspond to the gold transcription sequence when repeated labels are collapsed.

The use of an underlying recurrent neural network allows the model to implicitly model context via the parameters of the LSTM, despite the independent frame-wise label predictions of the CTC network. It is this feature of the architecture that makes it a promising tool for tonal prediction, since tonal information is suprasegmental, spanning many frames (Mortensen et al., 2016). Context beyond the immediate local signal is indispensable for tonal prediction, and long-ranging context is especially important in the case of morphotonologically rich languages such as Na and Chatino.

Past work distinguishes between *embedded* tonal modelling, where phoneme and tone labels are jointly predicted, and *explicit* tonal modelling, where they are predicted separately (Lee et al., 2002). We compare several training objectives for the purposes of phoneme and tone prediction. This includes separate prediction of 1) phonemes and 2) tones, as well as 3) jointly predict phonemes and tones using one label set. Figure 1 presents an example sentence from the Na corpus described in §3.1, along with an example of these three objectives.

---

[1]https://github.com/oadams/mam

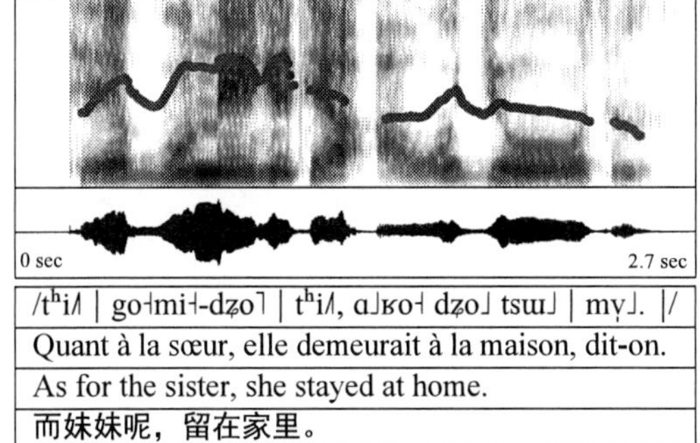

/tʰiʌ | go˧mi˧-dʐo˥ | tʰiʌ, a˩ʁo˧ dʐo˩ tsɯ˩ | my˩. |/

Quant à la sœur, elle demeurait à la maison, dit-on.

As for the sister, she stayed at home.

而妹妹呢，留在家里。

Target label sequence:

1.	tʰ i g o m i dʐ o tʰ i a ʁ o dʐ o t s ɯ m y
2.	˧˩ ˧˩ ˥ ˩ ˧ ˩ ˩ ˩ ˩
3.	tʰ i ʌ g o ˧ m i ˧ dʐ o ˥ tʰ i ʌ a ˩ ʁ o ˧ dʐ o ˩ t s ɯ ˩ m y ˩

Figure 1: A sentence from the Na corpus. Top to bottom: spectrogram with F_0 in blue; waveform; phonemic transcription; English, French and Chinese translations; target label sequences: 1. phonemes only, 2. tones only, 3. phonemes and tones together.

3 Experimental Setup

We designed the experiments to answer these primary questions:

1. How do the error rates scale with respect to training data?

2. How effective is tonal modelling in a CTC framework?

3. To what extent does phoneme context play a role in tone prediction?

4. Does joint prediction of phonemes and tones help minimize error rates?

We assess the performance of the systems as training data scales from 10 minutes to 150 minutes of a single Na speaker, and between 12 and 50 minutes for a single speaker of Chatino. Experimenting with this extremely limited training data gives us a sense of how much a linguist needs to transcribe before this technology can be profitably incorporated into their workflow.

We evaluate both the phoneme error rate (PER) and tone error rate (TER) of models based on the same neural architecture, but with varying input features and output objectives. Input features include log Filterbank features[2] (fbank), pitch features of Ghahremani et al. (2014) (pitch), and a

combination of both (fbank+pitch). These input features vary in the amount of acoustic information relevant to tonal modelling that they include. The output objectives correspond to those discussed in §2: tones only (tone), phonemes only (phoneme), or jointly modelling both (joint). We denote combinations of input features and target labellings as ⟨input⟩⇒⟨output⟩.

In case of tonal prediction we explore similar configurations to that of phoneme prediction, but with two additional points of comparison. The first is predicting tones given one-hot phoneme vectors (phoneme) of the gold phoneme transcription (phoneme⇒tone). The second predicts tones directly from pitch features (pitch⇒tone). These important points of comparison serve to give us some understanding as to how much tonal information is being extracted directly from the acoustic signal versus the phoneme context.

3.1 Data

We explore application of the model to the Na corpus that is part of the Pangloss collection (Michailovsky et al., 2014). This corpus consists of around 100 narratives, constituting 11 hours of speech from one speaker in the form of traditional stories, and spontaneous narratives about life, family and customs (Michaud, 2017, 33). Several hours of the recordings have been phonemically transcribed, and we used up to 149 minutes of this for training, 24 minutes for validation and 23 minutes for testing. The total number of phoneme and tone labels used for automatic transcription was 78 and 7 respectively.

For Chatino, we used data of Ćavar et al. (2016) from the GORILLA language archive for Eastern Chatino of San Juan Quiahije, Oaxaca, Mexico for the purposes of comparing phoneme and tone prediction with Na when data restriction is in place. We used up to 50 minutes of data for training, 8 minutes for validation and 7 minutes for testing. The phoneme inventory we used consists of 31 labels along with 14 tone labels. For both languages, preprocessing involved removing punctuation and any other symbols that are not phonemes or tones such as tone group delimiters and hyphens connecting syllables within words.

4 Quantitative Results

Figure 2 shows the phoneme and tone error rates for Na and Chatino.

---

[2] 41 log Filterbank features along with their first and second derivatives

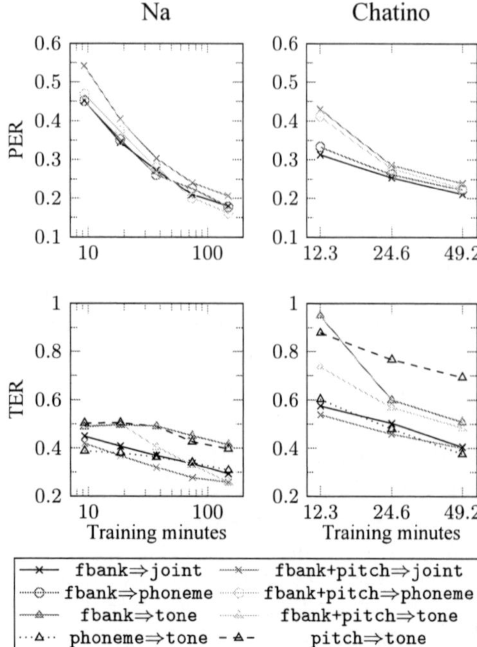

Figure 2: Phoneme error rate (PER) and tone error rate (TER) on test sets as training data is scaled for Na (left) and Chatino (right). The legend entries are formatted as ⟨input⟩ ⇒ ⟨output⟩ to indicate input features to the model and output target labels.

Error rate scaling   Error rates decrease logarithmically with training data. The best methods reliably have a lower than 30% PER with 30 minutes of training data. We believe it is reasonable to expect similar trends in other languages, with these results suggesting how much linguists might need to transcribe before semi-automation can become part of their workflow.

In the case of phoneme-only prediction, use of pitch information does help reduce the PER, which is consistent with previous work (Metze et al., 2013).

Tonal modelling   TER is always higher than PER for the same amount of training data, despite there being only 7 tone labels versus 78 phoneme labels in our Na experiment. This is true even when pitch features are present. However, it is unsurprising since the tones have overlapping pitch ranges, and can be realized with vastly different pitch over the course of a single sentence. This suggests that context is more important for predicting tones than phonemes, which are more context-independent.

fbank⇒tone and pitch⇒tone are vastly in-

ferior to other methods, all of which are privy to phonemic information via training labels or input. However, combining the fbank and pitch input features (fbank+pitch⇒tone) makes for the equal best performing approach for tonal prediction in Na at maximum training data. This indicates both that these features are complementary and that the model has learnt a representation useful for tonal prediction that is on par with explicit phonemic information.

Though tonal prediction is more challenging than phoneme prediction, these results suggest automatic tone transcription is feasible using this architecture, even without inclusion of explicit linguistic information such as constraints on valid tone sequences which is a promising line of future work.

Phoneme context   To assess the importance of context in tone prediction, phoneme⇒tone gives us a point of comparison where no acoustic information is available at all. It performs reasonably well for Na, and competitively for Chatino. One likely reason for its solid performance is that long-range context is modelled more effectively by using phoneme input features, since there are vastly fewer phonemes per sentence than speech frames. The rich morphotonology of Na and Chatino means context is important in the realisation of tones, explaining why phoneme⇒tone can perform almost as well as methods using acoustic features.

Joint prediction   Interestingly, joint prediction of phonemes and tones does not outperform the best methods for separate phoneme and tone prediction, except in the case of Chatino tone prediction, if we discount phoneme⇒tone. In light of the celebrated successes of multitask learning in various domains (Collobert et al., 2011; Deng et al., 2013; Girshick, 2015; Ramsundar et al., 2015; Ruder, 2017), one might expect training with joint prediction of phonemes and tones to help, since it gives more relevant contextual information to the model.

Na versus Chatino   The trends observed in the experimentation on Chatino were largely consistent with those of Na, but with higher error rates owing to less training data and a larger tone label set. There are two differences with the Na results worth noting. One is that phoneme⇒tone is more competitive in the case of Chatino, suggest-

	M	L	H	LH	MH
M	0	69.8	18.6	7.4	4.2
L	77	0	14.6	6.1	2.3
H	56.1	27.3	0	10.6	6.1
LH	38.6	31.8	25	0	4.5
MH	41.4	22.4	17.2	19	0

Figure 3: Confusion matrix showing the rates of substitution errors between tones (as a percentage, normalized per row).

ing that phoneme context plays a more important role in tonal prediction in Chatino. The second is that fbank⇒tone outperforms pitch⇒tone, and that adding pitch features to Filterbank features offers less benefit than in Na.

4.1 Error Types

Figure 3 shows the most common tone substitution mistakes for fbank+pitch⇒joint in the test set. Proportions were very similar for other methods. The most common tonal substitution errors were those between between M and L. Acoustically, M and L are neighbours; as mentioned above, in Na the same tone can be realised with a different pitch at different points in a sentence, leading to overlapping pitch ranges between these tones. Moreover, M and L tones were by far the most common tonal labels.

5 Qualitative Discussion

The phoneme error rates in the above quantitative analysis are promising, but is this system actually of practical use in a linguistic workflow? We discuss here the experience of a linguist in applying this model to Na data to aid in transcription of 9 minutes and 30 seconds of speech.

5.1 Recognition Errors

The phonemic errors typically make linguistic sense: they are not random added noise and often bring the linguist's attention to phonetic facts that are easily overlooked because they are not phonemically contrastive.

One set of such errors is due to differences in articulation between different morphosyntactic classes. For example, the noun 'person' /hĩ˩/ and the relativizer suffix /-hĩ˩/ are segmentally identical, but the latter is articulated much more weakly than the former and it is often recognized as /ĩ/ in automatic transcription, without an initial /h/. Likewise, in the demonstrative /ʈʂʰɯ˩/ the initial

consonant /ʈʂʰ/ is often strongly hypo-articulated, resulting in its recognition as a fricative /ʂ/, /ʐ/, or /ʐ̩/ instead of an aspirated affricate. As a further example, the negation that is transcribed as /mõ˧/ in *Housebuilding2.290* instead of /mɤ˧/. This highlights that the vowel in that syllable is probably nazalised, and acoustically unlike the average /ɤ/ vowel for lexical words. The extent to which a word's morphosyntactic category influences the way it is pronounced is known to be language-specific (Brunelle et al., 2015); the phonemic transcription tool indirectly reveals that this influence is considerable in Na.

A second set is due to loanwords containing combinations of phonemes that are unattested in the training set. For example /ʐu˩pe˧/, from Mandarin *riběn* (日本, 'Japan'). /pe/ is otherwise unattested in Na, which only has /pi/; accordingly, the syllable was identified as /pi/. In documenting Na, Mandarin loanwords were initially transcribed with Chinese characters, and thus cast aside from analyses, instead of confronting the issue of how different phonological systems coexist and interact in language use.

A third set of errors made by the system result in an output that is not phonologically well formed, such as syllables without tones and sequences with consonant clusters such as /kgɣ/. These cases are easy for the linguist to identify and amend.

The recognition system currently makes tonal mistakes that are easy to correct on the basis of elementary phonological knowledge: it produces some impossible tone sequences such as M+L+M inside the same tone group. Very long-ranging tonal dependencies are not harnessed so well by the current tone identification tool. This is consistent with quantitative indications in §4 and is a case for including a tonal language model or refining the neural architecture to better harness long-range contextual information.

5.2 Benefits for the Linguist

Using this automatic transcription as a starting point for manual correction was found to confer several benefits to the linguist.

Faithfulness to acoustic signal The model produces output that is faithful to the acoustic signal. In casual oral speech there are repetitions and hesitations that are sometimes overlooked by the transcribing linguist, who is engrossed in a holistic process involving interpretation, translation, annotation, and communication with the language consultant. When using an automatically generated transcription as a canvas, there can be full confidence in the linearity of transcription, and more attention can be placed on linguistically meaningful dialogue with the language consultant.

Typographical errors and the transcriber's mindset Transcriptions are made during fieldwork with a language consultant and are difficult to correct down the line based only on auditory impression when the consultant is not available. However, such typographic errors are common, with a large number of phoneme labels and significant use of combinations of keys (Shift, Alternative Graph, etc). By providing a high-accuracy first-pass automatic transcription, much of this manual data entry is entirely avoided. Enlisting the linguist solely for correction of errors also allows them to embrace a critical mindset, putting them in "proofreading mode", where focus can be entirely centred on assessing the correctness of the system output without the additional distracting burden of data entry.

Speed Assessing automatic transcription's influence on the speed of the overall language documentation process is beyond the scope of this paper and is left to future work. Language documentation is a holistic process. Beyond phonemic transcription, documentation of Na involves other work that happens in parallel: translating, discussing with a native speaker, copying out new words into the Na dictionary, and being constantly on the lookout for new and unexpected linguistic phenomena. Further complicating this, the linguist's proficiency of the language and speed of transcription is dynamic, improving over time. This makes comparisons difficult.

From this preliminary experiment, the efficiency of the linguist was perceived to be improved, but the benefits lie primarily in the advantages of providing a transcript faithful to the recording, and allowing the linguist to minimize manual entry, focusing on correction and enrichment of the transcribed document.

The snowball effect More data collection means more training data for better ASR performance. The process of improving the acoustic model by training on such semi-automatic transcriptions has begun, with the freshly transcribed *Housebuilding2* used in this investigation now available for subsequent Na acoustic modelling training.

As a first example of output by incorporating automatic transcription into the Yongning Na documentation workflow, transcription of the recording *Housebuilding* was completed using automatic transcription as a canvas; this document is now available online.[3]

6 Conclusion

We have presented the results of applying a CTC-based LSTM model to the task of phoneme and tone transcription in a resource-scarce context: that of a newly documented language. Beyond comparing the effects of various training inputs and objectives on the phoneme and tone error rates, we reported on the application of this method to linguistic documentation of Yongning Na. Its applicability as a first-pass transcription is very encouraging, and it has now been incorporated into the workflow. Our results give an idea of the amount of speech other linguists might aspire to transcribe in order to bootstrap this process: as little as 30 minutes in order to obtain a sub-30% phoneme error rate as a starting point, with further improvements to come as more data is transcribed in the semi-automated workflow. There is still much room for modelling improvement, including incorporation of linguistic constraints into the architecture for more accurate transcriptions.

References

Laurent Besacier, Etienne Barnard, Alexey Karpov, and Tanja Schultz. 2014. Automatic speech recognition for under-resourced languages: A survey. *Speech Communication* 56:85–100.

Marc Brunelle, Daryl Chow, and Thụy Nhã Uyên Nguyễn. 2015. Effects of lexical frequency and lexical category on the duration of Vietnamese syllables. In The Scottish Consortium for ICPhS 2015, editor, *Proceedings of 18th International Congress of Phonetic Sciences*. University of Glasgow, Glasgow, pages 1–5.

Lukáš Burget, Petr Schwarz, Mohit Agarwal, Pinar Akyazi, Kai Feng, Arnab Ghoshal, Ondřej Glembek, Nagendra Goel, Martin Karafiát, Daniel Povey, and Others. 2010. Multilingual acoustic modeling for speech recognition based on subspace Gaussian mixture models. In *Acoustics Speech and Signal Processing (ICASSP), 2010 IEEE International Conference on*. IEEE, pages 4334–4337.

---

[3] http://lacito.vjf.cnrs.fr/pangloss/corpus/show_text_en .php?id=crdo-NRU_F4_HOUSEBUILDING2_SOUND &idref=crdo-NRU_F4_HOUSEBUILDING2

Małgorzata E. Ćavar, Damir Cavar, and Hilaria Cruz. 2016. Endangered Language Documentation: Bootstrapping a Chatino Speech Corpus, Forced Aligner, ASR. In *LREC*. pages 4004–4011.

Chatino Language Documentation Project. 2017. Chatino Language Documentation Project Collection.

Ronan Collobert, Jason Weston, and Michael Karlen. 2011. Natural Language Processing (almost) from Scratch 1:1–34.

Emiliana Cruz. 2011. *Phonology, tone and the functions of tone in San Juan Quiahije Chatino*. Ph.D., University of Texas at Austin, Austin. http://hdl.handle.net/2152/ETD-UT-2011-08-4280.

Emiliana Cruz and Tony Woodbury. 2006. El sandhi de los tonos en el Chatino de Quiahije. In *Las memorias del Congreso de Idiomas Indígenas de Latinoamérica-II*, Archive of the Indigenous Languages of Latin America.

Li Deng, Geoffrey Hinton, and Brian Kingsbury. 2013. New types of deep neural network learning for speech recognition and related applications: an overview. In *2013 IEEE International Conference on Acoustics, Speech and Signal Processing*. IEEE, pages 8599–8603. https://doi.org/10.1109/ICASSP.2013.6639344.

Thi-Ngoc-Diep Do, Alexis Michaud, and Eric Castelli. 2014. Towards the automatic processing of Yongning Na (Sino-Tibetan): developing a 'light' acoustic model of the target language and testing 'heavyweight' models from five national languages. In *4th International Workshop on Spoken Language Technologies for Under-resourced Languages (SLTU 2014)*. St Petersburg, Russia, pages 153–160. https://halshs.archives-ouvertes.fr/halshs-00980431.

Yan-Mei Feng, Li Xu, Ning Zhou, Guang Yang, and Shan-Kai Yin. 2012. Sine-wave speech recognition in a tonal language. *The Journal of the Acoustical Society of America* 131(2):EL133–EL138. https://doi.org/10.1121/1.3670594.

Pegah Ghahremani, Bagher BabaAli, Daniel Povey, Korbinian Riedhammer, Jan Trmal, and Sanjeev Khudanpur. 2014. A pitch extraction algorithm tuned for automatic speech recognition. In *Acoustics, Speech and Signal Processing (ICASSP), 2014 IEEE International Conference on*. IEEE, pages 2494–2498.

Ross Girshick. 2015. Fast R-CNN. In *2015 IEEE International Conference on Computer Vision (ICCV)*. IEEE, pages 1440–1448. https://doi.org/10.1109/ICCV.2015.169.

Alex Graves, Santiago Fernandez, Faustino Gomez, and Jurgen Schmidhuber. 2006. Connectionist Temporal Classification : Labelling Unsegmented Sequence Data with Recurrent Neural Networks. *Proceedings of the 23rd international conference on Machine Learning* pages 369–376. https://doi.org/10.1145/1143844.1143891.

Nikolaus Himmelmann. 2006. Language documentation: what is it and what is it good for? In J. Gippert, Nikolaus Himmelmann, and Ulrike Mosel, editors, *Essentials of language documentation*, de Gruyter, Berlin/New York, pages 1–30.

Geoffrey Hinton, Li Deng, Dong Yu, George E Dahl, Abdel-rahman Mohamed, Navdeep Jaitly, Andrew Senior, Vincent Vanhoucke, Patrick Nguyen, Tara N Sainath, and Others. 2012. Deep neural networks for acoustic modeling in speech recognition: The shared views of four research groups. *Signal Processing Magazine, IEEE* 29(6):82–97.

Sepp Hochreiter and Jürgen Schmidhuber. 1997. Long short-term memory. *Neural computation* 9(8):1735–1780.

Viet-Bac Le and Laurent Besacier. 2009. Automatic speech recognition for under-resourced languages: application to Vietnamese language. *Audio, Speech, and Language Processing, IEEE Transactions on* 17(8):1471–1482.

Tan Lee, Wai Lau, Yiu Wing Wong, and P C Ching. 2002. Using tone information in Cantonese continuous speech recognition. *ACM Transactions on Asian Language Information Processing (TALIP)* 1(1):83–102.

Florian Metze, Zaid A.W. W Sheikh, Alex Waibel, Jonas Gehring, Kevin Kilgour, Quoc Bao Nguyen, and Van Huy Nguyen. 2013. Models of tone for tonal and non-tonal languages. *2013 IEEE Workshop on Automatic Speech Recognition and Understanding, ASRU 2013 - Proceedings* pages 261–266. https://doi.org/10.1109/ASRU.2013.6707740.

Boyd Michailovsky, Martine Mazaudon, Alexis Michaud, Séverine Guillaume, Alexandre François, and Evangelia Adamou. 2014. Documenting and researching endangered languages: the Pangloss Collection. *Language Documentation and Conservation* 8:119–135.

Alexis Michaud. 2017. *Tone in Yongning Na: lexical tones and morphotonology*. Number 13 in Studies in Diversity Linguistics. Language Science Press, Berlin. http://langsci-press.org/catalog/book/109.

David R Mortensen, Patrick Littell, Akash Bharadwaj, Kartik Goyal, Chris Dyer, and Lori Levin. 2016. PanPhon: A Resource for Mapping IPA Segments to Articulatory Feature Vectors. *Proceedings of COLING 2016, the 26th International Conference on Computational Linguistics: Technical Papers* pages 3475–3484. http://aclweb.org/anthology/C16-1328.

Markus Müller, Sebastian Stüker, and Alex Waibel. 2017. Language Adaptive Multilingual CTC Speech Recognition. In Alexey Karpov, Rodmonga Potapova, and Iosif Mporas, editors, *Speech and Computer: 19th International*

Conference, SPECOM 2017, Hatfield, UK, September 12-16, 2017, Proceedings, Springer International Publishing, Cham, pages 473–482. https://doi.org/10.1007/978-3-319-66429-3_47.

Bharath Ramsundar, Steven Kearnes, Patrick Riley, Dale Webster, David Konerding, and Vijay Pande. 2015. Massively Multitask Networks for Drug Discovery http://arxiv.org/abs/1502.02072.

Sebastian Ruder. 2017. An Overview of Multi-Task Learning in Deep Neural Networks http://arxiv.org/abs/1706.05098.

Mike Schuster and Kuldip K Paliwal. 1997. Bidirectional recurrent neural networks. *IEEE Transactions on Signal Processing* 45(11):2673–2681.

Gary F. Simons and Charles D. Fennig, editors. 2017. *Ethnologue: languages of the world*. SIL International, Dallas, twentieth edition edition. http://www.ethnologue.com.

Nick Thieberger. 2016. Documentary linguistics: methodological challenges and innovatory responses. *Applied Linguistics* 37(1):88–99. https://doi.org/10.1093/applin/amv076.

Ngoc Thang Vu, David Imseng, Daniel Povey, Petr Motlicek, Tanja Schultz, and Hervé Bourlard. 2014. Multilingual deep neural network based acoustic modeling for rapid language adaptation. In *Proceedings of the 39th IEEE International Conference on Acoustics, Speech and Signal Processing (ICASSP)*. Florence, Italy, pages 7639–7643.

Haihua Xu, Hang Su, Chongjia Ni, Xiong Xiao, Hao Huang, Eng-Siong Chng, and Haizhou Li. 2016. Semi-supervised and Cross-lingual Knowledge Transfer Learnings for DNN Hybrid Acoustic Models under Low-resource Conditions. In *Proceedings of the Annual Conference of the International Speech Communication Association, (INTERSPEECH)*. San Francisco, USA, pages 1315–1319.

Ping Xu and Pascale Fung. 2013. Cross-lingual language modeling for low-resource speech recognition. *IEEE Transactions on Audio, Speech and Language Processing* 21(6):1134–1144. https://doi.org/10.1109/TASL.2013.2244088.

A Comparative Study of Two Statistical Modelling Approaches
for Estimating Multivariate Likelihood Ratios
in Forensic Voice Comparison

Shunichi Ishihara
The Australian National University
Department of Linguistics
shunichi.ishihara@anu.edu.au

Abstract

The acoustic features used in forensic voice comparison (FVC) are correlated in almost all cases. A sizeable proportion of FVC studies and casework has relied, for statistical modelling, on the multivariate kernel density likelihood ratio (MVKDLR) formula, which considers the correlations between the features and computes an overall combined likelihood ratio (LR) for the offender-suspect comparison. However, following concerns over the robustness of the MVKDLR, in particular its computational weakness and numerical instability specifically when a large number of features are employed, the principal component analysis kernel density likelihood ratio (PCAKDLR) approach was developed as an alternative. In this study, the performance of the two approaches is investigated and compared using Monte Carlo-simulated synthetic data based on the 16th-order Mel Frequency Cepstrum Coefficients extracted from the long vowel /e:/ segments of spontaneous speech uttered by 118 native Japanese male speakers. Performance is assessed in terms of validity (= accuracy) and reliability (= precision), with the log-likelihood ratio cost (C_{llr}) being used to assess validity and the 95% credible interval (95%CI) to assess reliability.

1 Introduction

In many branches of the forensic sciences, including fingerprint (Neumann et al., 2007), handwriting (Marquis et al., 2011), voice (Morrison, 2009a), DNA (Evett et al., 1993), glass fragments (Curran, 2003), earmarks and footwear marks (Evett et al., 1998), strength of evidence is widely measured using the LR framework, increasingly accepted as the standard framework for forensic inference and statistics. Calculating an LR for *voice* evidence requires, as a first step, that each individual's evidence (e.g. offender and suspect recordings) be modelled using various acoustic features (e.g. formant frequencies) that are correlated almost without exceptions. However, estimating an LR based on correlated variables is not a simple problem; it was addressed by Aitken and Lucy (2004), resulting in the development of the multivariate kernel density likelihood ratio (MVKDLR) approach. The MVKDLR has been extensively used, especially in acoustic-phonetic based forensic voice comparison (FVC) (Kinoshita et al., 2009; Morrison, 2009b), but was recently shown to be prone to instability, in particular when the number of features for modelling is too high (e.g. features $\geq$ 5-6). The MVKDLR formula has the propensity to collapse when some of the covariance matrices of the offender and suspect data are ill-conditioned (e.g. sparse data, large number of input features) (Nair et al., 2014, pp. 90-91). This has motivated the development of an alternative, known as the principal component analysis kernel density likelihood ratio (PCAKDLR) approach (Nair et al., 2014).

To date, FVC studies in which the PCAKDLR is used to estimate LRs are limited; thus we don't know how the PCAKDLR performs in comparison to the MVKDLR (cf. Enzinger, 2016). To address this gap in our knowledge, the current study seeks to compare the performance of the MVKDLR and PCAKDLR approaches when the number of features for modelling changes, using synthetic data generated by Monte Carlo simulations (Fishman, 1995). The outcomes (scores) of the two approaches are calibrated using the logistic-regression calibration technique proposed

Shunichi Ishihara. 2017. A Comparative Study of Two Statistical Modelling Approaches for Estimating Multivariate Likelihood Ratios in Forensic Voice Comparison. In *Proceedings of Australasian Language Technology Association Workshop*, pages 61–69.

by Brümmer and du Preez (2006). The performance of the approaches is assessed in terms of validity (= accuracy), for which the metric is the log-likelihood-ratio cost (C_{llr}) (Brümmer & du Preez, 2006), as well as reliability (= precision), for which the metric is the 95% credible interval (95%CI) (Morrison, 2011).

2 Likelihood Ratio

The likelihood ratio (LR), a measure of the quantitative strength of evidence, is a ratio of two conditional probabilities: one is the probability (p) of observed evidence (E) assuming that one hypothesis (e.g. prosecution = H_p) is true; the other is the probability of the same observed evidence assuming that the alternative hypothesis (e.g defence = H_d) is true (Robertson & Vignaux, 1995). Thus, the LR can be expressed as 1).

$$LR=\frac{p(E|H_p)}{p(E|H_d)} \qquad 1)$$

In the case of FVC, the LR will be the probability of observing the difference between the offender's and the suspect's speech samples (referred to as the evidence, E) if they had been produced by the same speaker (H_p) relative to the probability of observing the same evidence (E) if they had been from different speakers (H_d). The relative strength of the given evidence with respect to the competing hypotheses (H_p vs. H_d) is reflected in the magnitude of the LR. The more the LR deviates from unity (LR = 1; logLR = 0), the greater support for either the prosecution hypothesis (LR > 1; logLR > 0) or the defence hypothesis (LR < 1; logLR < 0).

The important point is that the LR is concerned with the probability of the evidence, given the hypothesis (either H_p or H_d), which is the province of forensic scientists, while the trier-of-fact is concerned with the probability of the hypothesis, given the evidence. That is, the ultimate decision as to whether the suspect is guilty or not does not lie with the forensic expert, but with the court. The role of the forensic scientist is to estimate the strength of evidence (= LR) with a view to help the trier-of-fact make a final decision (Morrison, 2009a, p. 229).

3 Database, target segment, and speakers

In this study, monologues from the Corpus of Spontaneous Japanese (CSJ) (Maekawa et al., 2000) are used for FVC experiments. The recordings are 10-25 minutes long.

For this study, it was decided to target fillers. Fillers are sounds or words (e.g. *um*, *you know*, *like* in English) uttered by a speaker to signal that he/she is thinking or hesitating. The filler /e:/ and the /e:/ segment of the filler /e:to:/ were chosen because i) they are two of the most frequently used fillers in Japanese (many monologues contain at least ten of them) (Ishihara, 2010), ii) the vowel /e/ reportedly has the strongest speaker-discriminatory power out of the five Japanese vowels /i,e,a,o,u/ (Kinoshita, 2001), and iii) the segment /e:/ is significantly long so that it is easy to extract stable spectral features from this segment. It is also considered that fillers are uttered unconsciously or semiconsciously by the speaker and carry no lexical meaning. They are thus not likely to be affected by the pragmatic focus of the utterance.

For the experiments, speakers were selected from the CSJ based on five criteria: i) availability of two non-contemporaneous recordings per speaker (n.b. suspect and offender recordings are non-contemporaneous in real cases), ii) high spontaneity of speech (e.g. not reading), iii) exclusive use of standard modern Japanese, iv) presence of at least ten /e:/ segments, and v) availability of complete annotation of the data. As the researchers had real casework in mind, only male speakers were chosen for experiments. This is because males are more likely to commit crimes than females (Kanazawa & Still, 2000). The five criteria combined resulted in 236 recordings (118 speakers x 2 non-contemporaneous recordings), all of which were used in our experiments.

The 118 speakers were divided into three mutually exclusive sub-databases: the test database (40 speakers), the background database (39 speakers) and the development database (39 speakers). Each speaker in these databases has two recordings that are non-contemporaneous. The first ten /e:/ segments were annotated in each recording. Thus, for example, there are 800 annotated /e:/ segments in the test database (= 40 speakers x 2 sessions x 10 segments). Data sparsity is a common issue in FVC. Ten samples for each recording can be judged as a realistic setting. All statistics required for conducting Monte Carlo simulations were calculated using these databases.

The speaker comparisons derived from the test database were used to assess the performance of the FVC system. The background database was used as a background reference population, and the development database was for obtaining the logistic-regression weight, which was used to calibrate the scores of the test database (refer to §4.5 for a detailed explanation of calibration).

4 Experiments

4.1 Features

We used 16 Mel Frequency Cepstrum Coefficients (MFCC) in the experiments as feature vectors. MFCC is a standard spectral feature used in many voice-related applications, including automatic speaker recognition. All original speech samples were downsampled to 16kHz before MFCC values were extracted from the mid-duration-point of the target segment /e:/ with a 20 ms wide hamming window.

4.2 General experimental design

There are two types of tests for FVC. One relies on so-called *Same Speaker Comparisons* (SS comparisons), where two speech samples produced by the same speakers are compared. They are expected to receive LR values > 1 given the same-origins. The other type of test relies on *Different Speaker Comparisons* (DS comparisons), where two speech samples produced by different speakers are compared. They are expected to receive LR values < 1 given the different-origins.

For example, the 40 speakers of the test database enable us to undertake 40 SS comparisons and 1560 (= $_{50}C_2$ x 2) independent (e.g. not-overlapping) DS comparisons. Theoretically speaking, origin being identical, the 40 SS comparisons should receive an LR > 1 ($\log_{10}$LR > 0); on the other hand, origin being different, the 1560 DS comparisons should receive an LR < 1 (or $\log_{10}$LR < 0).

4.3 Likelihood ratio calculation

MVKDLR Approach

The MVKDLR formula computes a single LR from multiple variables (e.g. 16th-order MFCC), considering the correlations among them (Aitken & Lucy, 2004).

The numerator of the MVKDLR formula calculates the probability of evidence, which is the difference between the offender and suspect speech samples, when it is assumed that both samples have the same origin (in other words, that the persecution hypothesis H_p is true). For this calculation, the feature vectors of the offender and suspect samples and the within-speaker variance, which is given in the form of a variance/covariance matrix, are needed. The same feature vectors of the offender and suspect samples and the between-speaker variance are used in the denominator of the formula to estimate the probability of getting the same evidence when it is assumed that they have different origins (i.e. that the defence hypothesis H_d is true). These within- and between-speaker variances are estimated from the background database. The MVKDLR formula assumes normality for within-speaker variance while it uses a kernel-density model for between-speaker variance.

In the MVKDLR formula, the covariance matrices for offender and suspect data are used extensively. The inverses of these matrices are required at some stages in the process, and there are also some instances of these inverted matrices being re-inverted. All of these processes contribute to the decorrelation of the original features and the equalisation of their contribution. However, in return, the MVKDLR formula has the propensity to collapse when some of the covariance matrices of the offender and suspect data are ill-conditioned due to, for example, sparse data and large input parameters.

PCAKDLR Approach

In the PCAKDLR approach, in particular when high-dimensional features are used, the issue of the instability described for the MVKDLR is handled by decorrelating the features through principal component analysis (PCA), and then estimating LRs as the product of the univariate LRs of the resultant uncorrelated features. Thus, PCA is merely used to decorrelate the features (not to reduce feature dimensionality). With the resultant orthogonal features, a univariate LR was estimated separately for each feature using the modified kernel density model (Nair et al., 2014, pp. 88-90); the independent LRs were multiplied to generate an overall LR.

4.4 Repeated experiments using Monte Carlo simulations

As explained earlier, each speaker has two sets of ten /e:/ segments, and 16 MFCC values were extracted from each of them. That is, each session of each speaker can be modelled maximally with ten sets of 16th-order feature vectors. From these ten sets of vectors for each session of each speaker, we also obtained the basic statistics (the mean vector µ and variance/covariance matrix ε) needed for the Monte Carlo simulations. In this study, we randomly generated, for each session of each speaker, ten feature vectors, each of which consists of 16 MFCC values. We repeated this procedure 150 times using the normal distribution function modelled with the basic statistics.

Figure 1 is an example of the Monte Carlo simulation showing 150 randomly generated first two MFCC values (c1 and c2) from the normal distribution function based on the statistics (μ and ε) obtained from the first session of the first speaker in the test database.

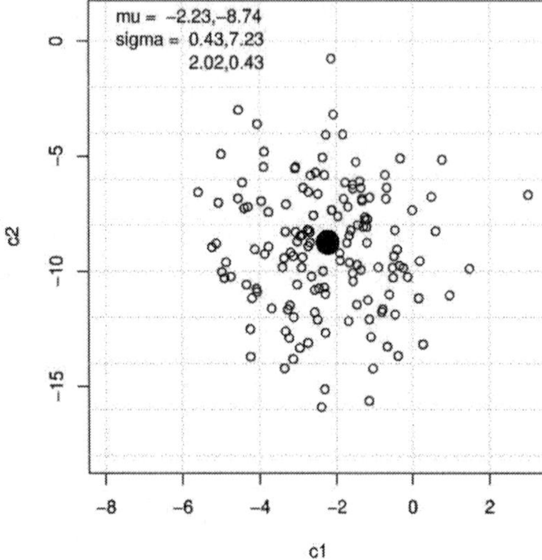

Figure 1: 150 randomly generated values (c1 and c2) from the statistics (μ and ε) obtained from the first session of the first speaker in the test database (only the first and second MFCC). The filled black circle = μ.

Experiments were repeatedly conducted using randomly generated synthetic feature vectors with different dimensions (= {2,4,6,8,10,12,14,16}). For example, a feature dimension of {2} means that the first two MFCC values were used for experiments, and a feature dimension of {14} means that the first 14 MFCC were used.

4.5 Calibration

A logistic-regression calibration (Brümmer & du Preez, 2006) was applied to the outputs (scores) of the MVKDLR and PCAKDLR approaches. Given two sets of scores derived from the SS and DS comparisons and a decision boundary, calibration is a normalisation procedure involving linear monotonic shifting and scaling of the scores relative to the decision boundary, so as to minimise a cost function, resulting in LRs. The FoCal toolkit [1] was used for the logistic-regression calibration in this study (Brümmer & du Preez, 2006). The logistic-regression weight was obtained from the development database.

4.6 Evaluation of performance: validity and reliability

The performance of the LR-based FVC system needs to be assessed in terms of its validity (= accuracy) and reliability (= precision). To explain the concepts of validity and reliability, we will look at an example. Let us imagine we have speech samples collected from two speakers at four different sessions denoted as S1.1, S1.2, S1.3, S1.4, S2.1, S2.2, S2.3 and S2.4, where S = speaker, and 1, 2, 3 and 4 = the first, second, third and fourth sessions (e.g. S1.1 refers to the first session recording collected from (S)peaker1, and S1.4 to the fourth session from that same speaker). From these speech samples, four independent (not overlapping) DS comparisons are possible: S1.1 vs. S2.1, S1.2 vs. S2.2, S1.3 vs. S2.3 and S1.4 vs. S2.4. Let us further suppose that we conducted two separate FVC tests using two different systems (Systems 1 and 2), and that we obtained the $\log_{10}$LRs given in Table 1 for these four DS comparisons.

DS comparison	System 1	System 2
S1.1 vs. S2.1	-8.3	-5.1
S1.2 vs. S2.2	-7.9	-1.2
S1.3 vs. S2.3	-8.0	-3.1
S1.4 vs. S2.4	-8.2	-0.1

Table 1: Example $\log_{10}$LRs explaining the concepts of validity and reliability.

Since the comparisons given in Table 1 are all DS comparisons, the desired $\log_{10}$LR value needs to be lower than 0, and the greater the negative $\log_{10}$LR value is, the better the system is, as it more strongly supports the correct hypothesis. For both Systems 1 and 2, all of the comparisons received $\log_{10}$LR < 0. That is, all of these $\log_{10}$LR values correctly single out the defence hypothesis. However, System 1 performs better than System 2 in that its $\log_{10}$LR values are further away from unity ($\log_{10}$LR = 0) than the $\log_{10}$LR values of System 2. This means that the $\log_{10}$LR values estimated by System 1 provide greater support for the correct hypothesis than System 2. Thus, it can be said that the validity (=

---

[1] https://sites.google.com/site/nikobrummer/focal

accuracy) of System 1 is higher than that of System 2. This is the basic concept of validity.

In this study, the log-likelihood-ratio cost (C_{llr}), which is a gradient metric based on LR, was used as the metric for validity. The calculation of C_{llr} is given in 2) (Brümmer & du Preez, 2006).

$$C_{llr}=\frac{1}{2}\left(\begin{array}{l}\frac{1}{N_{H_p}}\sum_{i\ \text{for}H_p=\text{true}}^{N_{H_p}}\log_2\left(1+\frac{1}{LR_i}\right)+\\\frac{1}{N_{H_d}}\sum_{j\ \text{for}H_d=\text{true}}^{N_{H_d}}\log_2\left(1+LR_j\right)\end{array}\right)\quad 2)$$

In 2), N_{H_p} and N_{H_d} are the number of SS and DS comparisons, and LR_i and LR_j are the linear LRs derived from the SS and DS comparisons, respectively. Given the same origins, all the SS comparisons should produce LRs greater than 1, and given the different origins, the DS comparisons should produce LRs less than 1. C_{llr} takes into account the magnitude of derived LR values, and assigns them appropriate penalties. In C_{llr}, LRs that support counter-factual hypotheses or, in other words, contrary-to-fact LRs (LR < 1 for SS comparisons and LR > 1 for DS comparisons) are heavily penalised and the magnitude of the penalty is proportional to how much the LRs deviate from unity. The lower the C_{llr} value, the better the performance.

The C_{llr} measures the overall performance of a system in terms of validity based on a cost function in which there are two main components of loss: namely discrimination loss (C_{llr}^{min}) and calibration loss (C_{llr}^{cal}) (Brümmer & du Preez, 2006). The former is obtained after the application of the so-called pooled-adjacent-violators (PAV) transformation – an optimal non-parametric calibration procedure. The latter is obtained by subtracting the former from the C_{llr}. In this study, besides C_{llr}, C_{llr}^{min} and C_{llr}^{cal} are also referred to. Once again, the FoCal toolkit[1] was used in this study for calculating C_{llr} (including both C_{llr}^{min} and C_{llr}^{cal}) (Brümmer & du Preez, 2006).

Let us now move to the concept of reliability. All of the DS comparisons given in Table 1 are comparisons of the same speaker pair (S1 vs. S2). Thus, it can be expected that the LR values obtained for these four DS comparisons should be similar as they are comparing the same speaker pair. However, the $\log_{10}LR$ values based on System 1 are closer to each other (-8.3, -7.9, -8.0 and -8.2) than those based on System 2 (-5.1, -1.2, -3.1 and -0.1). In other words, the reliability (= preci-

sion) of System 1 is higher than that of System 2. This is the basic concept of reliability.

As a metric of reliability, we used 95% credible intervals, the Bayesian analogue of frequentist confidence intervals (Morrison, 2011). In this study, we calculated 95% credible intervals (95%CI) in the parametric manner based on the deviation-from-mean values collected from all of the DS comparison pairs. For example, 95%CI = 1.23 and $\log_{10}LR = 2$ means, for this particular comparison, that it is 95% certain that $\log_{10}LR \geq 0.77$ (= 2-1.23) and $\log_{10}LR \leq 3.23$ (= 2+1.23). The smaller the 95%CI, the better the reliability. The 95%CI is obtainable only from the DS comparisons in the present study.

5 Experiment with Original Data

Before presenting the results of the experiments using synthetic data, we conducted experiments using the full 16th-order MFCC values from the original databases with the two different approaches. The results of these experiments are given as Tippett plots in Figure 2 with the C_{llr} and 95%CI values. Figure 2a is for the MVKDLR and Figure 2b is for the PCAKDLR. In these Tippett plots, the solid black curve indicates the cumulative proportion of the SS comparison $\log_{10}LRs$ (40) that are equal or smaller than the value indicated on the x-axis, and the solid grey curve indicates the cumulative proportion of the DS comparison $\log_{10}LRs$ (1560) that are equal or greater than the value indicated on the x-axis. Tippett plots graphically show how strongly the derived LRs not only support the correct hypothesis but also misleadingly support the contrary-to-fact hypothesis. In Figure 2, the $\log_{10}LRs$ for the DS comparisons are plotted together with ±95%CI band.

In terms of validity, the MVKDLR ($C_{llr} = 0.396$) marginally outperforms the PCAKDLR ($C_{llr} = 0.418$), but in terms of reliability, the PCAKDLR (95%CI = 3.536) outperforms the MVKDLR (95%CI = 4.026). As far as the Tippett plots are concerned, it can be seen from Figure 2a and Figure 2b that the magnitude of the derived LRs is very similar and comparable between the MVKDLR and PCAKDLR approaches. In terms of the discrimination (C_{llr}^{min}) and calibration (C_{llr}^{cal}) losses, although the MVKDLR ($C_{llr}^{min} = 0.253$ and $C_{llr}^{cal} = 0.143$) is slightly better than the PCAKDLR ($C_{llr}^{min} = 0.267$ and $C_{llr}^{cal} = 0.151$) in

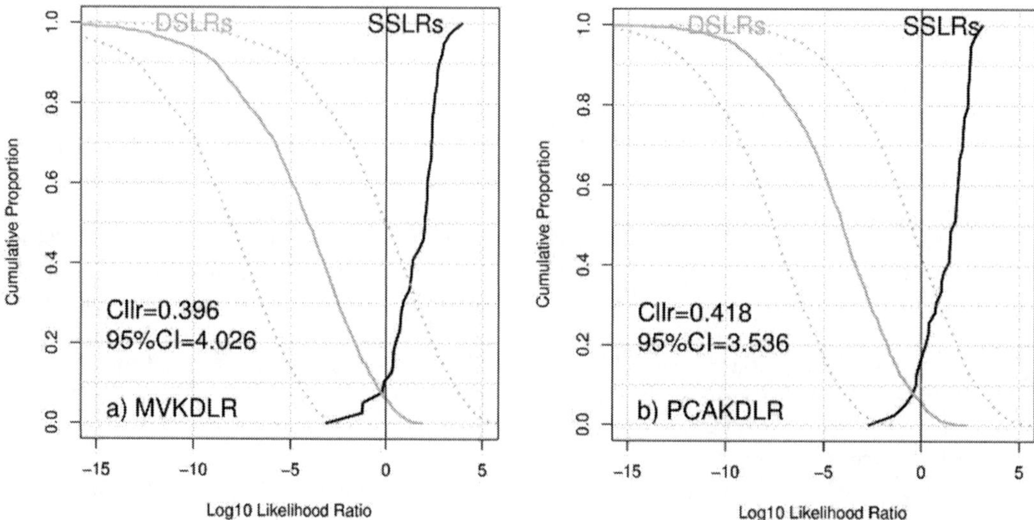

Figure 2: Tippett plots showing the magnitude of the derived LRs plotted separately for the SS (black) and DS (grey) comparisons. ±95%CI bands (grey dotted lines) are superimposed on the DS LRs. Panel a = MVKDLR and Panel b = PCAKDLR. C_{llr} value was calculated from the calibrated LRs and 95%CI value was calculated only for the calibrated DS LRs.

metric value, they are virtually the same and therefore comparable.

6   Experimental Results and Discussions

It was shown in §5 that, in terms of the C_{llr} (including both C_{llr}^{min} and C_{llr}^{cal}), the MVKDLR performed marginally better than the PCAKDLR (they performed equally well in a practical sense), but that the PCAKDLR outperformed the MVKDLR in terms of the 95%CI. It will be investigated in this section whether the observation made in §5 is a general observation that retains its validity when synthetic data are used. It will also be investigated how the number of features affects the performance of the two different approaches because the MVKDLR reportedly has an issue of instability when high-dimensional features are used.

Before the results of the experiments are displayed, it needs to be pointed out that the C_{llr} (MVKDLR = 0.396 and PCAKDLR = 0.418) and 95%CI values (MVKDLR = 4.026 and PCAKDLR = 3.536) with the 16th-order MFCC feature vector of the original data, which were given in §5, are similar to the mean C_{llr} (MVKDLR = 0.439 and PCAKDLR = 0.465) and 95%CI values (MVKDLR = 0.3348 and PCAKDLR = 2.689) of the 150 simulations with the synthetic 16th-order MFCC feature vector. This

suggests the appropriateness of the Monte Carlo simulation.

In Figure 3, the mean C_{llr} (Panel a), C_{llr}^{min} (Panel b) and C_{llr}^{cal} (Panel c) values of the 150 simulations are plotted for the different feature numbers (= {2,4,6,8,10,12,14,16}) against the mean 95%CI values (y-axis), but separately for the MVKDLR (filled circles) and PCAKDLR (empty circles) approaches. The numerical information of Figure 3 is given in Table 2.

It can be seen from Figure 3a that the overall performance of the MVKDLR in terms of validity (C_{llr}) improves as the number of features increases in that there is substantial improvement when moving from two to four features (from C_{llr} = 0.939 for {2} to C_{llr} = 0.674 for {4}), after which the improvement still continues, yet to a substantially lesser degree. The general trend of the reliability (95%CI) for the MVKDLR is that it deteriorates as the feature number increases. Thus, the trade-off between validity and reliability is fairly clearly observable in the case of the MVKDLR. Although, in terms of validity, the PCAKDLR shows a more or less similar trend compared to the MVKDLR, some exceptions (e.g. the feature number = {6,8}) can also be observed in that the inclusion of additional features did not contribute to an improvement in validity (from C_{llr} = 0.712 for {6} to C_{llr} = 0.736 for {8}). These exceptions

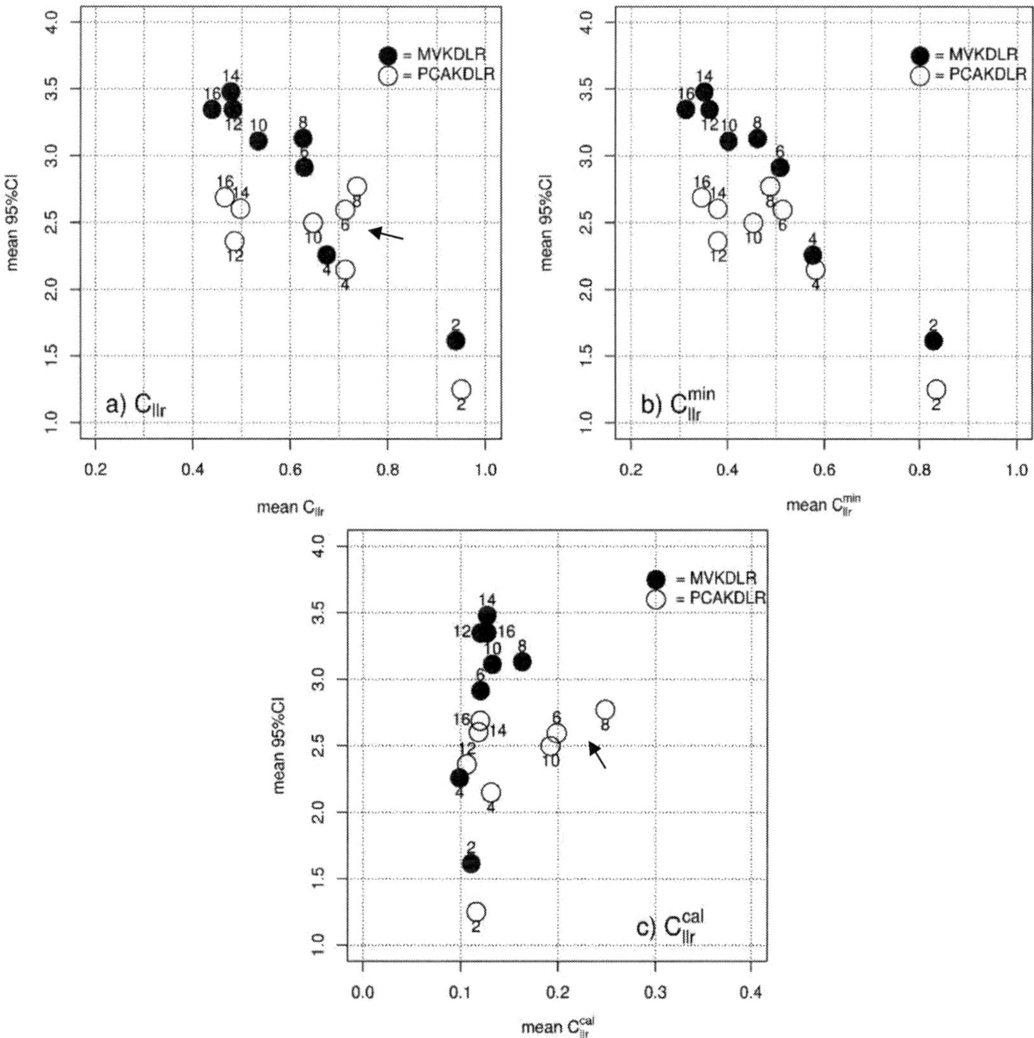

Figure 3: Mean C_{llr} (Panel a), C_{llr}^{min} (b) and C_{llr}^{cal} (c) values (x-axis) plotted against mean 95%CI values (y-axis). Filled and empty circles = MVKDLR and PCAKDLR, respectively. The number attached to each circle indicates the dimension of the feature vector. Note that the range of the x-axis scale is narrower for Panel c) than for Panels a) and b).

will be further investigated below with reference to calibration loss (C_{llr}^{cal}).

The main difference between the two approaches that can be observed from Figure 3a is that the inverse-correlation identified between validity and reliability for the MVKDLR is *not* clearly observable in the case of the PCAKDLR; the 95%CI values stay relatively constant around a 95%CI = 2.5 when six or more features are used for the experiments. As a result, although the PCAKDLR is constantly better in reliability (95%CI) than the MVKDLR, reliability is considerably better for the former than for the latter, in particular when the feature number is large (fea-

ture number $\geq$ 5-6). The observations derived from Figure 3a above more or less coincide with Enzinger (2016) finding that the MVKDLR is superior to the PCAKDLR in terms of validity, but inferior in terms of reliability.

Close observation of Figure 3b, which plots the discriminability of the system (C_{llr}^{min}) against its reliability shows an even clearer difference between the MVKDLR and PCAKDLR approaches described on the basis of Figure 3a in that the 95%CI values seem to hit a ceiling with six features or more for the PCAKDLR, while the 95%CI value continues to increase for the MVKDLR as a function of the feature number.

Metrics	Approaches	2	4	6	8	10	12	14	16
C_{llr}	MVKDLR	0.939	0.674	0.628	0.626	0.534	0.482	0.477	0.439
	PCAKDLR	0.950	0.712	0.712	0.736	0.646	0.485	0.497	0.465
C_{llr}^{min}	MVKDLR	0.828	0.576	0.508	0.462	0.401	0.361	0.350	0.312
	PCAKDLR	0.834	0.581	0.513	0.488	0.454	0.379	0.379	0.345
C_{llr}^{cal}	MVKDLR	0.110	0.098	0.120	0.163	0.132	0.120	0.127	0.127
	PCAKDLR	0.115	0.131	0.198	0.248	0.192	0.106	0.118	0.120
95%CI	MVKDLR	1.615	2.258	2.915	3.132	3.112	3.348	3.478	3.348
	PCAKDLR	1.250	2.148	2.595	2.771	2.498	2.360	2.603	2.689

Table 2: Numerical information of Figure 3. 2~16 = number of features

Figure 3b shows that i) system discriminability improves as a function of the number of features both for the MVKDLR and PCAKDLR approaches, ii) discriminability is marginally but constantly better for the MVKDLR, and iii) reliability is constantly better for the PCAKDLR; the former is considerably better than the latter when the feature number is large (feature number $\geq$ 6).

From Figure 3c, it can be seen that calibration performance is fairly constant and comparable (ca. C_{llr}^{min} = 0.125) between the MVKDLR and PCAKDLR approaches across different feature numbers, except for feature number = {6,8,10} for the PCAKDLR, which is indicated by an arrow in Figure 3c. The poor performance in calibration for feature numbers = {6,8,10} of the PCAKDLR contributes to the overall poor C_{llr} values of the PCAKDLR for the same feature numbers, which can be clearly seen in Figure 3a (as indicated by the arrow). As a result, the C_{llr} values of feature numbers = {6,8,10} are fairly better for the MVKDLR than for the PCAKDLR, while the former approach is only marginally better than the latter for the other feature numbers. However, it is not clear at this stage whether these poor calibrations are due to the PCAKDLR approach or other intrinsic or extrinsic reasons.

It has been reported in some studies that validity and reliability are often (but not always) negatively correlated (Frost, 2013; Ishihara, 2017; Morrison, 2011). That is, the better performance of the PCAKDLR in reliability may be merely due to the trade-off between validity and reliability because the MVKDLR performs better than the PCAKDLR in terms of validity. Although the effect of the trade-off should not be neglected, it is true that the PCAKDLR is substantially better in reliability than the MVKDLR, while the MVKDLR only marginally performed better than the PCAKDLR in terms of discriminability. The general trend for the 95%CI value to continue to increase as the feature number increases is another aspect of the MVKDLR that the PCAKDLR does not exhibit; the 95%CI values become saturated with a feature number $\geq$ 6. Thus, it is a sensible conclusion that the PCAKDLR is better than the MVKDLR in terms of reliability.

7   Conclusions and Future Directions

The outcomes of the experiments with the simulated data demonstrate some general characteristics of the PCAKDLR approach as compared to the MVKDLR approach: i) the PCAKDLR approach marginally underperforms the MVKDLR approach in terms of discriminability (C_{llr}^{min}), ii) the PCAKDLR approach performs constantly better than the MVKDLR in terms of reliability, and iii) a substantial difference in reliability performance can be observed in particular when the feature number is six or more. In some cases, the MVKDLR performed noticeably (not marginally) better than the PCAKDLR (e.g. feature number = {6,8,10}) with respect to C_{llr}, but it was pointed out that this is due to the poor calibration performance of the PCAKDLR. However, it is not clear whether these poor calibrations are indeed caused by the PCAKDLR or by other unrelated factors.

In the current study, the maximum number of /e:/ tokens, which is ten, was used to model each session of each speaker. It would be interesting to explore how a different number of tokens for modelling will influence the performance of the MVKDLR and PCAKDLR approaches because, in real cases, one is less likely to have many comparable tokens for modelling.

Acknowledgments

The author thanks the three reviewers for their valuable comments.

References

Aitken, C. G. G., & Lucy, D. (2004). Evaluation of trace evidence in the form of multivariate data. *Journal of the Royal Statistical Society, Series C (Applied Statistics), 53*(1), 109-122.

Brümmer, N., & du Preez, J. (2006). Application-independent evaluation of speaker detection. *Computer Speech and Language, 20*(2-3), 230-275.

Curran, J. M. (2003). The statistical interpretation of forensic glass evidence. *International Statistical Review, 71*(3), 497-520.

Enzinger, E. (2016). Likelihood ratio calculation in acoustic-phonetic forensic voice comparison: Comparison of three statistical modelling approaches. *Proceedings of the Interspeech 2016*, 535-539.

Evett, I. W., Lambert, J. A., & Buckleton, J. S. (1998). A Bayesian approach to interpreting footwear marks in forensic casework. *Science & Justice, 38*(4), 241-247.

Evett, I. W., Scranage, J., & Pinchin, R. (1993). An illustration of the advantages of efficient statistical-methods for RFLP analysis in forensic-science. *American Journal of Human Genetics, 52*(3), 498-505.

Fishman, G. S. (1995). *Monte Carlo: Concepts, Algorithms, and Applications*. New York: Springer.

Frost, D. (2013). *Likelihood Ratio-based Forensic Voice Comparison on L2 Speakers: A Case of Hong Kong Male Production of English Vowels*. (Unpublished Honours thesis), The Australian National University, Canberra.

Ishihara, S. (2010). Variability and consistency in the idiosyncratic selection of fillers in Japanese monologues: Gender differences. *Proceedings of the Australasian Language Technology Association Workshop 2010*, 9-17.

Ishihara, S. (2017). Strength of forensic text comparison evidence from stylometric features: A multivariate likelihood ratio-based analysis. *The International Journal of Speech, Language and the Law, 24*(1), 67-98.

Kanazawa, S., & Still, M. C. (2000). Why men commit crimes (and why they desist). *Sociological Theory, 18*(3), 434-447.

Kinoshita, Y. (2001). *Testing Realistic Forensic Speaker Identification in Japanese: A Likelihood Ratio Based Approach Using Formants*. (Unpublished PhD thesis), The Australian National University, Canberra.

Kinoshita, Y., Ishihara, S., & Rose, P. (2009). Exploring the discriminatory potential of F0 distribution parameters in traditional forensic speaker recognition. *International Journal of Speech Language and the Law, 16*(1), 91-111.

Maekawa, K., Koiso, H., Furui, S., & Isahara, H. (2000). Spontaneous speech corpus of Japanese. *Proceedings of the 2nd International Conference of Language Resources and Evaluation*, 947-952.

Marquis, R., Bozza, S., Schmittbuhl, M., & Taroni, F. (2011). Handwriting evidence evaluation based on the shape of characters: Application of multivariate likelihood ratios. *Journal of forensic sciences, 56*(Supplement 1), S238-242.

Morrison, G. S. (2009a). Forensic voice comparison and the paradigm shift. *Science & Justice, 49*(4), 298-308.

Morrison, G. S. (2009b). Likelihood-ratio forensic voice comparison using parametric representations of the formant trajectories of diphthongs. *Journal of the Acoustical Society of America, 125*(4), 2387-2397.

Morrison, G. S. (2011). Measuring the validity and reliability of forensic likelihood-ratio systems. *Science & Justice, 51*(3), 91-98.

Nair, B., Alzqhoul, E., & Guillemin, B. J. (2014). Determination of likelihood ratios for forensic voice comparison using principal component analysis. *International Journal of Speech Language and the Law, 21*(1), 83-112.

Neumann, C., Champod, C., Puch-Solis, R., Egli, N., Anthonioz, A., & Bromage-Griffiths, A. (2007). Computation of likelihood ratios in fingerprint identification for configurations of any number of minutiae. *Journal of forensic sciences, 52*(1), 54-64.

Robertson, B., & Vignaux, G. A. (1995). *Interpreting Evidence: Evaluating Forensic Science in the Courtroom*. Chichester: John Wiley.

Automatic Negation and Speculation Detection in Veterinary Clinical Text

Katharine Cheng   **Timothy Baldwin**   **Karin Verspoor**

School of Computing and Information Systems

The University of Melbourne

Australia

`katharinec@student.unimelb.edu.au`

`tb@ldwin.net`

`karin.verspoor@unimelb.edu.au`

Abstract

The automatic detection of negation and speculation in clinical notes is vital when searching for genuine instances of a given phenomenon. This paper describes a new corpus of negation and speculation data, in the veterinary clinical note domain, and describes a series of experiments whereby we port a CRF-based method across from the BioScope corpus to this novel domain.

1 Introduction

Negation and speculation are common in clinical texts, yet pose a challenge for natural language processing of these texts. Negation indicates the absence or opposite of something, and is defined within the previously released BioScope corpus (a collection of biomedical and clinical documents annotated for the task of negation/speculation detection) to be the "implication of the non-existence of something" (Szarvas et al., 2008). For example, the statement *no abnormalities were found in the patient* indicates the absence of abnormalities in the patient. Speculation is used to indicate uncertainty or the possibility of something, and is defined within BioScope to be statements of "the possible existence of something". For example, *there is possible bacterial infection* indicates that an infection might be present, without any certainty that it is. Both are commonly used in clinical texts as a means of ruling out diagnostic possibilities and hypothesising.

This paper will discuss a method for detecting negation and speculation over clinical records from the Veterinary Companion Animal Surveillance System (VetCompass) project.[1] The VetCompass project is a database of veterinary clinical records for tracking animal health. The database may be used for research on the effects and usage of a particular drug, or the prevalence and distribution of a disease. Such studies are typically performed by querying for terms relevant to a drug or disease of interest, and analysing the retrieved clinical records. However, results identified using keyword matching are often speculative or negated mentions rather than true occurrences. By automatically detecting negation and speculation, we aim to suppress these results, and provide a higher-utility set of documents to the user.

The task of negation/speculation detection is often defined in terms of two subtasks: (1) signal (or cue) detection; and (2) scope detection. Negation/speculation signal (or cue) detection involves determining which words in a sentence indicate that a negation/speculation is occurring. Negation/speculation scope detection involves determining which words in a sentence the negation/speculation applies to, under the constraints that: (a) the cue word is contained within the span of the scope; and (b) the span is contiguous. Consider two examples from the clinical notes subset of the BioScope corpus:

(1)   The lungs are well expanded, but [NEG <u>not</u> hyperinflated NEG].

(2)   Mild thoracic curvature, [SPEC <u>possibly</u> positional SPEC].

The cues here for negation and speculation are *not* and *possibly*, respectively, and the words inside the brackets are within the scope of the cues.

We apply this task formulation to the veterinary clinical notes of VetCompass. The VetCompass records (which mainly consists of notes from veterinary general practitioners) have a few important differences from the radiology clinical notes of the publicly available BioScope corpus. First, radiology notes are often shared between clinicians treating the same patient, and as such are generally written to be accessible to others. In notes from veterinary general practitioners, it is often the case that a single clinician treats the patient,

---

[1] `http://www.rvc.ac.uk/vetcompass`

Katharine Cheng, Timothy Baldwin and Karin Verspoor. 2017. Automatic Negation and Speculation Detection in Veterinary Clinical Text. In *Proceedings of Australasian Language Technology Association Workshop*, pages 70–78.

meaning that clinical notes are largely for personal consumption, and thus are highly idiosyncratic in nature. Second, while radiology clinical notes are often professionally transcribed from an oral account by the clinician, in the veterinary general practice context, notes are authored directly by the clinician as text. Inevitably, this is done under time pressure, meaning that the text is often ungrammatical and lacks punctuation. Examples (3) and (4) exemplify negation and speculation in Vet-Compass:

(3)   Mm - moist [NEG <u>no</u> skin tent NEG]

(4)   Adv [SPEC <u>poss</u> bacterial infection SPEC], adv [SPEC <u>can</u> be allergy in origin SPEC]

Such differences in usage between veterinary clinicians and other medical professionals such as radiologists are a major focus of this work, in adapting the annotation framework from BioScope to this new domain.

This paper attempts to address the following research questions: (1) Can the task of negation/speculation detection be applied to veterinary clinical records? (2) Are models trained over the human clinical records of the BioScope corpus applicable to veterinary clinical notes?

This paper describes the process of annotating negation and speculation in veterinary clinical records. We then demonstrate that the task of negation and speculation detection can be successfully applied to veterinary clinical notes using a simple conditional random field (CRF) model. We additionally show that models trained on a related out-of-domain corpus such as the BioScope have utility over veterinary clinical records, in particular for negation detection.

2 Literature Review

2.1 Previous Work in Negation and Speculation Detection

Most work on negation and speculation detection has focused on biomedical documents such as biological research papers and clinical notes, with the latter being most relevant to this research.

Early approaches to negation detection were primarily rule-based. One of the best-known systems for negation detection is NegEx (Chapman et al., 2001), which is based on regular expressions containing a negation cue term (such as *no* or *not*). Another rule-based negation detection system is NegFinder (Mutalik et al., 2001).

More recently, machine learning approaches have become popular. Morante et al. (2008) proposed a machine learning approach that consists of two phases: (1) classification of whether each token in a sentence is a negation cue, and (2) classification of whether each token is part of the negation scope of a given cue. Both phases used a memory-based classifier using features such as the the wordform of the token, part-of-speech (POS) tag, and chunk tags of the token and neighbouring tokens. The approach was also applied to speculation detection (Morante and Daelemans, 2009a), and incorporated into a meta-learning approach to the second phase of negation scope detection (Morante and Daelemans, 2009b). Other approaches that use machine learning include the work of Agarwal and Yu (2010a,b) that uses conditional random fields (CRFs) to detect negation and speculation, and Cruz Díaz et al. (2012) who experimented with the use of decision trees and support vector machines.

Most work on negation and speculation detection has focused on a specific corpus and domain, with some exceptions. Wu et al. (2014) investigated the generalisability of different negation detection methods over different domains, and found that performance often suffers without in-domain training data. Miller et al. (2017) also investigated the use of different unsupervised domain adaptation algorithms for negation detection in the clinical domain and found that such algorithms only achieved marginal increase in performance compared to systems that use in-domain training data.

2.2 Veterinary NLP

We are only aware of a few papers that have applied natural language processing in the veterinary domain. Ding and Riloff (2015) conducted work on detecting mentions of medication usage in a discussion forum for veterinarians, and categorizing the usage of the medication. A classifier determines whether each word is part of a medication mention using features such as the POS tags and neighbouring words The output of the medication mention detector is used by another classifier to determine its usage category such as whether the clinician prescribed the medication or changed it.

Text classification is a task that had been previously applied to veterinary clinical records. Anholt et al. (2014) performed classification of a collection of veterinary medical records to identify cases of enteric syndrome. Lam et al. (2007) used clinical records of racing horses to categorise their reason for retirement. Duz et al. (2017) used classification to identify cases of certain conditions and drug use in clinical records from equine veterinary practices. In each of these studies, a dictionary was compiled to identify and detect phrases that indicate a certain category.

2.3 BioScope Corpus

Currently, there is no publicly available corpus for training models over veterinary clinical notes. However, the BioScope corpus (Szarvas et al., 2008) provides a relevant dataset from which to train out-of-domain models. It is a publicly available collection of biomedical documents that have been annotated for both negation and speculation, in the form of cue words and their scope (see Section 1). BioScope consists of three subcollections: clinical radiology notes, biological papers, and abstracts of biological papers from the GENIA corpus (Collier et al., 1999).

3 VetCompass Corpus

The VetCompass project is a collection of clinical records of veterinary consultations from several participating practices, to support analysis of animal health trends (McGreevy et al., 2017). To conduct these studies, clinicians use an information retrieval (IR) front-end to retrieve clinical records related to their particular information need, based on Boolean searches. A major bottleneck for the naive IR setup of returning all matching documents is the prevalence of term occurrences in negated or speculative contexts, which dominate the results for many queries. This is the primary motivation for this research: to improve the quality of the search results by filtering out document matches where the component term only occurs in negated or speculative context. The major challenge here is that the language used in the veterinary clinical notes of VetCompass differs from that used in related publicly available datasets such as the BioScope radiology clinical notes.

3.1 Discussion of VetCompass Corpus

The corpus used in this work was constructed from a random sample of 1 million clinical records from VetCompass UK.[2] VetCompass clinical records

---

²http://www.rvc.ac.uk/VetCOMPASS

contain a wide variety of text. Many records contain free text describing the clinician's observations, hypotheses, and descriptions of treatments and future actions. However, there are also records that contain only billing information, document the weight of the patient, or are reminders to perform certain actions like sending an invoice to the owner of the patient.

Compared to the BioScope radiology clinical notes, VetCompass clinical notes are much more informal, possibly due to the fact that they are largely "notes to self" (see Section 1). As such, ad hoc abbreviations and shortening of terms as shown in Examples (3) and (4) are very common, and informal speculative expressions such as *feels like* and *looks like* are prevalent:

(5) Skin [NEG <u>not</u> quite so erythematous NEG] but some scurf and [SPEC <u>looks like</u> superficial pyoderma SPEC].

(6) [SPEC <u>Feels like</u> lipoma SPEC], but [NEG <u>cannot</u> confirm without lab tests NEG].

(7) Adv [SPEC <u>sounds like</u> colitis SPEC] so disp emds btu adv o if no improvement resee and bring in sample.

There are certain negation and speculation cue terms that appear only in the VetCompass corpus such as:

(8) Examination: v lively, [NEG <u>nad</u> on oral exam NEG] and ghc all fine.

(9) Assessment: [SPEC gastritis<u>??</u> SPEC]

The term *nad* is often used in place of *no acute distress* or *no abnormalities detected*, and is an instance of negation. Question marks were often used as speculative cue terms such as in Example (9). The use of domain-specific cue terms presents a challenge for applying models that were trained on a corpus like BioScope clinical notes.

Misspellings, grammatical errors and lack of punctuation are also common in the text of the veterinary general practice clinical notes, e.g.:

(10) But depressed last 4 days and srop preds 2.5mg abruptly 4 days ago and sneezing [NEG <u>wuithout</u> nasla discharge NEG] 2 days too.

(11) Gave deepest sympathies; [SPEC <u>unsure</u> of cause SPEC] [SPEC <u>poss</u> underlying condition causing gut stasis <u>or</u> non-specific abdominal pain symptoms <u>or</u> acute embolus this morning SPEC]

In Example (10), the negation cue *without* is misspelled. In Example (11), punctuation is missing, making it hard to clearly separate the different statements in the sentence, and suggesting that pure parser-based approaches will struggle over this data.

In terms of annotation, while some abbreviations, shorthands, misspellings, and punctuation errors are easy to interpret, others are more difficult to understand:

(12)   - other poss: renal diz (given that had low sg + proteinuria, ^BUN/^Phosp BUT N - creat)/liver diz (given hepatomegally on rads + ^ALP, Bile acids, Cholest, ? low sod/K+ ratio - could be related to kids or addisonian crisis BUT no hx of pu/pd

Symbols like ^ require domain expertise to interpret. The appearance of terms like *poss* indicates that the sentence contains speculation but the irregular use of punctuation makes determining the correct boundaries of the speculation scope difficult. In fact, the absence of certain punctuation marks such as full stops can make it difficult for sentence tokenizers to work correctly.

In the VetCompass corpus, a single statement of speculation is sometimes expressed using multiple speculation cue terms, e.g.:

(13)   History- o concerned swollen lower lip, ⟦SPEC <u>thinks poss</u> stung SPEC⟧, been there 2d

Here, the clinician is reporting that the owner of the patient (shortened to *o*) speculated that the patient was stung, as indicated by two cue terms, *thinks* and *poss*, presumably to indicate their lack of confidence in the statement. Such instances of "double hedging" are very rare in BioScope, presenting an extra point of differentiation.

3.2   Annotation Guidelines

Here, we outline the annotation guidelines for the VetCompass corpus, which borrow heavily from the BioScope annotation guidelines. As per the BioScope annotation guidelines, sentences from VetCompass are annotated for speculation if they express uncertainty or speculation, and annotated for negation if they express the non-existence of something. The min-max strategy of BioScope annotation is also followed (Szarvas et al., 2008). Negation/speculation **cues** are annotated such that the minimal unit that expresses negation/speculation by itself is marked. **Scopes** are then annotated relative to cue words, to have maximal size or the largest syntactic unit possible. Below, we detail important deviations from the BioScope annotation guidelines, which are motivated in part by the usage of the negation/speculation detection system in an information retrieval context.

3.2.1   Annotation of Cues

The VetCompass annotation guidelines use the same set of cue words as BioScope, with the addition of *NAD* (a negation cue — see above), question marks (which are potentially speculation cues — see above), and shortened and misspelled variants of cue words (like *poss* for *possible*).

As with BioScope, not all occurrences of a negation or speculation keyword indicate negation or speculation. For instance, occurrences of negation or speculation keywords in descriptions of proposed actions are generally not annotated for negation or speculation. Examples of such cases are:

(14)   Advised to not give last onsior due to d+.

(15)   Suggested FNA if increase in size

In Example (14), *not* is not annotated as a negation cue since the sentence is stating a recommendation rather than expressing the absence or opposite of anything. In Example (15), *suggested* is not annotated since it is being used in the sense of proposing an action rather than hypothesising. These examples are also not annotated because of the utility they might provide for a clinician. If a clinician was researching *FNA*, the document containing Example (15) would be potentially useful for understanding situations where such a procedure was proposed. However, actions that were performed in the past that contains negation or speculation would be annotated such as *cannot* in Example (6) which is clearly expressing the opposite of the ability to perform that action.

Conditionals are another situation where negation or speculation keywords may not always be annotated as cues. If a negation or speculation keyword appears in the clause expressing the condition (clause containing the *if*), then they should not be annotated as cues as demonstrated in the following examples:

(16)   Adv if O not wanting to consider euthanasia then need to get a veterinary behaviourist involved ASAP

(17)   Stop treatment immediately if vomiting or diarrhoea occurs

Here, there is not clear negation or speculation, but rather the lack of something in the conditional (e.g. *consider euthanasia*) or consequent (e.g. *treatment*). While these two sentences may be annotated under the BioScope annotation guidelines, we chose not to do this for the VetCompass clinical records because of the utility they might provide for a clinician. Even if a certain term is negated inside of a conditional, there is usually other information in the clinical record that provides instructions about what to do in non-negated circumstances which is useful for a clinician. In the case of a term being speculated inside of a conditional, the consequences of the term occurring is certain even if the condition had not occurred.

3.2.2 Annotation of Scopes

In many cases, negation and speculation scopes start at cue terms and end at the end of the clause or sentence. However, punctuation is often omitted, meaning that boundaries of clauses and sentences can be unclear. The annotator must use their own judgement and interpretation of the sentence in order to create a suitable annotation. The following example demonstrates a sentence where an annotator must interpret the sentence to understand where the clause boundaries are:

(18) Abdo palpation ok [NEG _no_ pain NEG] [SPEC _poss_ a little bloated SPEC] [NEG _no_ fluid NEG] thrill abdominally temp normal has had ongoing GI issues occasional use of steroids.

Unlike the BioScope annotations, VetCompass clinical records were not annotated to contain nested speculation scopes, i.e. speculation scopes are never contained within other speculation scopes. This decision was motivated by the expected retrieval usage of the negation/speculation system: such information does not provide additional information to help filter out negated or speculated mentions of certain terms from search results. An example of the implication of this guideline is shown in the following sentence that is annotated with one negation scope and one speculation scope:

(19) [NEG _No_ obvious mass NEG], [SPEC _suspect_ _poss_ trichobezoars_?_ SPEC]

The above sentence would have been annotated as three nested speculation scopes under the BioScope annotation guidelines. However, using the VetCompass annotation guidelines, only a single speculation scope will be annotated, containing three separate speculations cues. If a user had wanted to search for documents with _trichobezoars_, this sentence will not be retrieved regardless of whether the nested structure is annotated or not. However, nested negation scopes in VetCompass are annotated. Moreover, speculation scopes that are nested within a negation scope and vice versa are also annotated.

	κ	F1-score
Negation Cue	0.80	80.3
Speculation Cue	0.65	65.5
Negation Scope	0.73	54.8
Speculation Scope	0.73	63.3

Table 1: Inter-annotator agreement rates

3.3 Annotation Process

1041 records were randomly selected for annotation. These were divided into a training set, development set and test set, comprising 624, 208 and 209 records, respectively. The data was single-annotated by the first author using the BRAT annotation tool (Stenetorp et al., 2012), in consultation with the other authors in instances of doubt.

100 records (containing 586 sentences) from the test set were selected and annotated by one of the other authors, following the guidelines in Section 3.1. The agreement between the two annotators was calculated using Cohen's kappa (κ) and F1-score (obtained by treating the annotations made by the main annotator as the gold-standard). We measure the amount that the two annotators agreed that a particular token is a negation/speculation cue or scope. The inter-annotator agreement is described in Table 1.

The κ values in Table 1 demonstrate a reasonable amount of agreement between the two annotators. However, there is still some subjectivity, particularly for the speculation cues.

There are several reasons for the discrepancy in annotations between the two annotators: (1) the limited experience in linguistics and text analysis on the part of the main annotator of VetCompass; (2) the lack of pre-training for annotating the VetCompass corpus for the other annotator, beyond receiving the annotation guidelines; and (3) the different levels of familiarity with the datasets of BioScope and VetCompass.

3.4 Preparation of corpus

Sentence tokenization was performed to prepare the corpus for usage, based on the findings of Read et al. (2012). The output of the sentence tokenizer was converted into the BRAT annotation format so that the output could be manually corrected if needed. However, the correction was not a systematic process. A sentence tokenization output was corrected only if it was clearly incorrect from a quick inspection during the annotation process. Most corrections only occurred when nega-

Total documents	1041
Total sentences	6582
Total words	50222
Avg. sentence length	10.06±8.38
% negated documents	41.59
% negated sentences	11.21
Avg. neg. span length	3.69±1.97
% speculated documents	20.65
% speculated sentences	5.15
Avg. spec. span length	5.60±3.57

Table 2: VetCompass NegSpec Corpus Statistics

tion/speculation scopes had the potential to cross sentence boundaries or in clear instances where correct sentence boundaries were not added. Only about 10% of the corpus underwent correction for sentence tokenization.

3.5 Summary of Corpus

Table 2 provides details of the annotated corpus. In general, large variations in sentence length can be observed: some sentences are as short as two words (e.g. reporting the patient weight), while others contain long detailed descriptions of the consultation.

The annotated VetCompass corpus contains a slightly lower proportion of negated sentences compared to those in the BioScope clinical notes (where 13.55% of the sentences were annotated as negated), and a much lower proportion of speculative sentences (compared to 13.39% in BioScope).

4 Methodology

4.1 Model Description

To evaluate whether the task of negation and speculation detection can be applied to the veterinary clinical notes of VetCompass, a simple linear-chain conditional random field (CRF: Lafferty et al. (2001)) model was trained, in the form of a re-implementation of the negation and speculation detection methods proposed by Agarwal and Yu (2010a,b).

The negation detection system consists of two parts: a cue detection system, and a scope detection system. The cue detection system is a CRF that classifies whether or not a given token is a negation cue. A CRF was used for cue detection to be able to model contexts in which cues appear in both negation and non-negation contexts, and to model multiword cues. The scope detection system is also a CRF, and classifies whether or not a token in a sentence is part of a negation scope.

The negation cue CRF uses only the words of the sentence as features. For the negation scope CRF, both the words of the sentence and the POS tags were used. When POS tags are used, the words that are part of a negation cue (that were detected by the negation cue CRF model) were either retained or replaced with a special CUE tag. The speculation detection system has a similar setup, except the system classifies a token as being the inside or outside of a speculation cue or scope.

The cue detection system is based on the following features: the target word, and the two words to the left and right of the target word. The scope detection system determines if a token is inside or outside a negation or speculation signal using either the words and POS tags of the token, five tokens to the left and right.

Our experiments are based on the corpus described in Section 3.4. The size of the context window for the CRF model was selected based on preliminary experiments with the development set. The parameter that achieved the best F-score over that set was chosen. NLTK[3] was used to tokenise the sentence and obtain the POS tags. As our CRF learner, we used CRF++ v0.58.[4] In our experiments, CRF models were either trained on BioScope clinical dataset, VetCompass, or both.

4.2 Baselines

We used NegEx system and LingScope as baselines. LingScope is a Java implementation of the CRF models developed by Agarwal and Yu (2010a,b). It contains models that were pre-trained using the BioScope clinical data. Though our CRF model and LingScope were based on the same paper, LingScope differs from our models through the use of a different CRF implementation (using the CRF model provided by the Abner tool (Settles, 2005)), the size of context window used for the classification, and the POS tagger (the Stanford POS tagger).

We used a Python implementation of NegEx.[5] This version of NegEx detects negation scopes to be between a trigger term/phrase identified by NegEx and either a conjunction, start or end of a sentence (which can be longer than the limit of five tokens in the original version of NegEx by Chapman et al. (2001)).

4.3 Experimental Setup

Our experiments were based on the fixed split of the corpus described in Section 3.3. We evaluate both the cue detection and scope detection system using precision ($\mathcal{P}$), recall ($\mathcal{R}$) and micro-average F-score ($\mathcal{F}$). Evaluation was performed on a token-level based on whether it is inside or outside of any negation/speculation cue or scope.

We experimented with using different training data to determine whether models trained on out-of-domain data such as BioScope clinical data are suitable for veterinary clinical notes. Since Bio-Scope clinical dataset is much larger than Vet-Compass, we also experimented with oversampling of instances from the VetCompass training data when both corpora were used for training (at oversampling rates of 1, 2 and 5). When an oversampling rate of 2 is used, we use two duplicates of each VetCompass training record during the training process, and similarly for oversampling rate of 5.

5 Results

Results for negation cue detection and negation scope detection are presented in Table 3 and Table 4, respectively. Results for speculation cue detection and speculation scope detection are presented in Table 5 and Table 6, respectively.

When trained only on BioScope clinical data, the CRF systems (for both cue detection and scope detection) performed worse than their respective baselines. The model only outperforms the baselines when VetCompass training data is used. For negation cue detection and scope detection, incorporating both BioScope clinical data with VetCompass records as training instances helps improves the F-scores for most cases. Further marginal improvements can be achieved with oversampling of the VetCompass training instances as well in most cases.

However, for speculation cue and scope detection, the inclusion of BioScope clinical data with VetCompass training data helps improve the recall but reduces the precision, leading to only marginal improvements in F-scores. Oversampling Vet-Compass helps to improve the precision, recall and F-score slightly, but the precision is still lower than when the BioScope clinical data was not included in the training set. In both speculation cue detection and scope detection results, the recall is consistently much lower than the precision. The re-

	$\mathcal{P}$	$\mathcal{R}$	$\mathcal{F}$
NegEx	73.2	73.2	73.2
LingScope	89.1	71.1	79.1
CRF (VC)	89.3	78.5	83.6
CRF (BIO)	75.2	63.1	68.6
CRF (BIO + VC)	90.2	80.5	85.1
CRF (BIO + VC×2)	89.4	85.2	87.3
CRF (BIO + VC×5)	89.5	85.9	87.7

Table 3: Results for Negation Cue Detection Training data used for CRF models are either Bio-Scope (BIO) and VetCompass (VC) or both

System	Training Set	$\mathcal{P}$	$\mathcal{R}$	$\mathcal{F}$
NegEx	—	56.3	75.4	64.4
LingScope (word)	—	79.3	52.4	63.1
LingScope (POS; keep cue)	—	66.8	64.4	65.6
LingScope (POS; replace cue)	—	65.9	62.6	64.2
CRF (word)	VC	87.9	64.4	74.4
	BIO	70.3	57.8	63.4
	BIO + VC	86.8	68.1	76.3
	BIO + VC×2	87.4	68.0	76.5
	BIO + VC×5	88.1	68.3	77.0
CRF (POS; keep cue)	VC	86.6	68.0	76.1
	BIO	78.2	51.1	61.8
	BIO + VC	84.8	71.3	77.5
	BIO + VC×2	85.1	74.3	79.3
	BIO + VC×5	85.5	73.3	79.0
CRF (POS; replace cue)	VC	81.5	67.0	73.6
	BIO	63.6	55.7	59.4
	BIO + VC	82.2	70.7	76.0
	BIO + VC×2	82.4	74.4	78.2
	BIO + VC×5	82.1	73.9	77.8

Table 4: Results for Negation Scope Detection Training data used for CRF models are either Bio-Scope (BIO) and VetCompass (VC) or both

	$\mathcal{P}$	$\mathcal{R}$	$\mathcal{F}$
LingScope	43.3	27.6	33.7
CRF (VC)	88.7	44.8	59.5
CRF (BIO)	19.7	24.8	21.9
CRF (BIO + VC)	76.5	49.5	60.1
CRF (BIO + VC×2)	79.7	52.4	63.2
CRF (BIO + VC×5)	81.4	54.3	65.1

Table 5: Results for Speculation Cue Detection Training data used for CRF models are either Bio-Scope (BIO) and VetCompass (VC) or both

sults achieved for speculation detection are also much lower than those achieved for negation detection.

5.1 Error Analysis

Unsurprisingly, when the cue detection system does not incorporate VetCompass data, cues that appear only in VetCompass records were usually not detected. For negation, these cues in-

System	Training Set	$\mathcal{P}$	$\mathcal{R}$	$\mathcal{F}$
LingScope (word)	—	27.4	27.4	27.4
LingScope (POS; keep cue)	—	35.9	28.9	32.0
LingScope (POS; replace cue)	—	40.6	28.2	33.3
	VC	91.4	27.8	42.6
	BIO	28.1	28.0	28.1
CRF (word)	BIO + VC	78.1	33.5	46.9
	BIO + VC×2	79.9	33.9	47.6
	BIO + VC×5	81.7	35.2	49.2
	VC	80.7	30.2	43.9
	BIO	30.0	18.8	23.1
CRF (POS; keep cue)	BIO + VC	67.7	34.4	45.6
	BIO + VC×2	71.5	37.4	49.1
	BIO + VC×5	73.3	40.9	52.5
	VC	84.2	33.9	48.4
	BIO	27.6	25.8	26.7
CRF (POS; replace cue)	BIO + VC	71.5	40.0	51.3
	BIO + VC×2	72.2	40.9	52.2
	BIO + VC×5	75.0	43.3	54.9

Table 6: Results for Speculation Scope Detection. Training data used for CRF models are either Bio-Scope (BIO) and VetCompass (VC) or both

clude *NAD*, *unable*, and contractions such as *doesn't*. For speculation, these cues include question marks, *poss* and *think*. In speculation cue detection, it was particularly important to have in-domain training data as there are more domain-specific speculation cues.

However, even with VetCompass training data, the cue detection systems (particularly speculation cue detection) still have difficulty detecting all of the cues. Some of this was caused by cue words being misspelled (e.g. *doestn* instead of *doesn't*) or a variant not seen in the training data (such as *susp* for *suspect*). A useful feature could be to use word or string similarity to known cue terms to overcome this issue. Author or patient metadata could also be useful, since some of this is consistent across consultations for a given individual. Such data could be used as additional features for a classifier or by having separate models for different authors/patients.

However, even cues where the form appears in the training data are still sometimes not detected by our system, particularly for speculation cues. This may be because the system was not able to generalise from the limited training data. There was also a greater variety of speculation cues than negation cues. This observation, combined with the smaller proportion of sentences that were speculative, means that there were less training instances for each possible speculation cue.

Both negation and speculation cues also have

false-positives that resulted from identifying negation-like or speculation-like terms, such as *not bad*. The speculation cue detection system also often did not detect speculation cues that contained negation-like terms such as *not sure*, while the negation cue detection system incorrectly classifies the *not* in this example as a negation cue.

The errors in cue detection create further errors in the associated scope detection system. However, even with correctly detected cues, the scope detection system still has problems with recall. In most of these cases, the system does not correctly determine one token at the start or end of the scope as being part of it. If the scope is very long, the system will often only detect the first few tokens as being part of the scope and miss the remaining tokens. Scopes where the cues are question marks are also often smaller than the reference annotation, as the system usually only includes the token directly to the left or right of the question mark as part of the speculation scope.

6 Conclusions and Further Work

This paper describes the annotation of a new dataset for negation and speculation detection over veterinary clinical notes. We reimplemented a simple CRF approach for detecting negation and speculation cues and scope, and trained the model over VetCompass training data, BioScope, or both. Our results demonstrated that while datasets such as the BioScope clinical corpus have utility, in-domain training data is often necessary to attain reasonable performance levels, particularly for speculation detection.

Further work will focus on improving the recall of negation and speculation detection systems for veterinary clinical notes. Improving the recall is important for the IR use case that the system will be deployed in. We will also focus on expanding the features used for classification, and experiment with different classifiers. Another focus could be on learning features that are particular to the different authors of notes, and using these to improve negation and speculation detection.

References

Shashank Agarwal and Hong Yu. 2010a. Biomedical negation scope detection with conditional random fields. *Journal of the American Medical Informatics Association* 17(6):696–701.

Shashank Agarwal and Hong Yu. 2010b. Detecting hedge cues and their scope in biomedical text with conditional random fields. *Journal of Biomedical Informatics* 43(6):953–961.

R Michele Anholt, John Berezowski, Iqbal Jamal, Carl Ribble, and Craig Stephen. 2014. Mining free-text medical records for companion animal enteric syndrome surveillance. *Preventive Veterinary Medicine* 113(4):417–422.

Wendy W Chapman, Will Bridewell, Paul Hanbury, Gregory F Cooper, and Bruce G Buchanan. 2001. A simple algorithm for identifying negated findings and diseases in discharge summaries. *Journal of biomedical informatics* 34(5):301–310.

Nigel Collier, Hyun Seok Park, Norihiro Ogata, Yuka Tateishi, Chikashi Nobata, Tomoko Ohta, Tateshi Sekimizu, Hisao Imai, Katsutoshi Ibushi, and Jun-ichi Tsujii. 1999. The genia project: corpus-based knowledge acquisition and information extraction from genome research papers. In *Proceedings of the ninth conference on European chapter of the Association for Computational Linguistics*. Association for Computational Linguistics, pages 271–272.

Noa P Cruz Díaz, Manuel J Maña López, Jacinto Mata Vázquez, and Victoria Pachón Álvarez. 2012. A machine-learning approach to negation and speculation detection in clinical texts. *Journal of the Association for Information Science and Technology* 63(7):1398–1410.

Haibo Ding and Ellen Riloff. 2015. Extracting information about medication use from veterinary discussions. In *Human Language Technologies: The 2015 Annual Conference of the North American Chapter of the ACL*. pages 1452–1458.

Marco Duz, John F Marshall, and Tim Parkin. 2017. Validation of an improved computer-assisted technique for mining free-text electronic medical records. *JMIR Medical Informatics* 5(2):e17.

John Lafferty, Andrew McCallum, and Fernando CN Pereira. 2001. Conditional random fields: Probabilistic models for segmenting and labeling sequence data. In *Proceedings of the 18th International Conference on Machine Learning*. pages 282–289.

K Lam, Tim Parkin, Christopher Riggs, and Kenton Morgan. 2007. Use of free text clinical records in identifying syndromes and analysing health data. *Veterinary Record* 161(16):547–51.

Paul McGreevy, Peter Thomson, Navneet Dhand, David Raubenheimer, Sophie Masters, Caroline Mansfield, Tim Baldwin, Ricardo Soares Magalhaes, Jacquie Rand, Peter Hill, Anne Peaston, James Gilkerson, Martin Combs, Shane Raidal, Peter Irwin, Peter Irons, Richard Squires, David Brodbelt, and Jeremy Hammond. 2017. VetCompass Australia: Big data and real-time surveillance for veterinary science. *Animals* 7(10).

Timothy Miller, Steven Bethard, Hadi Amiri, and Guergana Savova. 2017. Unsupervised domain adaptation for clinical negation detection. *BioNLP 2017* pages 165–170.

Roser Morante and Walter Daelemans. 2009a. Learning the scope of hedge cues in biomedical texts. In *Proceedings of the Workshop on Current Trends in Biomedical Natural Language Processing*. Association for Computational Linguistics, pages 28–36.

Roser Morante and Walter Daelemans. 2009b. A metalearning approach to processing the scope of negation. In *Proceedings of the Thirteenth Conference on Computational Natural Language Learning*. Association for Computational Linguistics, pages 21–29.

Roser Morante, Anthony Liekens, and Walter Daelemans. 2008. Learning the scope of negation in biomedical texts. In *Proceedings of the Conference on Empirical Methods in Natural Language Processing*. Association for Computational Linguistics, pages 715–724.

Pradeep G Mutalik, Aniruddha Deshpande, and Prakash M Nadkarni. 2001. Use of general-purpose negation detection to augment concept indexing of medical documents: a quantitative study using the umls. *Journal of the American Medical Informatics Association* 8(6):598–609.

Jonathon Read, Rebecca Dridan, Stephan Oepen, and Lars Jørgen Solberg. 2012. Sentence boundary detection: A long solved problem? *COLING (Posters)* 12:985–994.

Burr Settles. 2005. Abner: an open source tool for automatically tagging genes, proteins and other entity names in text. *Bioinformatics* 21(14):3191–3192.

Pontus Stenetorp, Sampo Pyysalo, Goran Topić, Tomoko Ohta, Sophia Ananiadou, and Jun'ichi Tsujii. 2012. Brat: a web-based tool for nlp-assisted text annotation. In *Proceedings of the Demonstrations at the 13th Conference of the European Chapter of the Association for Computational Linguistics*. Association for Computational Linguistics, pages 102–107.

György Szarvas, Veronika Vincze, Richárd Farkas, and János Csirik. 2008. The bioscope corpus: annotation for negation, uncertainty and their scope in biomedical texts. In *Proceedings of the Workshop on Current Trends in Biomedical Natural Language Processing*. Association for Computational Linguistics, pages 38–45.

Stephen Wu, Timothy Miller, James Masanz, Matt Coarr, Scott Halgrim, David Carrell, and Cheryl Clark. 2014. Negation's not solved: generalizability versus optimizability in clinical natural language processing. *PloS one* 9(11):e112774.

Medication and Adverse Event Extraction from Noisy Text

Xiang Dai[1,2], Sarvnaz Karimi[1], and Cecile Paris[1]

[1]CSIRO Data61, Marsfield, NSW, Australia
[2]School of Information Technologies, University of Sydney
{dai.dai, sarvnaz.karimi, cecile.paris}@data61.csiro.au

Abstract

We investigate the problem of extracting mentions of medications and adverse drug events using sequence labelling and non-sequence labelling methods. We experiment with three different methods on two different datasets, one from a patient forum with noisy text and one containing narrative patient records. An analysis of the output from these methods are reported to identify what types of named entities are best identified using these methods and, more specifically, how well the discontinuous and overlapping entities that are prevalent in our forum dataset are identified. Our findings can guide studies to choose different methods based on the complexity of the named entities involved, in particular in text mining for pharmacovigilance.

1 Introduction

An Adverse Drug Reaction (ADR) is an injury occurring after a drug (medication) is used at the recommended dosage, for recommended symptoms. The practice of monitoring the ADRs of pharmaceutical products is known as *pharmacovigilance* [Alghabban, 2004]. Different from controlled clinical trials which are mainly conducted before drugs are licensed for use, pharmacovigilance is especially concerned with identifying previously unreported adverse reactions. Text mining over different sources of information, such as electronic health records and patient reports on health forums, can be one way of finding such potential adverse reactions. This is the area to which our work contributes. We note that when causality between an adverse reaction and a medication is not known, it is referred to as Adverse Drug Event (ADE) [Karimi et al., 2015c].

Extracting mentions of drugs and adverse events from social media is difficult for two main reasons. First, social media text contains colloquial language and typographical mistakes. References to the names of drugs, diseases, and ADEs are particularly prone to misspellings. Second, a medical concept can be considered both an ADE or a symptom in different contexts. For example, *aches and pains* is a symptom in the context of "*I am only taking 75 mg a day and it is wonderful for relieving all of my aches and pains*", while it is an ADE in another post complaining of *severe fatigue with aches and pains*. We cast this concept extraction problem as a supervised Named Entity Recognition (NER) task, with drugs and ADEs as entity types.

Named entity recognition itself has long been studied in different domains, including the biomedical domain. There are a number of challenges that are associated with how named entities are expressed in text. These include entities expressed as *multiwords*, especially if the entities are *overlapping, discontinuous,* or *nested*. Table 1 lists some examples of entity types of different complexities. Entities that consist of a discontinuous sequence of tokens are one of the more challenging ones to recognise correctly, yet they constitute a large portion (over 10%) of adverse event mentions in the forum posts that we studied.

We are interested in the extraction of two named entities from free-text: medications or drugs, and adverse drug events. We divide named entities into two sets of complex and simple entities. *Complex* entities are those belonging to one of the categories of *nested, discontinuous,* and *overlapping* entities. *Multiword* entities that are continuous are also more difficult to identify than the single word ones. We therefore refer to the entities that are single words, as *simple* regardless of what class of entity, drug or ADE, they represent. Extraction of complex entities is particularly important in the

Xiang Dai, Sarvnaz Karimi and Cecile Paris. 2017. Medication and Adverse Event Extraction from Noisy Text. In *Proceedings of Australasian Language Technology Association Workshop*, pages 79–87.

Complexity of Entity	Entity	Sentence
Simple and multiword (Continuous, non-overlapping)	1. *Disorentatation*, 2. *trouble brathing*, 3. *extreme hot*, 4. *readness and sweeling*, 5. *itching*, and 6. *abominal cramps*	Disorentatation, trouble brathing, extreme hot, readness and sweeling, itching, later abominal cramps.
Continuous, overlapping	*pain in knee* (overlapping with *pain in foot*)	pain in knee and foot.
Discontinuous, non-overlapping	*liver blood test mildly elevated*	My Liver blood test are also mildly elevated.
Discontinuous, overlapping	*pain in foot*	Pain in knee and foot.

Table 1: Examples of complexities in entities. Note the misspellings and irregular text in the sentences.

biomedical domain where these entities are more popular [Kilicoglu et al., 2016].

In this paper, we evaluate three NER methods, one most popular and two most recent ones, for their capabilities in extracting the complex entities that exist in our noisy dataset of reports of adverse drug events. Our aim is to identify which of these methods more accurately extracts these entities, and whether the differences in complexity or type of entities guide what method to choose.

2 Related Work

Related studies are categorised into two: (1) methods for named entity recognition, both in general and in the biomedical area, and (2) approaches to concept extraction for pharmacovigilance. NER has a very long history in the area of natural language processing, going back to early 90s and information extraction tasks in the Message Understanding Conferences. Below we only review those methods that are directly relevant to our work. Concept extraction in the biomedical area also has been studied extensively, with some of the early work for biological concepts such as genes and proteins in the context of GENIA [Ohta et al., 2002]. We only review a subset of these, focusing on medications and their adverse events.

2.1 Named Entity Recognition

Named Entity Recognition (NER), the problem of identifying named entities in free-text, was originally and long focused on entity classes of person, location, organisation, and time. It then expanded to a large variety of entities, depending on the application domains, including biomedical [Ramakrishnan et al., 2008, Leaman and Gonzalez, 2008, Verspoor et al., 2012] and social media [Ritter et al., 2011].

NER is traditionally seen as a sequence labelling task. One of the most competitive models is Conditional Random Fields (CRF). It is applied in a number of NER systems, such as Stanford NER. Finkel et al. [2005], who propose one of the methods underlying Stanford NER, modify CRF by adding non-local structure using Gibbs sampling. This method maintains a sequence model structure and, at the same time, adds long-distance conditioning influences. This way, there is no need to enforce no-overlap constraints as some of the other NER methods do. We note that, in the biomedical domain, similar CRF-based NER tools have been developed that incorporate some of the biomedical ontologies. BANNER [Leaman and Gonzalez, 2008] is one example of such publicly available tools.

In one of the early studies where the complexity of named entities is specifically investigated, Downey et al. [2007] propose a Web NER method to locate a diverse set of entities that can be found from the web. They consider the task of NER as an n-gram detection of multiword units. Their method starts unsupervised and therefore does not bound itself to pre-defined entities. It then uses CRFs and Conditional Markov Models, and is tested on both simple and complex named entities. In that work, complex named entities are defined as entities such as names of books and movies, where then baseline systems used to fail. Their proposed method, called *LEX*, is particularly high performing for finding the continuous multiword entities on web pages since it is designed for such cases.

In the biomedical domain, entities can be complicated. Ramakrishnan et al. [2008] highlight the problem of dealing with *compound* entities which they define as those NEs that are composed of simpler entities, such as names of diseases, body parts, processes and substances. Another class of complex entities is *nested* entities which has received attention from the biomedical NLP community. Alex et al. [2007] study nested and discontinuous entities in the biomedical domain in the context of two corpora: GENIA [Ohta et al., 2002] and BioInfer [Pyysalo et al., 2007]. For example, the name of a DNA can be nested inside the name of an RNA protein. Alex et al. [2007] identify the problem to be how NEs used to be represented using the IOB (Inside, Outside, Beginning) representation. This representation does not allow tokens to belong to more than one entity. They experiment with extending this representation as well as with cascading and joint learning models. Their method, however, is unable to identify nested entities of the same type. Finkel and Manning [2009] propose a discriminative parsing-based method for nested named entity recognition, employing CRFs as its core.

Kilicoglu et al. [2016] identify the lack of training data for NER in biomedical domain for consumer health questions. They create an annotated corpus where entities can be ambiguous by having multiple types, being nested, multi-part or discontinuous. They recognise the problem of evaluating systems using some of these entity types and provide some recommendations on how to deal with them by using different entity representations.

Most recently, neural networks have been applied to the NER task. Crichton et al. [2017] investigate NER in biomedical area using convolutional neural networks. They experiment with a variety of models–such as single-task, multi-task, dependent multi-task and multi-output models–on 15 different datasets. They show that, on average, multi-task models were superior to single-task ones.

Liu et al. [2017] investigate entity recognition from the Informatics on the Integrating Biology and the Bedside (i2b2) corpora (2010, 2012, and 2014 NLP challenges) using Long-Short Term Memory (LSTM). For the concept extraction task of the i2b2 challenge 2010, they show improvements over CRF methods using an LSTM-based method that uses character embeddings. NEs are represented using BIOES (B-beginning of an entity, I-insider of an entity, O-outsider of an entity, E-end of an entity, S-a single-token entity). This is close to one of the methods we use in our

work. However they do not provide any insight on extracting complex entities (if there were any) in their datasets.

2.2 Concept Extraction for Pharmacovigilance

Safety signal detection for pharmacovigilance from medical literature, electronic health records and medical forums have been studied in the past decade [Kuhn et al., 2010, Leaman et al., 2010, Benton et al., 2011, Liu and Chen, 2013, Karimi et al., 2015c, Henriksson et al., 2015, Zhao et al., 2015, Pierce et al., 2017]. One of the problems in generating such signals from text is the extraction of relevant concepts, such as medications, adverse events, and patient information. Named entity recognition therefore has been studied as one of the methods to extract these relevant concepts.

Nikfarjam et al. [2015] investigate ADE extraction from a medical forum, DailyStrength, and Twitter, using Conditional Random Fields (CRFs). To train the CRFs, they use word embeddings as one of the features created based on the forum and Twitter data. The entity representation method in their study is IOB (Inside, Outside, and Beginning).

Sarker and Gonzalez [2015] consider ADE extraction as a classification task using multiple corpora: a patient forum, Twitter, and medical case reports. They use these datasets for training classifiers, including SVM, Maximum Entropy and Naïve Bayes. The combination of different corpora for training leads to improved classification accuracy. Klein et al. [2017] also extend the work by providing classification baselines as well as making the Twitter data available for further research. This dataset however does not contain discontinuous, overlapping or nested entities and therefore is not used in our study. Another problem with using the Twitter dataset is that it changes as based on the availability of tweets at the time of crawling, making it difficult for comparisons of the reported results in the literature.

[Karimi et al., 2015b, Metke-Jimenez and Karimi, 2016] investigate both dictionary-based and machine learning approaches based on CRFs for the identification of medical concepts, including drugs and ADEs. Their CRF models outperform most lexicon-based methods popular in this domain on a corpus from medical forums, called CADEC [Karimi et al., 2015a]. They argue that some of the discontinuous entities in the corpus are responsible for a portion of their errors.

Cocos et al. [2017] develop an BiLSTM model that used word embeddings from a large Twitter corpus to identify ADEs in tweets. They compare their method to CRFs (from CRFSuite software [Okazaki, 2007]) and lexicon-based methods showing improvements using BiLSTMs. We note improvements are seen in recall values, as opposed to higher precision that is achieved using CRFs. Their experiments show that static semantic information learned from a large, generic dataset through word embeddings is the only setting in BiLSTM that leads to higher F-Score. Since their focus is not on identifying complex entities such as discontinuous ones, they use a straightforward IO schema (Inside, Outside) for representing the named entities. Their error analysis identifies constituent phrases (multiword ADEs) as one source of errors made by their method.

3 Datasets

We use two datasets for our evaluations: *CADEC* [Karimi et al., 2015a] and the *i2b2 2009 medication challenge* [Uzuner et al., 2010]. CADEC consists of 1,250 posts from the medical forum AskaPatient. These posts were manually annotated by medical experts and a clinical terminologist for drugs, ADEs, diseases, symptoms, and findings. Among all 9,111 annotated entities, there are 1,800 drug entities and 6,318 ADE entities. The rest of the entities are ignored in this study.

Table 2 lists the overall statistics of the entities in the two datasets. In CADEC, many of the entities, especially ADEs, consist of discontinuous and overlapping spans. Different from other NER corpus, where the longest possible spans are identified as single entities, CADEC has many fine-grained entities, each of which can be referred to a specific medical concept in medicine terminology vocabularies. For example, in the sentence *Pain in hip, lower back, knees & elbow*, there are four ADEs: *Pain in lower back*, *Pain in knees*, *Pain in elbow*, and *Pain in hip*, corresponding to four different concepts in SNOMED Clinical Terms (SNOMED CT)[1].

The i2b2 medication extraction challenge dataset focuses on the identification of medications and medication-related information, such as

their dosages, modes of administration, frequencies, durations, and reasons for administration, in discharge summaries. In our work, we identify only medication mentions. These include names, brand names, generics, and collective names of prescription substances, over-the-counter medications, and other biological substances.

There is a total of 1,249 discharge summaries in the i2b2 dataset. The i2b2 organisers first released a detailed annotation guideline along with a small set of ten annotated summaries. They then challenged the participants to collectively develop the gold standard annotations for 251 summaries which were used as test data. This was to encourage the development of unsupervised or semi-supervised methods. Here, we combine all these 261 summaries as labelled data.

4 Methods

4.1 Extended BIO Representation

To deal with discontinuous and overlapping spans, we use an extended version of the standard BIO chunking representation proposed by [Metke-Jimenez and Karimi, 2016]. In this representation, four additional prefixes are used: DB, DI, HB, and HI. The following details all the prefixes used in our work together with examples from our data.

O Outside concept. All tokens outside the concepts in which we are interested are labelled as *O*.

B- Begin of concept, for continuous and non-overlapping spans.

I- Continuation of concept, for continuous and non-overlapping spans.

DB- Begin of concept, for discontinuous and non-overlapping spans. For example, in the sentence *every joint in my body is in pain*, the ADE *joint pain* is a discontinuous span, so the label for the token *joint* is *DB-ADE*.

DI- Continuation of concept, for discontinuous and non-overlapping spans. The label for the token *pain* in the previous example is *DI-ADE*.

HB- Begin of concept, for discontinuous and overlapping spans that share one or more tokens with other concepts. For example, in the sentence *it has left me feeling exausted,*

---

[1] https://www.snomed.org/snomed-ct

	CADEC		i2b2
Entity	Drug	ADE	Drug
All	1800	6318	8850
Discontinuous, non-overlapping	1 (0.05)	82 (1.30)	0 (0.00)
Discontinuous, overlapping	1 (0.05)	593 (9.38)	0 (0.00)
Continuous, non-overlapping	1797 (99.83)	5311 (84.06)	8850 (100.00)
Continuous, overlapping	1 (0.05)	332 (5.25)	0 (0.00)
Multiword	141 (7.83)	4574 (72.40)	2181 (24.64)
Single word	1659 (92.17)	1744 (27.60)	6669 (75.36)

Table 2: Overall statistics of the number of entities and their breakdown based on their complexity in the datasets. Numbers in brackets are percentages.

and depressed, two ADEs *feeling exausted* and *feeling depressed* overlap and share one common token *feeling*, so the label of token *feeling* is *HB-ADE*.

HI- Continuation of concept, for discontinuous and overlapping spans. The label for the token *exausted* and *depressed* in the previous example are both *HI-ADE*.

4.2 Sequence Labelling: CRF and Bi-LSTM Model

We used two different sequence labelling methods: one based on conditional random fields as implemented in Stanford NER (version 3.8.0) [Finkel et al., 2005] and another based on a deep learning method implemented in NeuroNER [Dernoncourt et al., 2017a]. NeuroNER uses Bidirectional LSTM (Bi-LSTM) neural networks. It contains three layers: a character-enhanced token-embedding layer, a label prediction layer, and a label sequence optimisation layer [Dernoncourt et al., 2017b]. BiLSTMs are known to take into account context from both left and right of a token, and they can handle sequences of variable size.

Word embeddings can be provided as input to NeuroNER. To create the embedding, the documents are first tokenised using the spaCy tokeniser [2]. A token will be taken as input of the word embedding layer, and its vector representation will be generated as the output.

4.3 Non-Sequence Labelling

A recent work by Xu et al. [2017] propose a non-sequence labelling based on the FOFE (Fixed-Size Ordinally-Forgetting Encoding) representa-

tion [Zhang et al., 2015] which they call FOFE-NER. This is using a local detection approach where the left and right contexts of tokens created using FOFE are represented to a deep feedforward neural network. This method is very powerful in capturing immediate dependencies in the tokens and therefore should recognise multiword entities well. We directly apply this method to our problem with all the features that are proposed including character and word level features, to examine its effectiveness in our problem.

5 Experiments

We experiment using the three methods (CRF, Bi-LSTM, and non-sequence labelling) on the two datasets (CADEC, i2b2 2009) in two settings: (1) an overall comparison of the methods; and (2) an in-depth comparison based on the complexity of the named entities.

These methods are employed using a strategy called one-vs-all in which we train separate models for each entity type. For example, a model to identify *drug* is created yielding only two kinds of results: *drug* and *not-a-drug*.

Different methods of generating word embeddings using Wikipedia, MEDLINE, same corpus, and random embeddings are investigated. In our experiments they all generate similar results given our embeddings were used in a dynamic setting. Dynamic embeddings are re-calculated during the training phase. This is in line with the findings reported in [Karimi et al., 2017]. In the experimental results, we report on random word embeddings.

To evaluate, we run 10-fold cross-validation and report the average scores. Evaluation metrics used here are precision, recall, and F-score, all calculated based on the exact matches of extracted entities with the gold data.

---

[2] `https://spacy.io/` (Version 2.0, accessed 15 Nov 2017)

Dataset	Entity	Method	Precision	Recall	F-Score
CADEC	Drug	CRF	**95.1 $\pm$ 2.5**	79.1 $\pm$ 16.1	85.5 $\pm$ 11.4
		Bi-LSTM	92.9 $\pm$ 2.0	**92.2 $\pm$ 1.5**	**92.5 $\pm$ 0.7**[†]
		Non-sequence Labelling	88.6 $\pm$ 4.9	89.8 $\pm$ 1.8	89.1 $\pm$ 2.1
	ADE	CRF	67.5 $\pm$ 5.1	57.7 $\pm$ 2.9	62.1 $\pm$ 3.6
		Bi-LSTM	**73.4 $\pm$ 3.9**	**64.9 $\pm$ 4.4**	**68.7 $\pm$ 2.1**[†]
		Non-sequence Labelling	62.9 $\pm$ 3.8	61.6 $\pm$ 1.8	62.1 $\pm$ 1.0
i2b2	Drug	CRF	**93.5 $\pm$ 1.0**	85.7 $\pm$ 2.5	89.4 $\pm$ 1.7
		Bi-LSTM	93.2 $\pm$ 1.2	89.7 $\pm$ 1.3	**91.4 $\pm$ 0.6** [†]
		Non-sequence Labelling	84.4 $\pm$ 4.2	**90.2 $\pm$ 2.4**	87.1 $\pm$ 2.7

Table 3: Effectiveness of the different methodologies with their standard deviations over 10-fold cross-validations. Significant differences are shown with a [†] (p-value< 0.05).

		Bi-LSTM	
		✓	✗
CRF	✓	2811	498
	✗	885	2124

		Bi-LSTM	
		✓	✗
Non-Seq	✓	2315	198
	✗	1321	2484

		CRF	
		✓	✗
Non-Seq	✓	2333	180
	✗	916	2889

Table 4: Comparisons of different methods on the CADEC dataset (ADE entities) based on extracted entities that were correct (✓) or incorrect (✗).

		Bi-LSTM	
		✓	✗
CRF	✓	7378	233
	✗	498	741

		Bi-LSTM	
		✓	✗
Non-Seq	✓	7561	406
	✗	315	568

		CRF	
		✓	✗
Non-Seq	✓	7317	649
	✗	296	588

Table 5: Comparisons of different methods on the i2b2 dataset (drug entities) based on extracted entities that were correct (✓) or incorrect (✗).

5.1 Sequence Labelling versus Non-Sequence Labelling NER

We compare the two sequence labelling methods, CRF model using Stanford NER and Bi-LSTM-based NER implemented in NeuroNER. We also compare them with a non-sequence labelling method [Xu et al., 2017] that uses the FOFE representation [Zhang et al., 2015] (FOFE-NER). Results are shown in Table 3.

On the CADEC dataset, NeuroNER using Bi-LSTMs perform best for both drug and ADE entities. The only exception is precision for drugs, where the CRF model outperform Bi-LSTM by 2.2%. This is not however statistically significant (Kruskal-Wallis H-test and T-test). For the i2b2 dataset, again the Bi-LSTM's overall F-score is higher than that of the other two methods, except that CRF and Non-sequence labelling methods show slightly higher results in precision and recall, respectively. The differences, again, are not statistically significant.

We then further breakdown these results to identify the overlap between the three methods in terms of correctly identifying NEs, incorrectly identifying them or missing them. This is to determine whether there is the potential in these systems to be used together if the errors they make are different. We show these confusion matrices in Tables 4 and 5. For CADEC ADEs, there was an almost equal number of both correct and both incorrect cases for all the combinations. This shows the difficulty of extracting the ADEs. The non-sequence labelling method has a larger number of incorrect entities extracted compared to the other two approaches. In the i2b2 dataset (drug entities only), non-sequence labelling makes fewer mistakes that the other systems. We can also infer that these systems are similar (correct or incorrect) in approximately 90% of the time. There is thus a ceiling of 10% that combining the two methods could improve the effectiveness.

5.2 Complex Named Entities

In both the CADEC and i2b2 datasets, drug names rarely have overlapping or discontinuous properties. In contrast, it is common for ADEs to be discontinuous or overlapped. 925 out of 6318 ADEs in CADEC are overlapped, while 675 ones are discontinuous. In this section, we focus on the analysis of the effectiveness of the different methods on identifying these discontinuous or overlapped ADEs.

For the first set of experiments, we separate entities based on their complexity: overlapping, discontinuous, continuous multiword, and simple (single word). We then evaluate the output of the NER systems only based on those entities that fall into those categories. Results are shown in Table 6. Note that we mix both entity types of drugs and ADEs. Surprisingly, the CRF method is more successful in identifying overlapping and discontinuous entities. We note that the evaluations are strict: if two entities are overlapped, we expect both to be found to consider the system successful. We use the same strict criteria for the discontinuous entities: If a system only finds one of the two entities, it is not. For CADEC, continuous multiwords are more successfully identified by the non-sequence labelling model, while Bi-LSTM outperforms the other methods for simple entities. Multiwords for the i2b2 dataset do not differentiate the three methods as much, with CRF being slightly better than BiLSTM. Simple entities are equally identifiable for all the three methods too, with a slight win for non-sequence labelling.

One problem for the non-sequence labelling method is its tendency to extract long strings as one entity. For example, in the sentence *HORRIBLE muscle pains, horrible back spasms, spasms in leg muscles, nausea, vomitting, pain so bad that I could hardly walk or sit*, the ADE entities are: (1) *HORRIBLE muscle pains*, (2) *horrible back spasms*, (3) *spasms in leg muscles*, (4) *nausea*, (5) *vomitting* and (6) *pain*. These should be extract as separate entities. However, the non-sequence labelling method extracts the sequence of them as one entity which contributes to both one false positive and several false negatives.

6 Conclusions and Future Work

We presented a comparison of three named entity recognition (NER) methods for extraction of medications and adverse drug events. This is a task important in the context of pharmacovigilance, especially to extract information from consumer reports in health forums. Three methods–CRF, Bi-LSTM, and a non-sequence labelling method– were chosen based on their popularity, availability, and recency, as well as representing three different approaches to the NER task. We compared these methods based on how they deal with complexity in named entities, that is how they handle entity overlaps and discontinuity, as well as multiwords. Our experiments showed that the non-sequence labelling method can best extract continuous multiword entities, while CRF using Stanford NER is more successful for discontinuous entities.

Our next steps are to verify these results using other biomedical datasets, with different entity and document types. We are also interested in comparing these methods on nested entities which CADEC and i2b2 2009 did not contain. There are other methods that we should investigate, including joint models. Incorporating medical ontologies such as SNOMED CT and MedDRA can also potentially inform a system that deal with biomedical concepts, and in particular adverse events. Other potential methods to investigate are those that incorporate syntactic and semantic parsing of the sentences as well as tree-structure of the entities into account [Finkel and Manning, 2009, Dinarelli and Rosset, 2011, 2012].

Acknowledgments

Authors would like to thank Anthony Nguyen and Hamed Hassanzadeh (CSIRO e-Health Research Centre) as well as Stephen Wan and Mac Kim (CSIRO Data61) for earlier discussions on this work.

Dataset	Complexity	Method	Precision	Recall	F-Score
CADEC	Overlapping	CRF	21.4	15.3	17.8
		Bi-LSTM	–	3.5	–
		Non-Seq.	–	0.0	–
	Discountinuous	CRF	21.4	1.5	2.8
		Bi-LSTM	13.8	2.3	3.9
		Non-Seq.	–	0.0	–
	Multiword	CRF	57.4	46.4	51.4
		Bi-LSTM	60.9	62.6	61.7
		Non-Seq.	62.3	66.5	64.3
	Simple	CRF	78.0	63	69.7
		Bi-LSTM	79.6	68.5	73.6
		Non-Seq.	61.9	51.8	56.4
i2b2	Multiword	CRF	91.1	82.6	86.7
		Bi-LSTM	85.0	86.8	85.9
		Non-Seq.	82.8	81.5	82.1
	Simple	CRF	94.4	86.8	90.4
		Bi-LSTM	94.9	89.6	92.2
		Non-Seq.	91.1	92.4	91.7

Table 6: Breakdown of the effectiveness of NER methods based on entity complexity.

References

B. Alex, B. Haddow, and C. Grover. Recognising nested named entities in biomedical text. In *BioNLP*, pages 65–72, Prague, Czech Republic, 2007.

A. Alghabban. *Dictionary Of Pharmacovigilance*. Pharmaceutical Press, 2004.

A. Benton, L. Ungar, S. Hill, S. Hennessy, J. Mao, A. Chung, C. Leonard, and J. Holmes. Identifying potential adverse effects using the web: A new approach to medical hypothesis generation. *J. Biomed. Inform.*, 44(6):989–996, 2011.

A. Cocos, A. Fiks, and A. Masino. Deep learning for pharmacovigilance: Recurrent neural network architectures for labeling adverse drug reactions in Twitter posts. *J Am Med Inform Assoc.*, 24(4):813–821, 2017.

G. Crichton, S. Pyysalo, B. Chiu, and A. Korhonen. A neural network multi-task learning approach to biomedical named entity recognition. *BMC bioinformatics*, 18(1):368, 2017.

F. Dernoncourt, J. Y. Lee, and P. Szolovits. NeuroNER: an easy-to-use program for named-entity recognition based on neural networks. In *EMNLP*, pages 97–102, Copenhagen, Denmark, 2017a.

F. Dernoncourt, J. Y. Lee, Ö. Uzuner, and P. Szolovits. De-identification of patient notes with recurrent neural networks. *J Am Med Inform Assoc.*, 24(3):596–606, 2017b.

M. Dinarelli and S. Rosset. Models cascade for tree-structured named entity detection. In *IJCNLP*, pages 1269–1278, Chiang Mai, Thailand, 2011.

M. Dinarelli and S. Rosset. Tree-structured named entity recognition on OCR data: Analysis, processing and results. In *LREC*, pages 1266–1272, Istanbul, Turkey, 2012.

D. Downey, M. Broadhead, and O. Etzioni. Locating complex named entities in web text. In *IJCAI*, pages 2733–2739, Hyderabad, India, 2007.

J. R. Finkel and C. Manning. Nested named entity recognition. In *EMNLP*, pages 141–150, Singapore, 2009.

J. R. Finkel, T. Grenager, and C. Manning. Incorporating non-local information into information extraction systems by Gibbs sampling. In *ACL*, pages 363–370, Ann Arbor, MI, 2005.

A. Henriksson, M. Kvistab, H. Dalianis, and M. Duneld. Identifying adverse drug event information in clinical notes with distributional semantic representations of context. *J. Biomed. Inform.*, 57: 333–349, 2015.

S. Karimi, A. Metke-Jimenez, M. Kemp, and C. Wang. CADEC: A corpus of adverse drug event annotations. *J. Biomed. Inform.*, 55:73–81, 2015a.

S. Karimi, A. Metke-Jimenez, and A. Nguyen. CADEminer: A system for mining consumer reports on adverse drug side effects. In *ESAIR*, pages 47–50, Melbourne, Australia, 2015b.

S. Karimi, C. Wang, A. Metke-Jimenez, R. Gaire, and C. Paris. Text and data mining techniques in adverse drug reaction detection. *ACM Comput. Surv.*, 47(4): 56:1–56:39, May 2015c.

S. Karimi, X. Dai, H. Hassanzadeh, and A. Nguyen. Automatic diagnosis coding of radiology reports: A comparison of deep learning and conventional classification methods. In *BioNLP*, pages 328–332, Vancouver, Canada, 2017.

H. Kilicoglu, A. B. Abacha, Y. Mrabet, K. Roberts, L. Rodriguez, S. E. Shooshan, and D. Demner-Fushman. Annotating named entities in consumer health questions. In *LREC*, Portorož, Slovenia, 2016.

A. Klein, A. Sarker, M. Rouhizadeh, K. O'Connor, and G. Gonzalez. Detecting personal medication intake in Twitter: An annotated corpus and baseline classification system. In *BioNLP*, pages 136–142, Vancouver, Canada, 2017.

M. Kuhn, M. Campillos, I. Letunic, L. Jensen, and P. Bork. A side effect resource to capture phenotypic effects of drugs. *Mol. Syst. Biol.*, 6(1):Article 343, 2010.

R. Leaman and G. Gonzalez. BANNER: An executable survey of advances in biomedical named entity recognition. In *Pac. Symp. Biocomput.*, pages 652–663, Hawaii, 2008.

R. Leaman, L. Wojtulewicz, R. Sullivan, A. Skariah, J. Yang, and G. Gonzalez. Towards Internet-age pharmacovigilance: Extracting adverse drug reactions from user posts to health-related social networks. In *BioNLP*, pages 117–125, Uppsala, Sweden, 2010.

X. Liu and H. Chen. AZDrugminer: An information extraction system for mining patient-reported adverse drug events in online patient forums. In *ICSH*, pages 134–150, Beijing, China, 2013.

Z. Liu, M. Yang, X. Wang, Q. Chen, B. Tang, Z. Wang, and H. Xu. Entity recognition from clinical texts via recurrent neural network. *BMC Med Inform Decis Mak.*, 17(2):53–61, 2017.

A. Metke-Jimenez and S. Karimi. Concept identification and normalisation for adverse drug event discovery in medical forums. In *workshop on Biomedical Data Integration and Discovery*, Kobe, Japan, 2016.

A. Nikfarjam, A. Sarker, K. O'Connor, R. E. Ginn, and G. Gonzalez. Pharmacovigilance from social media: mining adverse drug reaction mentions using sequence labeling with word embedding cluster features. *J Am Med Inform Assoc.*, 22(3):671–681, 2015.

T. Ohta, Y. Tateisi, and J.-D. Kim. The GENIA corpus: An annotated research abstract corpus in molecular biology domain. In *HLT*, pages 82–86, San Diego, CA, 2002.

N. Okazaki. CRFsuite: a fast implementation of conditional random fields (CRFs), 2007. URL `http://www.chokkan.org/software/crfsuite/`.

C. Pierce, K. Bouri, C. Pamer, S. Proestel, H. Rodriguez, H. Van Le, C. Freifeld, J. Brownstein, M. Walderhaug, R. Edwards, and N. Dasgupta. Evaluation of Facebook and Twitter monitoring to detect safety signals for medical products: An analysis of recent FDA safety alerts. *Drug Saf.*, 40(4): 317–331, 2017.

S. Pyysalo, F. Ginter, J. Heimonen, J. Björne, J. Boberg, J. Järvinen, and T. Salakoski. Bioinfer: a corpus for information extraction in the biomedical domain. *BMC bioinformatics*, 8(1):50, 2007.

C. Ramakrishnan, P. Mendes, R. d. Gama, G. Ferreira, and A. Sheth. Joint extraction of compound entities and relationships from biomedical literature. In *IEEE/WIC/ACM WI-IAT*, pages 398–401, 2008.

A. Ritter, S. Clark, Mausam, and O. Etzioni. Named entity recognition in tweets: An experimental study. In *EMNLP*, pages 1524–1534, Edinburgh, UK, 2011.

A. Sarker and G. Gonzalez. Portable automatic text classification for adverse drug reaction detection via multi-corpus training. *J. Biomed. Inform*, 53:196–207, 2015.

O. Uzuner, I. Solti, and E. Cadag. Extracting medication information from clinical text. *J Am Med Inform Assoc.*, 17(5):514–518, 2010.

K. Verspoor, K. B. Cohen, A. Lanfranchi, C. Warner, H. Johnson, C. Roeder, J. Choi, C. Funk, Y. Malenkiy, M. Eckert, N. Xue, W. Baumgartner, M. Bada, M. Palmer, and L. Hunter. A corpus of full-text journal articles is a robust evaluation tool for revealing differences in performance of biomedical natural language processing tools. *BMC Bioinformatics*, 13(207), 2012.

M. Xu, H. Jiang, and S. Watcharawittayakul. A local detection approach for named entity recognition and mention detection. In *ACL*, pages 1237–1247, Vancouver, Canada, 2017.

S. Zhang, H. Jiang, M. Xu, J. Hou, and L. Dai. The fixed-size ordinally-forgetting encoding method for neural network language models. In *ACL*, pages 495–500, Beijing, China, 2015.

J. Zhao, A. Henriksson, and H. Boström. Cascading adverse drug event detection in electronic health records. In *Data Science and Advanced Analytics*, pages 1–8, 2015.

Incremental Knowledge Acquisition Approach for Information Extraction on both Semi-structured and Unstructured Text from the Open Domain Web

Maria Myung Hee Kim
Defence Science Technology Group
Edinburgh, SA 5111, Australia
maria.kim@dst.defence.gov.au

Abstract

Extracting information from semi-structured text has been studied only for limited domain sources due to its heterogeneous formats. This paper proposes a Ripple-Down Rules (RDR) based approach to extract relations from both semi-structured and unstructured text in open domain Web pages. We find that RDR's 'case-by-case' incremental knowledge acquisition approach provides practical flexibility for (1) handling heterogeneous formats of semi-structured text; (2) conducting knowledge engineering on any Web pages with minimum start-up cost and (3) allowing open-ended settings on relation schema. The efficacy of the approach has been demonstrated by extracting contact information from randomly collected open domain Web pages. The rGALA system achieved 0.87 F1 score on a testing dataset of 100 Web pages, after only 7 hours of knowledge engineering on a training set of 100 Web pages.

1 Introduction

Open Information Extraction (Open IE) (Banko et al., 2007; Wu and Weld, 2010; Fader et al., 2011) was introduced to extract information from the open domain Web where the relations of interest cannot be pre-defined in advance due to its heterogeneity in domain. Its purpose is to avoid specifying target relations and developing extraction models for individual target relations. The Open IE systems focus on discovering a binary relation candidate tuple in the form of (**E1, RelText, E2**) by identifying two entities of interest **E1** and **E2**, and the salient textual cues **RelText** (*aka 'relational text'*) between the two entities. Then, they classify whether any binary relation **R** exists between the two entities in a given tuple to extract a binary relation tuple like (**E1, R, E2**).

To date extracting information from the open domain Web has mainly focused on the unstructured text (i.e., where text is formatted in paragraphs and expressed as full sentences). However, most Web pages generally contain information expressed in semi-structured text including tables, lists, isolated words or text snippets as well as unstructured text. Therefore, it is important to develop an IE capability that is able to process both semi-structured and unstructured text from the open domain Web.

Unlike unstructured text, semi-structured text usually includes HTML tags, which is primarily for formatting purposes. The variability in the way people use HTML tags impedes IE process. Above all, HTML tags have the following characteristics which hinder the IE task:
(1) HTML's tabular structure is often abused to arrange the graphical aspect instead of using cascading style sheets; and
(2) HTML tags can be deeply nested mixing relevant content with web noise in a loose manner.

Processing semi-structured text from the open domain Web is very challenging task as it needs to deal with heterogeneous formats as well as heterogeneous domains. It is difficult to create sufficient labelled data for semi-structured text in heterogeneous formats. Due to these difficulties, extracting information from semi-structured text has been studied only for specific domains (Chang et al., 2006). Moreover, existing semi-structured text IE approaches cannot be extended to the open domain Web sources as they usually require domain dependent inputs.

In summary, extracting information from semi-structured text in the open domain Web presents the following three main challenges:

Maria Myunghee Kim. 2017. Incremental Knowledge Acquisition Approach for Information Extraction on both Semi-structured and Unstructured Text from the Open Domain Web. In *Proceedings of Australasian Language Technology Association Workshop*, pages 88–96.

1. It is difficult to distinguish between the relevant content and web noise without domain knowledge. There is no explicit difference in HTML structure between them.

2. There are no clear linguistic markers (e.g., punctuation) to segment semi-structured text in the same manner as a *sentence* in unstructured text.

3. It is hard to create "sufficient" labelled training data and/or a complete ruleset for semi-structured text in open domain due to its heterogeneous formats.

Our rGALA system aims to extract information from both semi-structured and unstructured text in the open domain Web. To handle heterogeneous formats in semi-structured text, the rGALA system treats semi-structured text the same way as unstructured text in the Open IE task. The system filters out most of HTML tags and forms a binary relation candidate tuple (**E1**, **RelText**, **E2**); the system then extracts a binary relation tuple (**E1, R, E2**) if a relation R exists between the two given entities.

The rGALA system adopts a Ripple-Down Rules (RDR)' incremental knowledge acquisition approach; in RDR, the rule creation process is simple and rapid with ensured consistency in ruleset maintenance. The system does not require labelled training data or up-front knowledge for rule creation. Moreover, it supports open-ended settings on target relation definition by starting with a small set of relations and incrementally adding more relations as discovered during the extraction process.

2   Related Work

2.1   Open Information Extraction (Open IE)

Open Information Extraction (Open IE) aims to achieve domain-independent discovery of relations from the heterogeneous Web. Existing Open IE systems can be categorised into two groups based on the level of sophistication of the NLP techniques applied: (1) shallow syntactic parsing; and (2) dependency parsing. Shallow syntactic parsing based Open IE systems annotate sentences with Part-of-Speech (POS) tags and phrase chunk tags, then identify relations by matching patterns over these tags. The systems in this category include TextRunner (Banko et al., 2007), WOE*pos* (Wu and Weld, 2010), ReVerb (Fader et al., 2011) and R2A2 (Etzioni et al., 2011). Dependency parsing based Open IE systems utilise a dependency parser to identify whole subtrees connecting

the relation predicate and its arguments. The systems in this category include OLLIE (Mausam et al., 2012), ClausIE (Corro and Gemulla, 2013), Wanderlust (Akbik and Brob, 2009), WOE*parse* (Wu and Weld, 2010) and KrakeN (Akbik and Loser, 2012). Each of these systems makes use of various heuristics to obtain extractions from the dependency parses. They are generally more time consuming than the shallow parsing based systems. They trade efficiency for improved precision and recall.

2.2   Ripple-Down Rules (RDR)

The basic idea of RDR (Compton and Jansen, 1990) is that each case is processed by the system and when the outcome is incorrect or NULL, one or more rules are added to provide the correct outcome for that case. The system also stores *cornerstone cases*, cases which triggered the creation of new rules.

The RDR approach has been applied to a range of NLP applications. Pham and colleagues developed KAFTIE using the RDR approach to extract positive attributions from scientific papers (Pham and Hoffmann, 2004) and to extract temporal relations (Pham and Hoffmann, 2006). KAFTIE was noted to have outperformed machine learning based systems. The RDR Case Explore (RDRCE) system (Xu and Hoffmann, 2010) combined RDR with a Machine Learning method. RDRCE was applied for POS tagging task and achieved a slight improvement over a state-of-the-art POS tagging system after 60 hours of knowledge engineering. A hybrid RDR-based Open IE system (Kim and Compton, 2012) makes use of RDR's incremental knowledge acquisition technique as an add-on to the state-of-the-art ReVerb Open IE system. With this wrapper approach, the ReVerb system's performance is further improved using RDR's error correction for the domain of interest.

2.3   IE systems for Semi-structured Text

Early IE systems for semi-structured text have been studied largely with manual approaches (Hammer et al., 1997; Arocena and Mendelzon, 1999) and supervised approaches (Kushmerick, 1997; Hsu and Dung, 1998; Soderland, 1999; Muslea et al., 1999; Califf and Mooney, 1999; Freitag, 2000; Laender et al., 2002). In order to increase the level of automation and reduce manual efforts, most of recent work has focused on semi-supervised approaches (Chang and Lui, 2001; Chang and Kuo, 2004) and unsupervised approaches (Crescenzi et al., 2001; Arasu and Garcia-Molina, 2003; Zhai and Liu, 2005; Liu et al., 2010; Grigalis, 2013). Semi-supervised and unsupervised IE systems can be applied only to template based Web pages as they depend heavily on the existence of a common template (Chang et al., 2006).

In the same manner as the rGALA system, WHISK (Soderland, 1999) also aims to extract information from both semi-structured and unstructured text; but unlike rGALA, it targets specific domain Web pages and uses a supervised learning algorithm. To reduce the amount of manual labelling, WHISK interleaves learning new rules and annotating new instances (training examples) using selective sampling; thus, the learning and annotation process is iterative. It begins with an empty set of rules and at each iteration: (1) it presents to the user a batch of instances to be labelled via a graphical interface; (2) the labelled instances are added to a training set; (3) for each instance in a training set (not covered by the existing ruleset), WHISK learns the new rule using top-down induction, i.e., it finds the most general rule that covers the seed, then specialises the rule by adding terms incrementally until a stopping condition is met and finally (4) it prunes the rules.

3   rGALA System

3.1   rGALA Implementation

The rGALA system consists of the following three main components: (1) Preprocessor, (2) Tuple Extractor, and (3) RDR Engine.

(1) Preprocessor consists of the following four tools:

(a) Web transformer

A simple HTML transformation tool was built using JSOUP[1] to extract both semi-structured and unstructured text. To keep all potential information while minimising the amount of Web noise, the Web transformer tool conducts the following two steps:

Step1: removes most of HTML tags and attributes except <table>, <list> and <p> tags.

Step2: extracts text within <p> tags.

(b) Text segmenter

A text segmenter was built using the JFlex[2] (fast lexical analyser generator for Java) parser to identify text segments from both semi-structured and unstructured text. It takes a specification with a set of regular expressions and corresponding actions to identify a whole block of text for semi-structured text and a sentence for unstructured text.

(c) Tokeniser

Similar to the text segmenter a tokeniser was built using the JFlex parser to tokenise formal and informal multi-lingual text. It tokenises text based on its *semantic bearing* instead of white spaces. For example, a phone number in text such as *(08) 999 8888* is tokenised as a single token.

(d) generic Active Learning Application (gALA) system

The gALA[3] system identifies Part-of-Speech tags and Named Entity tags. The gALA incremental learning system is based on the Maximum Entropy (MaxEnt) algorithm. It is configurable and portable across domains with minimal or no NLP knowledge.

(2) Tuple Extractor extracts candidate tuples, [ENTITY_1, BETWEEN, ENTITY_2], which become *RDR cases* for binary relation classification task in the RDR Engine. A candidate tuple consists of two entities (ENTITY_1 and ENTITY_2) and a relational text (BETWEEN), which includes all the words between the two entities. The maximum number of tokens in the relational text is not limited by default but this value is configurable.

(3) RDR Engine follows these three steps:

(a) Step 1: The user checks the Relation Extraction (RE) result returned from the system.

For each RDR case, the system can return a correct or an incorrect RE result, or a NULL result when no rule was fired for the given case.

(b) Step 2: The user creates an RDR rule when the result returned is not correct or NULL.

If the system returns an incorrect RE result, a new rule is created under the rule which returned the incorrect result. If the system returns a NULL result, a new rule is created under the root rule.

(c) Step 3: The system evaluates the newly created RDR rule and the user refines it when required.

For the newly created rule, the system automatically evaluates it against the relevant cases (the parent rule's cases and the sibling

---

[1] https://jsoup.org/

[2] http://jflex.de/ - The JFlex parser uses Deterministic Finite Automata (DFA) to segment a text stream based on a set of user-defined rules.

[3] The gALA system was developed by Defence Science and Technology (DST) group.

rules' cases) in the system, which may conflict with the new rule. If the rule conflicts with these cases, the user can refine the rule's condition to make the rule more precise.

3.2 RDR Rule Description

An RDR rule has one or more conditions connected with an 'AND' operation, and a conclusion. Figure 1 shows the components of the RDR rule condition and conclusion. Note that '*Cond*' and '*Conc*' refer to 'Condition' and 'Conclusion' respectively.

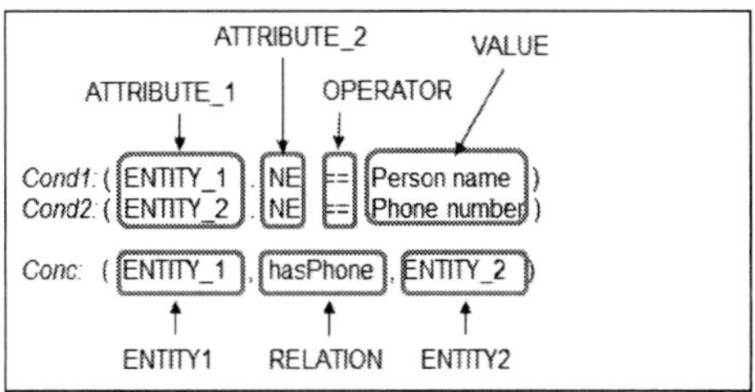

Figure 1: Components of RDR rule

(1) A *condition* consists of four components in the form of (**ATTRIBUTE_1.ATTRIBUTE_2 OPERATOR VALUE**).

(a) **ATTRIBUTE _1** refers to one of the 5 sections of a given text segment which is in the form of [E1BEFORE, ENTITY_1, BETWEEN, ENTITY_2, E2AFTER]. E1BEFORE and E2AFTER sections contain all the remaining tokens before the ENTITY_1 and after the ENTITY_2 sections, respectively.

(b) **ATTRIBUTE _2** refers to one of the NLP features; currently the following three NLP features are available:

- Lexical feature: token (TKN)
- Syntactic feature: Part-Of-Speech (POS)
- Semantic feature: Named Entity (NE)

(c) Currently the rGALA system supports nine **OPERATOR**s including '==', '!=', '*contains*', '*!contains*', '*regEx*', '*startsWith*', '*hasWordIn*', '*Pattern*' and '*NULL*'. Especially, the operator '*regEx*', '*hasWordIn*' and '*Pattern*' assist a single rule to handle multiple cases with similar patterns and words.

(d) **VALUE** is usually derived automatically in the system's GUI based on the choice made for the ATTRIBUTE_1 and ATTRIBUTE_2.

(2) A *conclusion* contains the relation extraction result in the form of (**ENTITY1, RELATION, ENTITY2**).

3.3 Rule Construction Example in Multiple Classification RDR (MCRDR)

A Multiple Classification RDR (MCRDR) is an 'n-ary' tree structure with only *except* edges. A case is evaluated by passing it to the root rule, which is always satisfied. An MCRDR evaluates all the first level rules which are direct children of the root rule. When a rule is satisfied, all its corresponding children rules are tested recursively where the children rules' conclusions overwrite the parent rule's conclusion. The inference process stops when there are no more children rules to evaluate.

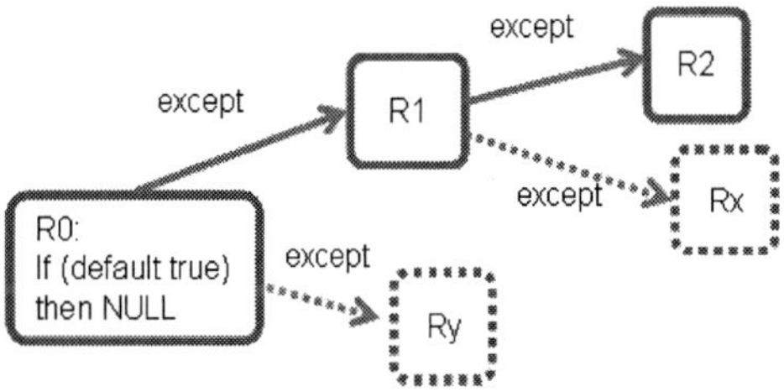

Figure 2: Rule construction example in MCRDR

The rGALA system applies an MCRDR for the single classification task as it is proved to be more efficient than a Single Classification RDR (SCRDR) even for single classification task (Kang et al., 1995). Figure 2 demonstrates MCRDR ruleset construction starting with an empty ruleset and the following three RDR cases described in the examples below.

Example 1. From the below text segment 1, RDR case 1 is identified. As the system returns a NULL result, a new rule is created.

Text segment 1:   *'Copies can be bought by contacting: Dr. John Smith at NCID Edinburgh and phone: 77778888.'*
RDR case1:   [**ENTITY_1: *'John Smith'***,   BETWEEN: *'at NCID Edinburgh and phone:'*,   **ENTITY_2: 77778888**]

RDR actions:
 1. The default rule **R0** is fired with a NULL result as there is no rule to handle the given case.
 2. A user creates a new rule **R1** under **R0** to extract 'hasPhone' relation from the given case.
 R1:
     Cond1:(ENTITY_1.NE == Person Name) AND
     Cond2:(ENTITY_2.NE == Phone Number) AND
     Cond3:(BETWEEN.NE !contains Person Name)
     Conc: (ENTITY_1, hasPhone, ENTITY_2)

Example 2. From the below text segment 2, RDR case 2 and RDR case 3 are identified. The system returns a correct result for the RDR case 2, but an incorrect result for the RDR case 3.

Text segment 2:
'<p>*Dr. Jane Smith* </p>
<p>*Postal Address*</p>
<p>*Elizabeth, East Ave., Australia*</p>
<p>*Phone: (618) 322 4444, Fax: (618)*
3115555</p>'

RDR case2:
[ENTITY_1: '*Jane Smith*',
BETWEEN: '<p>*Postal Address*</p>
<p>*Elizabeth, East Ave., Australia*</p>
<p>*Phone:*',
ENTITY_2: '*(618) 322 4444*']

RDR actions:
1. The rule **R1** is fired and returns the **[ENTITY_1, hasPhone, ENTITY_2]** result which is correct. The given case is saved under the rule **R1** and no further action is required.

RDR case3:
[ENTITY_1: '*Jane Smith*',
BETWEEN: '<p>*Postal Address*</p>
<p> *Elizabeth, East Ave., Australia*</p>
<p>*Phone: (618) 322 4444, Fax:*',
ENTITY_2: '*(618) 311 5555*']

RDR actions:
1. The rule **R1** is fired and returns the **[ENTITY_1, hasPhone, ENTITY_2]** result which is an incorrect result as the ENTITY_2 is a fax number rather than a phone number.
2. The user needs to create an exception rule **R2** under **R1** to extract 'hasFax' relation from the given case by adding one more condition to specify the given case and returns the **[ENTITY_1, hasFax, ENTITY_2]** result. R1's three conditions become pre-conditions of R2 automatically.
R2:
   Cond1: (BETWEEN.TKN contains '*Fax*')
   Conc: (ENTITY_1, hasFax, ENTITY_2)

In RDR's exception rule structure, a user needs to select only a few conditions which are enough to distinguish the current case from the cornerstone case of the parent rule.

3.4   rGALA Graphic User Interface (GUI)

Figure 3 presents the RDR Engine GUI of the rGALA system. The GUI allows a user to view each RDR case and the system's classification results, and to form a rule when required. The numbers in figure 3 describes the followings:

1. Displays a text segment;

2. Displays identified candidate tuples in the form of [ENTITY_1, BETWEEN, ENTITY_2];

3. Displays relation extraction result returned from the RDR ruleset in the form of [ENTITY1, RELATION, ENTITY2];

4. Displays NLP features in the form of [E1BEFORE, ENTITY_1, BETWEEN, ENTITY_2, E2AFTER] for the current case, cornerstone case and evaluated cases;

5. Selects rule's conditions and a conclusion;

6. Displays rule's pre-conditions, conditions and a conclusion; and

7. Displays the process log, the currently fired rule's path and the evaluation results.

4   Experiments

The experiments were conducted to demonstrate the efficacy of the rGALA system in creating rules and the effectiveness of its ruleset on both semi-structured and unstructured text in open domain Web pages.

4.1   Experiment Settings

In order to examine the efficacy of the rGALA system on open domain Web pages, a set of Web pages was collected from various educational institutions (e.g. '.*edu*'), commercial companies (e.g. '.*com*') and government organisations (e.g. '.*gov*') web sites based on their URL addresses (without domain specific keywords). Manual annotation of a gold standard data is the very time consuming process. Therefore, from 1351 collected Web pages, only two sets of 100 Web pages were randomly selected as training and testing datasets without duplication.

Five types of relations about contact information including '*hasPhone*', '*hasFax*', '*hasAddress*', '*hasEmail*' and '*hasDomainAddress*' were chosen as initial target relations because: (1) they are commonly observed information in both semi-structured and unstructured text in open domain Web pages; and (2) they are usually written in heterogeneous formats influenced by personal, organisational and cultural preferences.

In the experiments, these five types of relations were further categorised into ten target relations. For example, the '*hasPhone*' relation was further specified into two relations '*O_hasPhone*' and '*P_hasPhone*' to capture the different entity types (organisation and person).

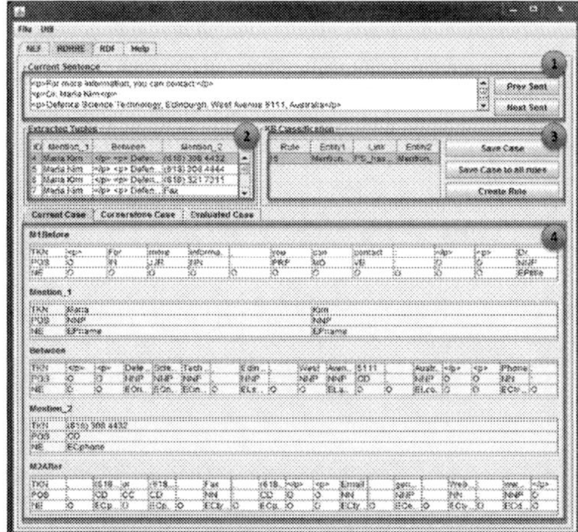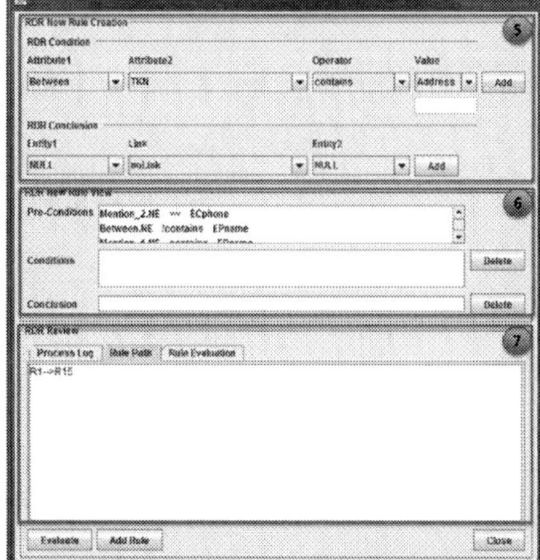

Figure 3: RDR Engine GUI for case-by-case incremental Knowledge Acquisition

Note that partially matched entities (esp. phone numbers) were evaluated as correct extractions in these experiments. For example, for '*+61 2 9999 5444/9999 1111*', the extracted entity '*9999 1111*' instead of '*+61 2 9999 1111*' was counted as a correct extraction.

4.2 Initial RDR Ruleset Construction

This section presents how the initial RDR ruleset was created to handle instances of the target relations from an empty ruleset.

To create the gold standard data, we manually analysed the post-processed 100 Web pages in the training dataset. As shown in the Table 1, a total of 325 instances of target relations were identified; 320 instances were found from semi-structured text written in 61 patterns and 5 instances were found from unstructured text written in 5 patterns.

To build the initial RDR ruleset, the rGALA system processed the 100 Web pages in the training dataset. It identified 1396 text segments and 5770 candidate tuples (*RDR cases*). In the tuple extraction process, 7 NE types were identified as entities' of interest including person, organisation, location, phone number, fax number, email address, postal address, and domain address.

The 5770 candidate tuples include 318 instances of the target relations and missed 7 target relation instances due to errors in detecting some phone number formatting. For example,

for '*Phone: (618) 322 4444/5555*', the current system can detect '*(618) 322 4444*' but it cannot detect the last shortened phone number '*5555*'.

Table 1 shows the number of RDR rules created for each type of target relations. In total, 22 rules were created; 21 rules were created to cover 67 patterns and 1 rule was created to reshape an overly generalised rule causing a false positive error. On average, for semi-structured text, one rule covered three or more patterns.

Some RDR rules created for unstructured text also handled semi-structured text, and vice versa. These are indicated using bold numbers in Table 1. For example, no rule was required to handle the 17 instances of '*P_hasPhone*' relation from semi-structured text as it was covered by one rule created from one instance in unstructured text. This arises because the rGALA system handles semi-structured text the same way as unstructured text; it filters out most of HTML tags and identifies candidate tuples in the form of (**E1, RelText, E2**).

The knowledge engineering of 5770 candidate tuples (*RDR cases*) took about 7 hours without any extra-preparation time for labelling data or understanding the data structure in advance. The initial RDR ruleset construction time starts when a case is called and finishes when a rule is accepted as complete. This construction time is logged automatically.

	Semi-structured text			Unstructured text		
	Ins	Pat	RDR	Ins	Pat	RDR
O_hasPhone	149	13	4	1	1	0
P_hasPhone	17	4	0	1	1	1
O_hasFax	92	11	4	0	0	0
P_hasFax	4	3	1	0	0	0
O_hasAddress	22	12	3	0	0	0
P_hasAddress	10	4	1	0	0	0
O_hasEmail	18	9	2	1	1	1
P_hasEmail	6	3	1	0	0	0
O_hasDomain Address	1	1	0	2	2	2
P_hasDomain Address	1	1	1	0	0	0
Total	320	61	17	5	5	4

Table 1: rGALA rule creation analysis on the training Dataset. ('*Ins*' and '*Pat*' refers to '*Instances*' and '*Patterns*' respectively)

	Both Semi-structured and Unstructured text			
	Ins	P	R	F1
O_hasPhone	74	0.87	0.78	0.82
P_hasPhone	0	0	0	0
O_hasFax	49	1.00	0.86	0.92
P_hasFax	0	0	0	0
O_hasAddress	13	1.00	0.85	0.92
P_hasAddress	0	0	0	0
O_hasEmail	5	0.8	0.8	0.8
P_hasEmail	0	0	0	0
O_hasDomain Address	0	0	0	0
P_hasDomain Address	0	0	0	0
Total	141	0.93	0.83	0.88

Table 2: The rGALA performance on the testing dataset. ('*Ins*' refers to '*Instances*')

4.3 rGALA System Performance

This section presents the performance of the rGALA system on the 100 Web pages in the testing dataset with the RDR ruleset constructed from the training dataset.

To create the gold standard data, the post-processed 100 Web pages in the testing dataset were also manually analysed. As shown in Table 2, a total of 141 instances of the target relations were identified; 137 instances were found from semi-structured text written in 26 patterns and 4 instances were found from unstructured text written in 4 patterns. Among the 26 patterns from semi-structured text, 10 patterns were the same as the patterns from semi-structured text in the training dataset.

As shown in Table 2, the testing dataset only included four target relations out of our ten target relations including 'O_hasPhone', 'O_hasFax', 'O_hasAddress' and 'O_hasEmail' due to the random selection of testing data. The testing dataset contained four out of five types of relations about contact information including 'hasPhone', 'hasFax', 'hasAddress' and 'hasEmail'.

When processing the testing dataset, the rGALA system identified 1386 text segments and 2818 candidate tuples (*RDR cases*). Overall, the rGALA system achieved reasonable and balanced performance of 0.88 F1 score with 0.93 precision and 0.83 recall. Total of 24 errors occurred including 4 False Positive (FP) errors and 20 False Negative errors (FN). All the 24 errors were caused from NE errors in the pre-processing phase; the 4 FP errors were due to incorrect NE types and the 20 FN errors were due to missed NEs. Among the 20 FN errors, the 8 FN errors were from missing shortened phone numbers format and 12 FN errors were from missing person and organisation named entities.

5 Discussion

As mentioned in section 4, the rGALA system achieved reasonable performance of 0.88 F1 score (with 0.93 precision and 0.83 recall) after only 7 hours of knowledge engineering on 100 open domain Web pages. No extra time was spent in analyzing the data, validating the rules or debugging.

In our experiment, the training dataset by chance contained more examples and patterns than the testing dataset. If the testing dataset were to contain more examples and patterns, the system may degrade. However, the rGALA system can quickly handle those uncovered examples in the testing dataset by adding rules incrementally.

The rGALA system cleans out HTML tags and treats semi-structured text in the same way as unstructured text. This approach brings out two main advantages shown in Table 1: (1) the rGALA system can handle various patterns of semi-structured text without any prior knowledge of the data structure/format and (2) its RDR rules work on both semi-structured and unstructured text. It is usually difficult to perfectly extract information from open domain Web pages in one go. Subsequent maintenance and evolution of the ruleset is of utmost importance. In the rGALA system, a new rule is automatically organised in an exception structure, with automatic checking for any potential conflicts. This effectively addresses the critical maintenance issue from which most manual approaches suffer.

Although the size of the experimental dataset was not large, it fully satisfied our initial scenario where IE is required from a collection of open domain Web pages without prior knowledge of the data. Experience suggests that knowledge acquisition with RDR remains very simple and rapid even for large rulesets with over 10,000 rules (Compton et al., 2011).

As mentioned in section 2.3, WHISK (Soderland, 1999) also aimed for information extraction from both semi-structured and unstructured text. While the rGALA system builds one ruleset which works for both semi-structured and unstructured text for open domain sources, WHISK builds separate rulesets for semi-structured and unstructured text; it requires specific inputs for different domains such as the exact phrase delimiters to be extracted from semi-structured text.

The rGALA system is simple but effective; its case-by-case incremental knowledge acquisition approach helps to efficiently capture human knowledge to handle heterogeneous formats of semi-structured text in the open domain Web without prior knowledge, a labelled dataset or pre-defined relation schema. Rules can be updated as errors are uncovered, or when new formats are discovered, or new target relations are defined. The rGALA system is not a system to extract *all* potential relations from the *whole* Web, but it is a system to extract *any* relations of interests from *any* given Web pages. To date no work has been published on IE from semi-structured text for open domain Web pages. We have demonstrated that treating semi-structured text the same way as unstructured text for this problem shows considerable promise.

References

Alan Akbik and Jugen Brob. 2009. Wanderlust: Extracting semantic relations from natural language text using dependency grammar patterns. In *Proceedings of the 18th International conference on World Wide Web*, pages 6-15.

Alan Akbik and Alexander Loser. 2012. Kraken: N-ary facts in open information extraction. In *Proceedings of the Joint Workshop on Automatic Knowledge Base Construction and Web-scale Knowledge Extraction*, pages 52-56.

Arvind Arasu and Hector Garcia-Molina. 2003. Extracting structured data from web pages. In *Proceedings of the 2003 ACM SIGMOD International Conference on Management of Data*, pages 337-348.

Gustavo O. Arocena and Alberto O. Mendelzon. 1999. WebOQL: Restructuring documents, databases and Webs. *Theory and Practice of Object Systems*, 5(3): 127-141.

Michele Banko, Michael J. Cafarella, Stephen Soderland, Matt Broadhead and Oren Etzioni. 2007. Open information extraction from the web. In *Proceedings of the 20th International Joint Conference on Artificial Intelligence*, pages 2670-2676.

Mary Elaine Califf and Raymond J. Mooney. 1999. Relational Learning of Pattern-Match Rules for Information Extraction. In *Proceedings of the 16th National Conference on Artificial Intelligence and 11th Conference on Innovative Applications of Artificial Intelligence.* pages 328-334.

Chia-Hui Chang and Shih-Chien Kuo. 2004. OLERA: Semisupervised Web-data extraction with visual support. *IEEE Intelligent Systems*, 19(6): 56-64.

Chia-Hui Chang, M. Kayed, M.R. Girgis and K.F. Shaalan. 2006. A Survey of Web Information Extractio Systems. *IEEE Transactiona on Knowledge and Data Engineering*, 18(10): 1411-1428.

Chia-Hui Chang and Shao-Chen Lui. 2001. IEPAD: informatio extraction based on pattern discovery. In *Proceedings of the 10th International World Wide Web Conference*, pages 681-688.

Paul Compton and Bob Jansen. 1990. A philosophical basis for knowledge acquisition. *Knowledge Acquisition*, 2(3): 241-258.

Paul Compton, Lindsay Peters, Timothy Lavers, Yang-Sok Kim. 2011. Experience with long-term knowledge acquisition. In *Proceedings of the 6th international conference on Knowledge capture*, pages 49-56.

Luciano Del Corro and Rainer Gemulla. 2013. ClausIE: Clause-Based Open Information Extraction. In *Proceedings of the 22nd International conference on World Wide Web*, pages 355-366.

Valter Crescenzi, Giansalvatore Mecca and Paolo Merialdo. 2001. RoadRunner: Towards Automatic Data Extraction from Large Web Sites. In *Proceedings of the 27th International Conference on Very Large Data Basaes*, pages 109-118.

Oren Etzioni, Anthony Fader, Janara Christensen, Stephen Soderland, and Mausam. 2011. Open information extraction: The second generation. In *Proceedings of the Conference on Artificial Intelligence*, pages 3-10.

Anthony Fader, Stephen Soderland and Oren Etzioni. 2011. Identifying relations for open information extraction. In *Proceedings of the Conference on Empirical Methods in Natural Language Processing*, pages 1535-1545.

Dayne Freitag. 2000. Machine Learning for Information Extraction in Informal Domains. *Machine Learning*, 39(2-3): 169-202.

Tomas Grigalis, Towards web-scale structured web data extraction. 2013. In *Proceedings of the 6th ACM International Conference on Web search and data mining,* pages 753-758.

Joachim Hammer, Jason McHugh and Hector Garcia-Molina. 1997. Semistructured Data: The TSIMMIS Experience. In *Proceedings of the 1st East-European conference on Advances in Databases and Information Systems,* pages 22-22.

Chun-Nan Hsu and Ming-Tzung Dung. 1998. Generating finite-state transducers for semi-structured data extraction from the Web. *Information systems*, 23(8): 521-538.

Byeong Ho Kang, Paul Compton and Phil Preston. 1995. Multiple classification ripple down rules: evaluation and possibilities. In *Proceedings of the 9th Banff Knowledge Acquisition for Knowledge Based Systems Workshop.*

Myung Hee Kim and Paul Compton. Improving Open Information Extraction for Informal Web Documents with Ripple-Down Rules. 2012. In *Proceedings of the 12th Pacific Rim conference on Knowledge Management and Acquisition for Intelligent Systems*, pages 160-174.

Nicholas Kushmerick. 1997. Wrapper induction for information extraction. PhD dissertation, University of Washington.

Alberto H.F. Laender, Berthier Ribeiro-Neto and Altigran S. da Silva. 2002. DEByE - Data Extraction By Example. *Data and Knowledge Engineering,* 40(2): 121-154.

Wei Liu, Xiaofeng Meng and Weiyi Meng. 2010. Vide: A vision-based approach for deep web data extraction. *IEEE Transactions on Knowledge and Data Engineering*, 22 (3), pages 447-460.

Mausam, Michael Schmitz, Robert Bart, Stephen Soderland and Oren Etzioni. 2012. Open Language Learning for Information Extraction. In *Proceedings of the 2012 Joint Conference on Empirical Methods in Natural Language Processing and Computational Natural Langauge Learning*, pages 523-534.

Ion Muslea, Steve Minton and Craig Knoblock. 1999. A hierarchical approach to wrapper induction. In *Proceedings of the 3rd Annual Conference on Autonomous Agents.* pages 190-197.

Son Bao Pham and Achim Hoffmann. 2004. Extracting Positive Attributions from Scientific papers. In *Proceedings of the 7th International conference on Discovery Science Conference,* pages 169-182.

Son Bao Pham and Achim Hoffmann. 2006. Efficient Knowledge Acquisition for Extracting Temporal Relations. In *Proceedings of the 17th European Conference on Artificial Intelligence,* pages 521-525.

Stephen Soderland. 1999. Learning Information Extraction Rules for Semi-structured and Free Text. *Machine Learning*, pages 1-44.

Fei Wu and Daniel S. Weld. 2010. Open information extraction using Wikipedia. In *Proceedings of the 48th Annual Meeting of the Association for Computational Linguistics*, pages 118-127.

Han Xu and Achim Hoffmann. 2010. RDRCE: Combining Machine Learning and Knowledge Acquisition. In *Proceedings of the 11th International Workshop,* pages 165-179.

Yanhong Zhai and Bing Liu. 2005. Web data extraction based on partial tree alignment. In *Proceedings of the 14th International Conference on World Wide Web.* pages 76-85.

Short papers

On Extending Neural Networks with Loss Ensembles for Text Classification

Hamideh Hajiabadi
Ferdowsi University of Mashhad (FUM)
Mashhad, Iran
hamideh.hajiabadi@mail.um.ac.ir

Diego Molla-Aliod
Macquarie University
Sydney, New South Wales, Australia
diego.molla-aliod@mq.edu.au

Reza Monsefi
Ferdowsi University of Mashhad (FUM)
Mashhad, Iran
monsefi@um.ac.ir

Abstract

Ensemble techniques are powerful approaches that combine several weak learners to build a stronger one. As a meta learning framework, ensemble techniques can easily be applied to many machine learning techniques. In this paper we propose a neural network extended with an ensemble loss function for text classification. The weight of each weak loss function is tuned within the training phase through the gradient propagation optimization method of the neural network. The approach is evaluated on several text classification datasets. We also evaluate its performance in various environments with several degrees of label noise. Experimental results indicate an improvement of the results and strong resilience against label noise in comparison with other methods.

1 Introduction

In statistics and machine learning, ensemble methods use multiple learning algorithms to obtain better predictive performance (Mannor and Meir, 2001). It has been proved that ensemble methods can boost weak learners whose accuracies are slightly better than random guessing into arbitrarily accurate strong learners (Bai et al., 2014; Zhang et al., 2016). When it could not be possible to directly design a strong complicated learning system, ensemble methods would be a possible solution. In this paper, we are inspired by ensemble techniques to combine several weak loss functions in order to design a stronger ensemble loss function for text classification.

In this paper we will focus on multi-class classification where the class to predict is encoded as a vector y with the one-hot encoding of the target label, and the output of a classifier $\hat{y} = f(x; \theta)$ is a vector of probability estimates of each label given input sample x and training parameters θ. Then, a loss function $L(y, \hat{y})$ is a positive function that measures the error of estimation (Steinwart and Christmann, 2008). Different loss functions have different properties, and some well-known loss functions are shown in Table 1. Different loss functions lead to different Optimum Bayes Estimators having their own unique characteristics. So, in each environment, picking a specific loss function will affect performance significantly (Xiao et al., 2017; Zhao et al., 2010).

In this paper, we propose an approach for combining loss functions which performs substantially better especially when facing annotation noise. The framework is designed as an extension to regular neural networks, where the loss function is replaced with an ensemble of loss functions, and the ensemble weights are learned as part of the gradient propagation process. We implement and evaluate our proposed algorithm on several text classification datasets.

The paper is structured as follows. An overview of several loss functions for classification is briefly introduced in Section 2. The proposed framework and the proposed algorithm are explained in Section 3. Section 4 contains experimental results on classifying several text datasets. The paper is concluded in Section 5.

2 Background

A typical machine learning problem can be reduced to an expected loss function minimization problem (Bartlett et al., 2006; Painsky and Rosset, 2016). Rosasco et al. (2004) studied the impact of choosing different loss functions from the viewpoint of statistical learning theory. In this section,

Hamideh Hajiabadi, Diego Mollá-Alliod and Reza Monsefi. 2017. On Extending Neural Networks with Loss Ensembles for Text Classification. In *Proceedings of Australasian Language Technology Association Workshop*, pages 98–102.

Name of loss function	$L(y, \hat{y})$
Zero-One (Xiao et al., 2017)	$L_{0-1} = \begin{cases} 0 & z \geq 0 \\ 1 & z < 0 \end{cases}$
Hinge Loss (Masnadi-Shirazi and Vasconcelos, 2009; Steinwart, 2002)	$L_H = \begin{cases} 0 & z \geq 1 \\ \max(0, 1 - z) & z < 1 \end{cases}$
Smoothed Hinge (Zhao et al., 2010)	$L_{S-H} = \begin{cases} 0 & z \geq 1 \\ \frac{1-z^2}{2} & 0 \leq z < 1 \\ \max(0, 1 - z) & z \leq 0 \end{cases}$
Square Loss	$L_S = \|y - \hat{y}\|_2^2$
Correntropy Loss (Liu et al., 2007, 2006)	$L_C = \exp \frac{\|y - \hat{y}\|_2^2}{\sigma^2}$
Cross-Entropy Loss (Masnadi-Shirazi et al., 2010)	$L_{C-E} = \log\left(1 + \exp\left(-z\right)\right)$
Absolute Loss	$L_A = \|y - \hat{y}\|_1$

Table 1: Several well-known loss functions, where $z = y \cdot \hat{y} \in \mathcal{R}$.

several well-known loss functions are briefly introduced, followed by a review of ensemble methods.

In the literature, loss functions are divided into margin-based and distance-based categories. Margin-based loss functions are often used for classification purposes (Steinwart and Christmann, 2008; Khan et al., 2013; Chen et al., 2017). Since we evaluate our work on classification of text datasets, in this paper we focus on margin-based loss functions.

A margin-based loss function is defined as a penalty function $L(y, \hat{y})$ based in a margin $z = y \cdot \hat{y}$. In any given application, some margin-based loss functions might have several disadvantages and advantages and we could not certainly tell which loss function is preferable in general. For example, consider the Zero-One loss function which penalizes all the misclassified samples with the constant value of 1 and the correctly classified samples with no loss. This loss function would result in a robust classifier when facing outliers but it would have a terrible performance in an application with margin focus (Zhao et al., 2010).

A loss function is margin enforcing if minimization of the expected loss function leads to a classifier enhancing the margin (Masnadi-Shirazi and Vasconcelos, 2009). Learning a classifier with an acceptable margin would increase generalization. Enhancing the margin would be possible if the loss function returns a small amount of loss for the correct samples close to the classification hyperplane. For example, Zero-One does not penalize correct samples at all and therefore it does not enhance the margin, while Hinge Loss is a margin enhancing loss function.

The general idea of ensemble techniques is to combine different expert ideas aiming at boosting the accuracy based on enhanced decision making. Predominantly, the underlying idea is that the decision made by a committee of experts is more reliable than the decision of one expert alone (Bai et al., 2014; Mannor and Meir, 2001). Ensemble techniques as a framework have been applied to a variety of real problems and better results have been achieved in comparison to using a single expert.

Having considered the importance of the loss function in learning algorithms, in order to reach a better learning system, we are inspired by ensemble techniques to design an ensemble loss function. The weight applied to each weak loss function is tuned through the gradient propagation optimization of a neural network working on a text classification dataset.

Other works (Shi et al., 2015; BenTaieb et al., 2016) have combined two loss functions where the weights are specified as a hyperparameter set prior to the learning process (e.g. during a fine-tuning process with crossvalidation). In this paper, we combine more than two functions and the hyperparameter is not set a-priory but it is learned during the training process.

3 Proposed Approach

Let (x, y) be a sample where $x \in \mathcal{R}^N$ is the input and $y \in \{0, 1\}^C$ is the one-hot encoding of the label (C is the number of classes). Let

θ be the parameters of a neural network classifier with a top softmax layer so that the probability estimates are $\hat{y} = softmax(f(x;\theta))$. Let $\{L_i(y,\hat{y})\}_{i=1}^{M}$ denote M weak loss functions. In addition to finding the optimal θ, the goal is to find the best weights , $\{\lambda_1, \lambda_2, \ldots, \lambda_M\}$, to combine M weak loss functions in order to generate a better application-tailored loss function. We need to add a further constraint to avoid yielding near zero values for all λ_i weights. The proposed ensemble loss function is defined as below.

$$L = \sum_{j=1}^{M} \lambda_j L_j(y,\hat{y}), \sum_{j=1}^{M} \lambda_j = 1 \quad (1)$$

The optimization problem could be defined as follows, given T training samples.

$$\underset{\theta,\lambda}{\text{minimize}} \sum_{i=1}^{T} \sum_{j=1}^{M} \lambda_j L_j(y_i, \hat{y}_i)$$
$$\text{s.t.} \sum_{j=1}^{M} \lambda_j = 1, \lambda_i \geq 0 \quad (2)$$

To make the optimization algorithm simpler, we use λ_i^2 instead of λ_i, so the second constraint $\lambda_i \geq 0$ can be omitted. We then incorporate the constraint as a regularization term based on the concept of Augmented Lagrangian. The modified objective function using Augmented Lagrangian is presented as follows.

$$\underset{\theta,\lambda}{\text{minimize}} \sum_{i=1}^{T} \sum_{j=1}^{M} \lambda_j^2 L_j(y_i, \hat{y}_i)+$$
$$\eta_1(\sum_{j=1}^{M} \lambda_j^2 - 1) + \eta_2(\sum_{j=1}^{M} \lambda_j^2 - 1)^2 \quad (3)$$

Note that the amount of η_2 must be significantly greater that η_1 (Nocedal and Wright, 2006) . The first and the second terms of the objective function cause λ_i^2 values to approach zero but the third term satisfies $\sum_{j=1}^{M} \lambda_j^2 = 1$.

Figure 1 illustrates the framework of the proposed approach with the dashed box representing the contribution of this paper. In the training phase, the weight of each weak loss function is trained through the gradient propagation optimization method. The accuracy of the model is calculated in a test phase not shown in the figure.

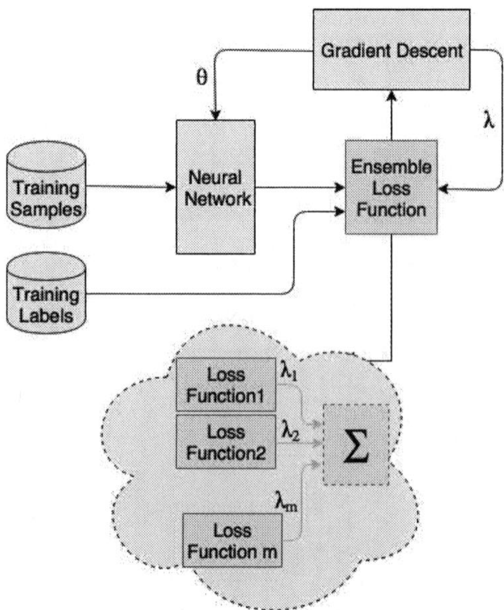

Figure 1: The proposed learning diagram

4 Experimental Results

We have applied the proposed ensemble loss function to several text datasets. Table 2 provides a brief description of the datasets. To reach a better ensemble loss function we choose three loss functions with different approaches in facing with outliers, as weak loss functions: Correntropy Loss which does not assign a high weight to samples with big errors, Hinge Loss which penalizes linearly and Cross-entropy Loss function which highly penalizes the samples whose predictions are far from the targets. We compared results with 3 loss functions which are widely used in neural networks: Cross-entropy, Square Loss, and Hinge Loss.

We picked η_1 near zero and $\eta_2 = 200$ in (3).

Since this work is a proof of concept, the neural networks of each application are simply a softmax of the linear combination of input features plus bias:

$$\hat{y} = \text{softmax}(x \cdot W + b)$$

where the input features x are the word frequencies in the input text. Thus, θ in our notation is composed of W and b. We use Python and its TensorFlow package for implementing the proposed approach. The results are shown in Table 3. The table compares the results of using individual loss functions and the ensemble loss.

Name of Datasets	Description
20-newsgroup	This data set is a collection of 20,000 messages,collected from 20 different net-news newsgroups.
Movie-reviews in corpus	The NLTK corpus movie-reviews data set has the reviews, and they are labeled already as positive or negative.
Email-Classification (TREC)	It is a collection of sample emails (i.e. a text corpus). In this corpus, each email has already been labeled as Spam or Ham.
Reuters-21578	The data was originally collected and labeled by Carnegie Group, Inc. and Reuters, Ltd. in the course of developing the CONSTRUE text categorization system

Table 2: Description of dataset

Dataset	Cross-entropy	Hinge	Square	Ensemble
20-newsgroups	0.80	0.69	0.82	**0.85**
Movie-review	0.83	0.81	**0.85**	0.83
Email-Classification (TREC)	0.88	0.78	0.96	**0.97**
Reuters	0.79	0.79	**0.81**	**0.81**

Table 3: Accuracy

We have also compared the robustness of the proposed loss function with the use of individual loss functions. In particular, we add label noise by randomly modifying the target label in the training samples, and keep the evaluation set intact. We conducted experiments with 10% and 30% of noise, where e.g. 30% of noise means randomly changing 30% of the labels in the training data. Tables 4 and 5 show the results, with the best results shown in boldface. We can observe that, in virtually all of the experiments, the ensemble loss is at least as good as the individual losses, and in only two cases the loss is (slightly) worse. And, in general, the ensemble loss performed comparatively better as we increased the label noise.

Dataset	Cross-entropy	Hinge	Square	Ensemble
20-newsgroups	0.79	0.67	0.69	**0.83**
Movie-reviews	0.75	0.74	0.73	**0.78**
Email-Classification (TREC)	0.86	0.57	0.82	**0.96**
Reuters	**0.76**	0.69	0.71	0.73

Table 4: Accuracy in data with 10% label noise

5 Conclusion

This paper proposed a new loss function based on ensemble methods. This work focused on text classification tasks and can be considered as an initial attempt to explore the use of ensemble loss functions. The proposed loss function shows an improvement when compared with the use of well-known individual loss functions. Furthermore, the approach is more robust against the presence of label noise. Moreover, according to our experiments, the gradient descent method quickly converged.

Dataset	Cross-entropy	Hinge	Square	Ensemble
20-newsgroups	0.57	0.64	0.55	**0.82**
movie-review	0.55	0.54	0.55	**0.6**
Email-Classification (TREC)	0.80	0.46	0.81	**0.93**
Reuters	0.64	0.54	0.53	**0.68**

Table 5: Accuracy in data with 30% label noise

We have used a very simple neural architecture in this work but in principle this method could be used for systems that use any neural networks. In future work we will explore the integration of more complex neural networks such as those using convolutions and recurrent networks. We also plan to study the application of this method to other tasks such as sequence labeling (e.g. for NER and PoS tagging). Another possible extension could focus on handling sparseness by adding a regularization term.

References

Qinxun Bai, Henry Lam, and Stan Sclaroff. 2014. A Bayesian framework for online classifier ensemble. In *Proceedings of the 31st International Conference on Machine Learning (ICML-14)*. pages 1584–1592.

Peter L Bartlett, Michael I Jordan, and Jon D McAuliffe. 2006. Convexity, classification, and risk bounds. *Journal of the American Statistical Association* 101(473):138–156.

Aïcha BenTaieb, Jeremy Kawahara, and Ghassan Hamarneh. 2016. Multi-loss convolutional networks for gland analysis in microscopy. In *Biomedical Imaging (ISBI 2016)*. pages 642–645.

Badong Chen, Lei Xing, Bin Xu, Haiquan Zhao, Nanning Zheng, and Jose C Principe. 2017. Kernel risk-sensitive loss: Definition, properties and application to robust adaptive filtering. *IEEE Transactions on Signal Processing* 65(11):2888–2901.

Inayatullah Khan, Peter M Roth, Abdul Bais, and Horst Bischof. 2013. Semi-supervised image classification with huberized Laplacian support vector machines. In *Emerging Technologies (ICET), 2013 IEEE 9th International Conference on*. IEEE, pages 1–6.

W. Liu, P. P. Pokharel, and J. C. Principe. 2007. Correntropy: Properties and applications in non-Gaussian signal processing. *IEEE Transactions on Signal Processing* 55(11):5286–5298. https://doi.org/10.1109/TSP.2007.896065.

Weifeng Liu, P. P. Pokharel, and J. C. Principe. 2006. Correntropy: A localized similarity measure. In *The 2006 IEEE International Joint Conference on Neural Network Proceedings*. pages 4919–4924. https://doi.org/10.1109/IJCNN.2006.247192.

Shie Mannor and Ron Meir. 2001. Weak learners and improved rates of convergence in boosting. In *Advances in Neural Information Processing Systems*. pages 280–286.

Hamed Masnadi-Shirazi, Vijay Mahadevan, and Nuno Vasconcelos. 2010. On the design of robust classifiers for computer vision. In *Computer Vision and Pattern Recognition (CVPR), 2010 IEEE Conference on*. IEEE, pages 779–786.

Hamed Masnadi-Shirazi and Nuno Vasconcelos. 2009. On the design of loss functions for classification: theory, robustness to outliers, and SavageBoost. In *Advances in neural information processing systems*. pages 1049–1056.

Jorge Nocedal and Stephen J Wright. 2006. Penalty and augmented Lagrangian methods. *Numerical Optimization* pages 497–528.

Amichai Painsky and Saharon Rosset. 2016. Isotonic modeling with non-differentiable loss functions with application to Lasso regularization. *IEEE transactions on pattern analysis and machine intelligence* 38(2):308–321.

Lorenzo Rosasco, Ernesto De Vito, Andrea Caponnetto, Michele Piana, and Alessandro Verri. 2004. Are loss functions all the same? *Neural Computation* 16(5):1063–1076.

Qinfeng Shi, Mark Reid, Tiberio Caetano, Anton Van Den Hengel, and Zhenhua Wang. 2015. A hybrid loss for multiclass and structured prediction. *IEEE Transactions on Pattern Analysis and Machine Intelligence* 37(1):2–12. https://doi.org/10.1109/TPAMI.2014.2306414.

Ingo Steinwart. 2002. Support vector machines are universally consistent. *Journal of Complexity* 18(3):768–791.

Ingo Steinwart and Andreas Christmann. 2008. *Support Vector Machines*. Springer Science & Business Media.

Yingchao Xiao, Huangang Wang, and Wenli Xu. 2017. Ramp loss based robust one-class SVM. *Pattern Recognition Letters* 85:15–20.

Peng Zhang, Tao Zhuo, Yanning Zhang, Hanqiao Huang, and Kangli Chen. 2016. Bayesian tracking fusion framework with online classifier ensemble for immersive visual applications. *Multimedia Tools and Applications* 75(9):5075–5092.

Lei Zhao, Musa Mammadov, and John Yearwood. 2010. From convex to nonconvex: A loss function analysis for binary classification. In *Data Mining Workshops (ICDMW), 2010 IEEE International Conference on*. IEEE, pages 1281–1288.

Towards the Use of Deep Reinforcement Learning with Global Policy For Query-based Extractive Summarisation[*]

Diego Mollá
Department of Computing
Macquarie University
Sydney
`diego.molla-aliod@mq.edu.au`

Abstract

Supervised approaches for text summarisation suffer from the problem of mismatch between the target labels/scores of individual sentences and the evaluation score of the final summary. Reinforcement learning can solve this problem by providing a learning mechanism that uses the score of the final summary as a guide to determine the decisions made at the time of selection of each sentence. In this paper we present a proof-of-concept approach that applies a policy-gradient algorithm to learn a stochastic policy using an undiscounted reward. The method has been applied to a policy consisting of a simple neural network and simple features. The resulting deep reinforcement learning system is able to learn a global policy and obtain encouraging results.

1 Introduction

Common supervised machine learning approaches to extractive summarisation attempt to label individual text extracts (usually sentences or phrases; in this paper we will use sentences). In a subsequent stage, a summary is generated based on the predicted labels of the individual sentences and other factors such as redundancy of information.

The process of obtaining the annotated data can be complex. Data sets often contain complete summaries written manually. Well-known examples of data sets of this type are the DUC and TAC data sets (Dang, 2006, 2008). In such cases the task of labelling individual sentences is not straightforward and needs to be derived from the full summaries. Alternatively, annotations can be

obtained through highlights made by the annotators (Woodsend and Lapata, 2010, for example).

Regardless of the means used to annotate individual sentences, the final evaluation of the system compares the output summary with a set of target summaries, either by using human judges or automatically by using packages such as ROUGE (Lin, 2004). However, machine learning approaches designed to minimise the prediction error of individual sentences would not necessarily minimise the prediction error of the final summary evaluation metric.

In this paper we propose a proof-of-concept method that uses reinforcement learning with global policy as a means to use the ROUGE-L evaluation of the final summary directly in the training process. Section 2 introduces reinforcement learning and mentions past work on the use of reinforcement learning for summarisation. Section 3 describes our proposal for the use of reinforcement learning for query-based summarisation. Section 4 presents the results of our experiments, and Section 5 concludes this paper.

2 Reinforcement Learning

Reinforcement Learning (RL) is a machine learning approach that is designed to train systems that aim to maximise a long-term goal, even when there is no knowledge (or little knowledge) of the impact of the individual decisions that are made to achieve the goal. A RL task (Figure 1) consists of an environment that can be observed and can be acted on, and an agent that makes a sequence of actions. The effect of undertaking an action (a) on the environment will result in an observed state (s) and a reward (r). The agent then needs to learn the sequence of actions that maximises the cumulative reward.

The task of query-based summarisation can be

___

[*] Code available at `https://github.com/dmollaaliod/alta2017-rl`

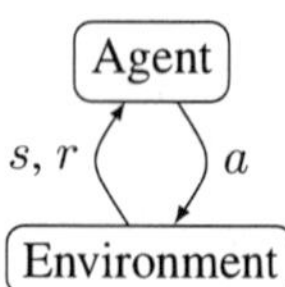

Figure 1: The reinforcement learning process.

reduced to a RL task by assigning null reward $r = 0$ to the decision of selecting each individual sentence or not, until the point at which a final summary has been extracted. At the moment that a final summary has been extracted, the reward r is the actual evaluation score of the full summary. The RL approach should learn a policy π such that the agent can determine how the individual decisions made at the time of selecting (or not) a sentence would impact on the evaluation score of the final summary.

Ryang and Abekawa (2012) and Rioux and Hasan (2014) propose the learning of a local policy π that is specific to each summary. For this purpose, the reward r of the entire summary is calculated based on measures of similarity between the summary and the source document. Thus, Ryang and Abekawa (2012) uses information such as coverage, redundancy, length and position. Rioux and Hasan (2014) uses a reward system that is more similar to the ROUGE set of metrics, but again using only information from the source text and the generated summary. Effectively, these approaches use RL as a means to search the space of possible selections of sentences by training a local policy that needs to be re-trained each time a new summary needs to be generated.

Ryang and Abekawa (2012) mentions the possibility of training a global policy in the section of further work provided that there is a mean to provide a feature representation of a summary. In this paper we show a simple way to represent the state of the environment, including the summary, such that the system can train a global policy. We use a training set annotated with target summaries to train a global policy that uses the direct ROUGE_L score as the reward. Once a global policy has been learnt, it is applied to unseen text for evaluation. By using a global policy instead of a local policy, the system can use the direct ROUGE_L score instead of an approximation, and the computational cost shifts to the training stage, enabling a faster generation of summaries after the system has been trained.

There is also research that use other mechanisms in order to train a summarisation system using the direct ROUGE score (Aker et al., 2010) or an approximation (Peyrard and Eckle-Kohler, 2016).

3 Reinforcement Learning for Query-based Extractive Summarisation

This section describes our proposal for the adaptation of query-based summarisation to RL with global policy.

3.1 Environment

After applying a decision whether sentence i is to be selected as a summary or not, the environment records the decision and issues a reward $r = 0$. After all decisions have been made, the environment builds the summary by concatenating all selected sentences in linear order. Then, the environment returns the ROUGE_L score of the summary as the reward. More formally, and assuming that the total number of sentences in the input text is n, the reward is computed as follows:

$$r = \begin{cases} 0 & \text{if } i < n \\ \text{ROUGE\_L} & \text{if } i = n \end{cases}$$

This process is inspired in Ryang and Abekawa (2012)'s framework, the difference being that, in our work, the reward returned when $i = n$ is the actual ROUGE_L score of the summary instead of an approximation.

For the purposes of this paper, the environment is implemented as an object `env` that allows the following operations:

- $s \leftarrow$ `env.reset(sample)`: reset to sample `sample` and return an initial state s.

- $s, r, \text{done} \leftarrow$ `env.step(a)`: perform action a and return state s, reward r, and a Boolean value $True$ if all input sentences have been processed.

3.2 Action Space

At each step of the RL process, the agent will decide whether a particular sentence is to be selected (1) or not (0).

3.3 State

The RL framework is greedy in the sense that, once a decision is made about sentence i, it cannot be undone. The agent should therefore have the information necessary to make the right decision, including information about what sentences are yet to process. Since the agent uses a global policy, the state should be able to encode information about any number of input sentences, and any number of remaining sentences. We resolved this by building vectors that represent sequences of sentences. In this paper we use *tf.idf*, but other methods could be used, such as sentence embeddings learnt by training deep neural networks.

In concrete, the environment provides the following state:

1. *tf.idf* of the candidate sentence i.

2. *tf.idf* of the entire input text to summarise.

3. *tf.idf* of the summary generated so far.

4. *tf.idf* of the candidate sentences that are yet to be processed.

5. *tf.idf* of the question.

Information 2. and 3. would be useful to determine whether the current summary is representative of the input text. Information 4. would be useful to determine whether there is still important information that could be added to the summary in future steps. The agent could then, in principle, contrast 1. with 2., 3., 4. and 5. to determine whether sentence i should be selected or not.

3.4 Global Policy

The global policy is implemented as a neural network that predicts the probability of each action a available in the action space $\{0, 1\}$. In practice, the system only needs to predict $Pr(a = 0)$. As a proof of concept, the neural network implemented in this paper is simply a multi-layer network with one hidden layer that uses a relu activation, and the output unit is a Bernoulli logistic unit. Thus, given a state s formed by concatenating all the items listed in Section 3.3, the network predicts $Pr(a = 0)$ as follows.

$$
\begin{aligned}
Pr(a = 0) &= \sigma(h \cdot W_h + b_h) \\
h &= \max(0, s \cdot W_s + b_s)
\end{aligned}
$$

In our experiments, the size of the hidden layer is 200.

3.5 Learning Algorithm

The learning algorithm for the global policy is a variant of the REINFORCE algorithm (Williams, 1992) that uses gradient descent with cross-entropy gradients that are multiplied with the reward (Géron, 2017, Chapter 16). This is shown in Algorithm 1.

Data: `train_data`
Result: θ
`sample` $\sim Uniform(\texttt{train\_data})$;
$s \leftarrow$ `env.reset(sample)`;
`all_gradients` $\leftarrow \emptyset$;
`episode` $\leftarrow 0$;
while *True* **do**
  $\xi \sim Bernoulli\left(\frac{Pr(a=0)+p}{1+2\times p}\right)$;
  $y \leftarrow 1 - \xi$;
  `gradient` $\leftarrow \frac{\nabla(\texttt{cross\_entropy}(y, Pr(a=0)))}{\nabla \theta}$;
  `all_gradients.append(gradient)`;
  $s, r, done \leftarrow$ `env.step(`ξ`)`;
  `episode` $\leftarrow$ `episode` $+ 1$;
  if *done* **then**
    $\theta \leftarrow$
    $\theta - \alpha \times r \times$ `mean(all_gradients)`;
    `sample` $\sim Uniform(\texttt{train\_data})$;
    $s \leftarrow$ `env.reset(sample)`;
    `all_gradients` $\leftarrow \emptyset$;
  end
end

Algorithm 1: Training by Policy Gradient, where $\theta = (W_h, b_h, W_s, b_s)$.

In Algorithm 1, the neural net predicts $Pr(a = 0)$. The action chosen during training is sampled from a Bernoulli distribution with probability $Pr(a = 0)$ that has a perturbation p, such that p slowly decreases at each training episode. By adding this perturbation the system explores the two possible actions in the early stages of training and delays locking in possible local minima. In our implementation, p is computed with an initial value of 0.2 and decreasing using the formula:

$$
p = 0.2 \times 3000/(3000 + \text{episode})
$$

Thus, $p = 0.1$ after 3000 episodes, and so on.

When a full summary has been produced, the mean of all cross-entropy gradients used in all the steps that lead to the summary is computed and multiplied by the summary reward to update the neural network trainable parameters. Using

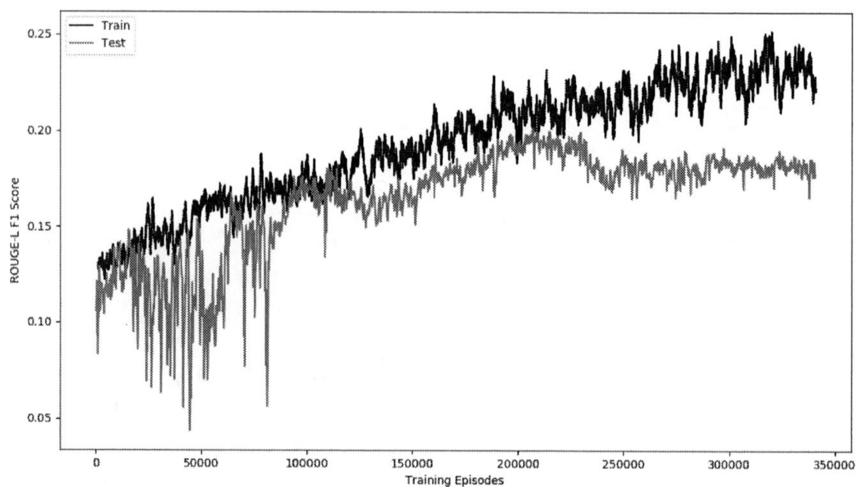

Figure 2: Results of the system. The results of training (black line) are the average ROUGE-L of the last 1000 chosen training samples at every point. The results of testing (red line) are the average ROUGE-L of the test set.

RL terminology, the method uses undiscounted reward.

At run time, the action a chosen is simply the action a with highest probability.

4 Experiments and Results

We have used the data provided by BioASQ 5b Phase B (Tsatsaronis et al., 2015). The dataset has 1799 questions together with input text and ideal answers. These ideal answers form the target summaries. We have split the data into a training an a test set.

Algorithm 1 updates the parameters θ by applying standard gradient descent. In our experiments, we have used the Adam optimiser instead, which has been shown to converge rapidly in many applications (Kingma and Ba, 2015). Also, due to computing limitations, our implementation only processes the first 30 sentences of the input text.

Figure 2 shows the progress of training and evaluation. We can observe that the neural net learns a global policy that improves the ROUGE-L results of the training data (black line). More importantly, it also improves the ROUGE-L results when presented with the test data (red line). It appears that the system starts overfitting after about 200,000 training steps.

Considering that the state does not have direct information about the sentence position or the length of the summary, and given the relatively small training data, these results are encouraging. It is well known that sentence position carries important information for the task of summarisation. Also, preliminary experiments adding summary length to the state showed quicker convergence to better values. In this paper we chose not to incorporate any of this information to test the capabilities of the use of reinforcement learning.

5 Conclusions

We have presented a reinforcement learning approach that learns a global policy for the task of query-based summarisation. Our experiments used fairly simple features to represent the state of the environment. Also, the neural network implemented to model the global policy is fairly simple. Yet, the system was able to effectively learn a global policy. In further work we will explore the use of more sophisticated features such as word or sentence embeddings, and more sophisticated neural networks.

Further work will also explore the use of variants of reinforcement learning algorithms in order to speed up the learning process.

References

Ahmet Aker, Trevor Cohn, and Robert Gaizauskas. 2010. Multi-document summarization using A* search and discriminative training. In *EMNLP 2010*. October, pages 482–491.

Hoa Trang Dang. 2006. Overview of DUC 2006. In *Proc. Document Understanding Workshop*. NIST.

Hoa Trang Dang. 2008. Overview of the TAC 2008 opinion question answering and summarization tasks. In *Proc. TAC 2008*.

Aurélien Géron. 2017. *Hands-on Machine Learning with Scikit-Learn and TensorFlow: Concepts, Tools, and Techniques to Build Intelligent Systems*. O'Reilly Media.

Diederik P. Kingma and Jimmy Ba. 2015. Adam: A method for stochastic optimization. In *ICLR 2015*. pages 1–15.

Chin-Yew Lin. 2004. ROUGE: A package for automatic evaluation of summaries. In *ACL Workshop on Tech Summarisation Branches Out*.

Maxime Peyrard and Judith Eckle-Kohler. 2016. Optimizing an approximation of ROUGE — a problem-reduction approach to extractive multi-document summarization. In *Proceedings of the 54th Annual Meeting of the Association for Computational Linguistics (Volume 1: Long Papers)*. pages 1825–1836.

Cody Rioux and Sadid A Hasan. 2014. Fear the REAPER: A system for automatic multi-document summarization with reinforcement learning. In *EMNLP 2014*. 2010, pages 681–690.

Seonggi Ryang and Takeshi Abekawa. 2012. Framework of automatic text summarization using reinforcement learning. In *EMNLP 2012*. July, pages 256–265.

George Tsatsaronis, Georgios Balikas, Prodromos Malakasiotis, Ioannis Partalas, Matthias Zschunke, Michael R Alvers, Dirk Weissenborn, Anastasia Krithara, Sergios Petridis, Dimitris Polychronopoulos, Yannis Almirantis, John Pavlopoulos, Nicolas Baskiotis, Patrick Gallinari, Thierry Artiéres, Axel-Cyrille Ngonga Ngomo, Norman Heino, Eric Gaussier, Liliana Barrio-Alvers, Michael Schroeder, Ion Androutsopoulos, and Georgios Paliouras. 2015. An overview of the BIOASQ large-scale biomedical semantic indexing and question answering competition. *BMC Bioinformatics* 16(1):138.

Ronald J. Williams. 1992. Simple statistical gradient-following algorithms for connectionist reinforcement learning. *Machine Learning* 8:229–256.

Kristian Woodsend and Mirella Lapata. 2010. Automatic generation of story highlights. In *Proceedings of the 48th Annual Meeting of the Association for Computational Linguistics*. July, pages 565–574.

From Word Segmentation to POS Tagging for Vietnamese

Dat Quoc Nguyen[1], **Thanh Vu**[2], **Dai Quoc Nguyen**[3], **Mark Dras**[1] and **Mark Johnson**[1]

[1]Department of Computing, Macquarie University, Australia

`{dat.nguyen, mark.dras, mark.johnson}@mq.edu.au`

[2]NIHR Innovation Observatory, Newcastle University, United Kingdom

`thanh.vu@newcastle.ac.uk`

[3]PRaDA Centre, Deakin University, Australia

`dai.nguyen@deakin.edu.au`

Abstract

This paper presents an empirical comparison of two strategies for Vietnamese Part-of-Speech (POS) tagging from unsegmented text: (i) a pipeline strategy where we consider the output of a word segmenter as the input of a POS tagger, and (ii) a joint strategy where we predict a combined segmentation and POS tag for each syllable. We also make a comparison between state-of-the-art (SOTA) feature-based and neural network-based models. On the benchmark Vietnamese treebank (Nguyen et al., 2009), experimental results show that the pipeline strategy produces better scores of POS tagging from unsegmented text than the joint strategy, and the highest accuracy is obtained by using a feature-based model.

1 Introduction

POS tagging is one of the most fundamental natural language processing (NLP) tasks. In English where white space is a strong indicator of word boundaries, POS tagging is an important first step towards many other NLP tasks. However, white space when written in Vietnamese is also used to separate syllables that constitute words. So for Vietnamese NLP, word segmentation is referred to as the key first step (Dien et al., 2001).

When applying POS tagging to real-world Vietnamese text where gold word-segmentation is not available, the pipeline strategy is to first segment the text by using a word segmenter, and then feed the word-segmented text—which is the output of the word segmenter—as the input to a POS tagger. For example, given a written text "thuế thu nhập cá nhân" (individual$_{cá_nhân}$ income$_{thu_nhập}$ tax$_{thuế}$) consisting of 5 syllables, the word seg-

menter returns a two-word phrase "thuế_thu_nhập cá_nhân."[1] Then given the input segmented text "thuế_thu_nhập cá_nhân", the POS tagger returns "thuế_thu_nhập/N cá_nhân/N."

A class of approaches to POS tagging from unsegmented text that has been actively explored in other languages, such as in Chinese and Japanese, is joint word segmentation and POS tagging (Zhang and Clark, 2008). A possible joint strategy is to assign a combined segmentation and POS tag to each syllable (Kruengkrai et al., 2009). For example, given the input text "thuế thu nhập cá nhân", the joint strategy would produce "thuế/B-N thu/I-N nhập/I-N cá/B-N nhân/I-N", where B refers to the beginning of a word and I refers to the inside of a word. Shao et al. (2017) showed that this joint strategy gives SOTA results for Chinese POS tagging by utilizing a BiLSTM-CNN-CRF model (Ma and Hovy, 2016).

In this paper, we present the first empirical study comparing the joint and pipeline strategies for Vietnamese POS tagging from unsegmented text. In addition, we make a comparison between SOTA feature-based and neural network-based models, which, to the best of our knowledge, has not done in any prior work on Vietnamese. On the benchmark Vietnamese treebank (Nguyen et al., 2009), we show that the pipeline strategy produces better scores than the joint strategy. We also show that the highest tagging accuracy is obtained by using a traditional feature-based model rather than neural network-based models.

2 Related work

2.1 Word segmentation

Nguyen et al. (2006), Dinh and Vu (2006) and

---

[1]In the traditional underscore-based representation in Vietnamese word segmentation (Nguyen et al., 2009), white space is only used to separate words while underscore is used to separate syllables inside a word.

Dat Quoc Nguyen, Thanh Vu, Dai Quoc Nguyen, Mark Dras and Mark Johnson. 2017. From Word Segmentation to POS Tagging for Vietnamese. In *Proceedings of Australasian Language Technology Association Workshop*, pages 108–113.

Tran et al. (2010) considered the Vietnamese word segmentation task as a sequence labeling task, using either a CRF, SVM or MaxEnt model to assign each syllable a segmentation tag such as B or I. In addition, Le et al. (2008), Pham et al. (2009) and Tran et al. (2012) used the maximum matching method (NanYuan and YanBin, 1991) to generate all possible segmentations for each input sentence; then to select the best segmentation, Le et al. (2008) and Tran et al. (2012) applied n-gram language model while Pham et al. (2009) employed POS information from an external POS tagger. Later, Liu and Lin (2014) and Nguyen and Le (2016) proposed approaches based on point-wise prediction, where a binary classifier is trained to identify whether or not there is a word boundary at each point between two syllables. Furthermore, Nguyen et al. (2017b) proposed a rule-based approach which gets the highest results to date in terms of both segmentation accuracy and speed.

2.2 POS tagging

Regarding Vietnamese POS tagging, Dien and Kiem (2003) projected POS annotations from English to Vietnamese via a bilingual corpus of word alignments. As a standard sequence labeling task, previous research has applied the CRF, SVM or MaxEnt model to assign each word a POS tag (Nghiem et al., 2008; Tran et al., 2009; Le-Hong et al., 2010; Nguyen et al., 2010; Tran et al., 2010; Bach et al., 2013). In addition, Nguyen et al. (2011) proposed a rule-based approach to automatically construct transformation rules for POS tagging in the form of a Ripple Down Rules tree (Compton and Jansen, 1990), leading to a development of the RDRPOSTagger (Nguyen et al., 2014a) which was the best system for the POS tagging shared task at the 2013 Vietnamese Language and Speech Processing (VLSP) workshop.

Nguyen et al. (2016a) and Nguyen et al. (2016b) later showed that SOTA accuracies at 94+% in the Vietnamese POS tagging task are obtained by simply retraining existing English POS taggers on Vietnamese data, showing that the MarMoT tagger (Mueller et al., 2013) and the Stanford POS tagger (Toutanova et al., 2003) obtain higher accuracies than RDRPOSTagger. Nguyen et al. (2016a) also showed that a simple lexicon-based approach assigning each word by its most probable POS tag gains a promising accuracy at 91%. Note that both Nguyen et al. (2016a) and Nguyen et al. (2016b)

did not experiment with neural network models. Pham et al. (2017) recently applied the BiLSTM-CNN-CRF (Ma and Hovy, 2016) for Vietnamese POS tagging, however, they did not experiment with SOTA feature-based models.

Previously, only Takahashi and Yamamoto (2016) carried out joint word segmentation and POS tagging for Vietnamese, to predicting a combined segmentation and POS tag to each syllable. In particular, Takahashi and Yamamoto (2016) experimented with traditional SVM- and CRF-based toolkits on a dataset of about 7k sentences and reported results of joint prediction only, i.e., they did not compare to the pipeline strategy. The CoNLL 2017 shared task on Universal Dependencies (UD) parsing from raw text (Zeman et al., 2017) provided some results to the pipeline strategy from word segmentation to POS tagging, however, the Vietnamese dataset in the UD project is very small, consisting of 1,400 training sentences. Furthermore, Nguyen et al. (2017a) provided a pre-trained jPTDP model for joint POS tagging and dependency parsing for Vietnamese,[2] which obtains a tagging accuracy at 93.0%, a UAS score at 77.7% and a LAS score at 69.5% when evaluated on the Vietnamese dependency treebank VnDT of 10k sentences (Nguyen et al., 2014b).

3 Experimental methodology

We compare the joint word segmentation and POS tagging strategy to the pipeline strategy on the benchmark Vietnamese treebank (Nguyen et al., 2009) using well-known POS tagging models.

3.1 Joint segmentation and POS tagging

Following Kruengkrai et al. (2009), Takahashi and Yamamoto (2016) and Shao et al. (2017), we formalize the joint word segmentation and POS tagging problem for Vietnamese as a sequence labeling task to assigning a combined segmentation and POS tag to each syllable. For example, given a manually POS-annotated training corpus "Cuộc/Nc diều_tra/V dường_như/X không/R tiến_triển/V ./CH" 'The investigation seems to be making no progress', we transform this corpus into a syllable-based representation as follows: "Cuộc/B-Nc diều/B-V tra/I-V dường/B-X như/I-X không/B-R tiến/B-V triển/I-V ./B-CH", where segmentation tags B and I denote beginning and in-

---

[2] https://drive.google.com/drive/
folders/0B5eBgc8jrKtpUmhhSmtFLWdrTzQ

side of a word, respectively, while Nc, V, X, R and CH are POS tags. Then we train sequence labeling models on the syllable-based transformed corpus.

3.2 Dataset

The Vietnamese treebank (Nguyen et al., 2009) is the largest annotated corpus for Vietnamese, providing a set of 27,870 manually POS-annotated sentences for training and development (about 23 words per sentence on average) and a test set of 2120 manually POS-annotated sentences (about 31 words per sentence).[3] From the set of 27,870 sentences, we use the first 27k sentences for training and the last 870 sentences for development.

3.3 Models

For both joint and pipeline strategies, we use the following models:

- RDRPOSTagger (Nguyen et al., 2014a) is a transformation rule-based learning model which obtained the highest accuracy at the VLSP 2013 POS tagging shared task.[4]

- MarMoT (Mueller et al., 2013) is a generic CRF framework and a SOTA POS and morphological tagger.[5]

- BiLSTM-CRF (Huang et al., 2015) is a sequence labeling model which extends the BiLSTM model with a CRF layer.

- BiLSTM-CRF + CNN-char, i.e. BiLSTM-CNN-CRF, is an extension of the BiLSTM-CRF, using CNN to derive character-based representations (Ma and Hovy, 2016).

- BiLSTM-CRF + LSTM-char is another extension of the BiLSTM-CRF, using BiLSTM to derive the character-based representations (Lample et al., 2016).

Here, for the pipeline strategy, we train these models to predict POS tags with respect to (w.r.t.) gold word segmentation. In addition, we also retrain the fast and accurate Vietnamese word segmenter RDRsegmenter (Nguyen et al., 2017b) using the training set of 27k sentences.[6]

Model	Pipeline	Joint
BiLSTM-CRF	100	200
+ CNN-char	100	250
+ LSTM-char	150	250

Table 1: Optimal number of LSTM units.

3.4 Implementation details

We use the original pure Java implementations of RDRPOSTagger and MarMoT with default hyper-parameter settings in our experiments. Instead of using implementations independently provided by authors of BiLSTM-CRF, BiLSTM-CRF + CNN-char[7] and BiLSTM-CRF + LSTM-char, we use a reimplementation which is optimized for performance of all these models from Reimers and Gurevych (2017).[8]

For three BiLSTM-CRF-based models, we use default hyper-parameters provided by Reimers and Gurevych (2017) with the following exceptions: we use a dropout rate at 0.5 (Ma and Hovy, 2016) with the frequency threshold of 5 for unknown word and syllable types. We initialize word and syllable embeddings with 100-dimensional pre-trained embeddings,[9] then learn them together with other model parameters during training by using Nadam (Dozat, 2016). For training, we run for 100 epochs. We perform a grid search of hyper-parameters to select the number of BiLSTM layers from $\{1, 2, 3\}$ and the number of LSTM units in each layer from $\{50, 100, 150, 200, 250, 300\}$. Early stopping is applied when no performance improvement on the development set is obtained after 5 contiguous epochs. For both pipeline and joint strategies, we find the highest performance on the development set is when using two stacked BiLSTM layers. Table 1 presents the optimal number of LSTM units.

Here the performance is evaluated by F1 score, based on the number of correctly segmented and tagged words (Zhang and Clark, 2008). In the case of gold word segmentation, F1 score for POS tagging is in fact the tagging accuracy.

---

[3] The data was officially used for the Vietnamese POS tagging shared task at the second VLSP 2013 workshop.

[4] http://rdrpostagger.sourceforge.net

[5] http://cistern.cis.lmu.de/marmot

[6] RDRsegmenter obtains a segmentation speed at 60k words per second, computed on a personal computer of Intel Core i7 2.2 GHz. RDRsegmenter is available at: https://github.com/datquocnguyen/RDRsegmenter

[7] https://github.com/XuezheMax/LasagneNLP

[8] https://github.com/UKPLab/emnlp2017-bilstm-cnn-crf

[9] Pre-trained word and syllable embeddings are learned by training the Word2Vec Skip-gram model (Mikolov et al., 2013) on a Vietnamese news corpus which is available at: http://mim.hus.vnu.edu.vn/phuonglh/corpus/baomoi.zip

Model	Accuracy	Speed
RDRPOSTagger	95.11	**180k**
MarMoT	**95.88**	25k
BiLSTM-CRF	95.06	3k
+ CNN-char	95.40	2.5k
+ LSTM-char	95.31	1.5k

Table 2: POS tagging accuracies (in %) on the test set w.r.t. gold word segmentation. "Speed" denotes the tagging speed, i.e. the number of words per second, computed on a personal computer of Intel Core i7 2.2 GHz (model loading time is not taken into account).

4 Main results

Table 2 presents POS tagging accuracy and tagging speed of each model on the test set w.r.t. gold word segmentation, in which MarMoT is the most accurate model while RDRPOSTagger is the fastest one. In particular, MarMoT obtains 0.5%+ higher accuracy than the three BiLSTM-based models. This is not surprising as the training set of 27k sentences is relatively small compared to the training data available in other languages such as English or Chinese.

Table 3 presents F1 scores for word segmentation and POS tagging in a real-world application scenario where the gold word-segmentation is not available. Comparing the results in Table 2 to results for the pipeline strategy, we observe a drop of about 2% for all models when using predicted segmentation instead of gold segmentation. Also, Table 3 clearly shows that the pipeline strategy helps produce better results than the joint strategy. In addition, pre-designed features in both RDRPOSTagger and MarMoT are designed to capture word-level information rather than syllable-level information, so it is also not surprising that for the joint strategy RDRPOSTagger is significantly lower while MarMoT is lower than the BiLSTM-CRF model with additional character-based representations.

Tables 2 and 3 suggest that for a practical application to Vietnamese where performance accuracy is preferred, we should consider using the pipeline strategy with a traditional SOTA feature-based tagger such as MarMoT. If speed is preferred such as in big data, RDRPOSTagger would be a superior alternative. With the current state of training data available in Vietnamese, future research should focus on incorporating Vietnamese linguistic features into the traditional feature-based sequence taggers.

	Model	WSeg	PTag
Pipeline	RDRPOSTagger	97.75	93.39
	MarMoT	97.75	**93.96**
	BiLSTM-CRF	97.75	93.25
	+ CNN-char	97.75	93.55
	+ LSTM-char	97.75	93.46
Joint	RDRPOSTagger	93.73	87.53
	MarMoT	96.50	92.78
	BiLSTM-CRF	96.15	92.43
	+ CNN-char	96.66	92.79
	+ LSTM-char	96.76	92.95

Table 3: F1 scores (in %) for word segmentation (**WSeg**) and POS tagging (**PTag**) from unsegmented text. The pipeline strategy uses RDRsegmenter for word segmentation. In preliminary experiments, where we also train the five models above to predict a segmentation tag B or I for each syllable, we then find that RDRsegmenter obtains better word segmentation score than those five models.

5 Conclusion

We have presented empirical comparisons between two strategies for Vietnamese POS tagging from unsegmented text and between SOTA feature- and neural network-based models. Experimental results on the benchmark Vietnamese treebank (Nguyen et al., 2009) show that the pipeline strategy produces higher scores of POS tagging from unsegmented text than the joint strategy. In addition, we also show that a traditional feature-based model (i.e. MarMoT) obtains better POS tagging accuracy than neural network-based models. We provide a pre-trained MarMoT model for Vietnamese POS tagging at `https://github.com/datquocnguyen/VnMarMoT`.

Acknowledgments

This research was partially supported by the Australian Government through the Australian Research Council's Discovery Projects funding scheme (project DP160102156). This research was also partially supported by NICTA, funded by the Australian Government through the Department of Communications and the Australian Research Council through the ICT Centre of Excellence Program.

References

Ngo Xuan Bach, Kunihiko Hiraishi, Nguyen Le Minh, and Akira Shimazu. 2013. Dual decomposition for Vietnamese part-of-speech tagging. In *Proceedings of the 17th International Conference on Knowledge Based and Intelligent Information and Engineering Systems*. pages 123–131.

P. Compton and R. Jansen. 1990. A Philosophical Basis for Knowledge Acquisition. *Knowledge Aquisition* 2(3):241–257.

Dinh Dien and Hoang Kiem. 2003. POS-Tagger for English-Vietnamese Bilingual Corpus. In *Proceedings of the HLT-NAACL 2003 Workshop on Building and Using Parallel Texts: Data Driven Machine Translation and Beyond*. pages 88–95.

Dinh Dien, Hoang Kiem, and Nguyen Van Toan. 2001. Vietnamese Word Segmentation. In *Proceedings of the Sixth Natural Language Processing Pacific Rim Symposium*. pages 749–756.

Dien Dinh and Thuy Vu. 2006. A Maximum Entropy Approach for Vietnamese Word Segmentation. In *Proceedings of the 2006 International Conference on Research, Innovation and Vision for the Future*. pages 248–253.

Timothy Dozat. 2016. Incorporating Nesterov Momentum into Adam. In *Proceedings of the ICLR 2016 Workshop Track*.

Zhiheng Huang, Wei Xu, and Kai Yu. 2015. Bidirectional LSTM-CRF models for sequence tagging. *arXiv preprint* arXiv:1508.01991.

Canasai Kruengkrai, Kiyotaka Uchimoto, Jun'ichi Kazama, Yiou Wang, Kentaro Torisawa, and Hitoshi Isahara. 2009. An Error-Driven Word-Character Hybrid Model for Joint Chinese Word Segmentation and POS Tagging. In *Proceedings of the 47th Annual Meeting of the ACL and the 4th IJCNLP of the AFNLP*. pages 513–521.

Guillaume Lample, Miguel Ballesteros, Sandeep Subramanian, Kazuya Kawakami, and Chris Dyer. 2016. Neural Architectures for Named Entity Recognition. In *Proceedings of the 2016 Conference of the North American Chapter of the Association for Computational Linguistics: Human Language Technologies*. pages 260–270.

Hong Phuong Le, Thi Minh Huyen Nguyen, Azim Roussanaly, and Tuong Vinh Ho. 2008. A hybrid approach to word segmentation of Vietnamese texts. In *Proceedings of the 2nd International Conference on Language and Automata Theory and Applications*. pages 240–249.

Phuong Le-Hong, Azim Roussanaly, Thi Minh Huyen Nguyen, and Mathias Rossignol. 2010. An empirical study of maximum entropy approach for part-of-speech tagging of Vietnamese texts. In *Proceedings of the Traitement Automatique des Langues Naturelles*.

Wuying Liu and Li Lin. 2014. Probabilistic Ensemble Learning for Vietnamese Word Segmentation. In *Proceedings of the 37th International ACM SIGIR Conference on Research & Development in Information Retrieval*. pages 931–934.

Xuezhe Ma and Eduard Hovy. 2016. End-to-end Sequence Labeling via Bi-directional LSTM-CNNs-CRF. In *Proceedings of the 54th Annual Meeting of the Association for Computational Linguistics (Volume 1: Long Papers)*. pages 1064–1074.

Tomas Mikolov, Ilya Sutskever, Kai Chen, Greg S Corrado, and Jeff Dean. 2013. Distributed Representations of Words and Phrases and their Compositionality. In *Advances in Neural Information Processing Systems 26*. pages 3111–3119.

Thomas Mueller, Helmut Schmid, and Hinrich Schütze. 2013. Efficient Higher-Order CRFs for Morphological Tagging. In *Proceedings of the 2013 Conference on Empirical Methods on Natural Language Processing*. pages 322–332.

Liang NanYuan and Zheng YanBin. 1991. A Chinese word segmentation model and a Chinese word segmentation system PC-CWSS. *Journal of Chinese Language and Computing* 1(1).

Minh Nghiem, Dien Dinh, and Mai Nguyen. 2008. Improving Vietnamese POS tagging by integrating a rich feature set and Support Vector Machines. In *Proceedings of the 2008 IEEE International Conference on Research, Innovation and Vision for the Future in Computing and Communication Technologies*. pages 128–133.

Cam-Tu Nguyen, Trung-Kien Nguyen, Xuan-Hieu Phan, Le-Minh Nguyen, and Quang-Thuy Ha. 2006. Vietnamese Word Segmentation with CRFs and SVMs: An Investigation. In *Proceedings of the 20th Pacific Asia Conference on Language, Information and Computation*. pages 215–222.

Dat Quoc Nguyen, Mark Dras, and Mark Johnson. 2017a. A Novel Neural Network Model for Joint POS Tagging and Graph-based Dependency Parsing. In *Proceedings of the CoNLL 2017 Shared Task: Multilingual Parsing from Raw Text to Universal Dependencies*. pages 134–142.

Dat Quoc Nguyen, Dai Quoc Nguyen, Dang Duc Pham, and Son Bao Pham. 2014a. RDRPOSTagger: A Ripple Down Rules-based Part-Of-Speech Tagger. In *Proceedings of the Demonstrations at the 14th Conference of the European Chapter of the Association for Computational Linguistics*. pages 17–20.

Dat Quoc Nguyen, Dai Quoc Nguyen, Dang Duc Pham, and Son Bao Pham. 2016a. A Robust Transformation-Based Learning Approach Using Ripple Down Rules for Part-of-Speech Tagging. *AI Communications* 29(3):409–422.

Dat Quoc Nguyen, Dai Quoc Nguyen, Son Bao Pham, Phuong-Thai Nguyen, and Minh Le Nguyen. 2014b. From Treebank Conversion to Automatic Dependency Parsing for Vietnamese. In *Proceedings of 19th International Conference on Application of Natural Language to Information Systems*. pages 196–207.

Dat Quoc Nguyen, Dai Quoc Nguyen, Son Bao Pham, and Dang Duc Pham. 2011. Ripple Down Rules for Part-of-Speech Tagging. In *Proceedings of the 12th International Conference on Intelligent Text Processing and Computational Linguistics - Volume Part I*. pages 190–201.

Dat Quoc Nguyen, Dai Quoc Nguyen, Thanh Vu, Mark Dras, and Mark Johnson. 2017b. A Fast and Accurate Vietnamese Word Segmenter. *arXiv preprint* arXiv:1709.06307.

Le Minh Nguyen, Xuan Bach Ngo, Viet Cuong Nguyen, Quang Nhat Minh Pham, and Akira Shimazu. 2010. A Semi-supervised Learning Method for Vietnamese Part-of-Speech Tagging. In *Proceedings of the International Conference on Knowledge and Systems Engineering*. pages 141–146.

Phuong Thai Nguyen, Xuan Luong Vu, Thi Minh Huyen Nguyen, Van Hiep Nguyen, and Hong Phuong Le. 2009. Building a Large Syntactically-Annotated Corpus of Vietnamese. In *Proceedings of the Third Linguistic Annotation Workshop*. pages 182–185.

Tuan-Phong Nguyen and Anh-Cuong Le. 2016. A Hybrid Approach to Vietnamese Word Segmentation. In *Proceedings of the 2016 IEEE RIVF International Conference on Computing and Communication Technologies: Research, Innovation, and Vision for the Future*. pages 114–119.

Tuan Phong Nguyen, Quoc Tuan Truong, Xuan Nam Nguyen, and Anh Cuong Le. 2016b. An Experimental Investigation of Part-Of-Speech Taggers for Vietnamese. *VNU Journal of Science: Computer Science and Communication Engineering* 32(3):11–25.

Dang Duc Pham, Giang Binh Tran, and Son Bao Pham. 2009. A Hybrid Approach to Vietnamese Word Segmentation using Part of Speech tags. In *Proceedings of the 2009 International Conference on Knowledge and Systems Engineering*. pages 154–161.

Thai-Hoang Pham, Xuan-Khoai Pham, Tuan-Anh Nguyen, and Phuong Le-Hong. 2017. NNVLP: A Neural Network-Based Vietnamese Language Processing Toolkit. In *Proceedings of the IJCNLP 2017 System Demonstrations*. page to appear.

Nils Reimers and Iryna Gurevych. 2017. Reporting Score Distributions Makes a Difference: Performance Study of LSTM-networks for Sequence Tagging. In *Proceedings of the 2017 Conference on Empirical Methods in Natural Language Processing*. pages 338–348.

Yan Shao, Christian Hardmeier, Jörg Tiedemann, and Joakim Nivre. 2017. Character-based Joint Segmentation and POS Tagging for Chinese using Bidirectional RNN-CRF. In *Proceedings of the 8th International Joint Conference on Natural Language Processing*. page to appear.

Kanji Takahashi and Kazuhide Yamamoto. 2016. Fundamental tools and resource are available for Vietnamese analysis. In *Proceedings of the 2016 International Conference on Asian Language Processing*. pages 246–249.

Kristina Toutanova, Dan Klein, Christopher D. Manning, and Yoram Singer. 2003. Feature-rich Part-of-speech Tagging with a Cyclic Dependency Network. In *Proceedings of the 2003 Conference of the North American Chapter of the Association for Computational Linguistics on Human Language Technology - Volume 1*. pages 173–180.

Ngoc Anh Tran, Thanh Tinh Dao, and Phuong Thai Nguyen. 2012. An effective context-based method for Vietnamese-word segmentation. In *Proceedings of First International Workshop on Vietnamese Language and Speech Processing*. pages 34–40.

Oanh Thi Tran, Cuong Anh Le, Thuy Quang Ha, and Quynh Hoang Le. 2009. An Experimental Study on Vietnamese POS Tagging. In *Proceedings of the 2009 International Conference on Asian Language Processing*. pages 23–27.

Thi Oanh Tran, Anh Cuong Le, and Quang Thuy Ha. 2010. Improving Vietnamese Word Segmentation and POS Tagging using MEM with Various Kinds of Resources. *Journal of Natural Language Processing* 17(3):41–60.

Daniel Zeman, Martin Popel, Milan Straka, Jan Hajic, Joakim Nivre, et al. 2017. CoNLL 2017 Shared Task: Multilingual Parsing from Raw Text to Universal Dependencies. In *Proceedings of the CoNLL 2017 Shared Task: Multilingual Parsing from Raw Text to Universal Dependencies*. pages 1–19.

Yue Zhang and Stephen Clark. 2008. Joint Word Segmentation and POS Tagging Using a Single Perceptron. In *Proceedings of the 46th Annual Meeting of the Association for Computational Linguistics: Human Language Technologies*. pages 888–896.

ALTA Shared Task papers

Overview of the 2017 ALTA Shared Task: Correcting OCR Errors

Diego Mollá and **Steve Cassidy**
Department of Computing
Macquarie University
Sydney, Australia
`diego.molla-aliod@mq.edu.au`
`steve.cassidy@mq.edu.au`

Abstract

This paper presents an overview of the 8th ALTA shared task that ran in 2017. The task was to correct OCR errors from scans of newspapers stored in the Trove database maintained by the National Library of Australia. We introduce the task, describe the data and present the results of the participating teams.

1 Introduction

Many digital documents are the result of scanning printed copies. These documents, although in digital form, are in fact images, and as such, standard natural language processing techniques such as text search cannot be applied to them.

The National Library of Australia[1] maintains an archive of scanned Australian publications in the Trove database[2]. Many of these scans have been processed through Optical Character Recognition (OCR) and form a searchable resource with over 500 million items. But the OCR output may contain errors which need to be corrected. Trove has corrected the errors through a process of collaborative editing of the output of the OCR system.

The goal of the 2017 ALTA Shared Task is to automatically correct errors of OCR from a subset of scans from the Trove database. Over 7,000 documents were downloaded from the Trove database. For each document, the original output of the OCR system was used as the input text to the shared task, and the corrected versions were used as the target text. A total of 6,000 documents and their corrected versions were provided as the training set, and the rest was used to evaluate the system results.

This paper is structured as follows. Section 2 describes the shared task. Section 3 briefly introduces related research on OCR. Section 4 describes the data set that was used. Section 5 details the evaluation process. Section 6 presents and discusses the results. Finally, Section 7 concludes this paper.

2 The 2017 ALTA Shared Task

The 2017 ALTA Shared Task is the 8th of the shared tasks organised by the Australasian Language Technology Association (ALTA). Like the previous ALTA shared tasks, it is targeted at university students with programming experience. The general objective of these shared tasks is to introduce university students to the sort of problems that are the subject of active research in a field of natural language processing.

There are no limitations on the size of the teams or the means that they can use to solve the problem, as long as the processing is fully automatic — there should be no human intervention.

As in past ALTA shared tasks, there are two categories: a student category and an open category.

- All the members of teams from the **student category** must be university students. The teams cannot have members that are full-time employed or that have completed a PhD.

- Any other teams fall into the **open category**.

The prize is awarded to the team that performs best on the private test set — a subset of the evaluation data for which participant scores are only revealed at the end of the evaluation period (see Section 5).

3 Related Work

OCR post-correction is a well established problem and has received some attention in particu-

---

[1] `https://www.nla.gov.au/`
[2] `http://trove.nla.gov.au/`

Diego Mollá and Steve Cassidy. 2017. Overview of the 2017 ALTA Shared Task: Correcting OCR Errors. In *Proceedings of Australasian Language Technology Association Workshop*, pages 115–118.

```
{
  "id":"64154501",
  "titleId":"131",
  "titleName":"The Broadford Courier (Broadford,
  "date":"1917-02-02",
  "firstPageId":"6187953",
  "firstPageSeq":"4",
  "category":"Article",
  "state":["Victoria"],
  "has":[],
  "heading":"Rather.",
  "fulltext":"Rather. The scarcity of servant gi
engage a farmer's daughter from a rural distri
of familiarity with town ways and language led
  One afternoon a lady called at the Vaughan re
   Kathleen answered the call.' \"Can Mrs. Vaug
   asked. \"Can she be seen?\" sniggered Kathle
   she can. She's six feet hoigh, and four feet
   Sorrah a bit of anything ilse can ye see whi
   man's love for his club is due to the fact t
   gives her tongue a rest",
  "wordCount":118,
  "illustrated":false
  }
```

Figure 1: An example Trove news article showing the JSON representation overlaid with an image of the original scanned document

lar with reference to historical texts. Afli et al. (2016) describe two approaches to the problem. The first based on the application of a statistical machine translation system, treating the problem as one of translating the uncorrected OCR text into the corrected version. The second approach uses a language model to rank alternate corrections for words in the original OCR text. A *Noisy Channel Model* is used to model the errors introduced by the OCR process and the most probable correction is selected. Results on a corpus of ancient French manuscripts showed the best performance for the SMT based system with an word error rate of around 20%.

In contrast (Eger et al., 2016) make use of *character level* models of sequence mapping to correct OCR errors in Latin texts - interestingly they also apply the same methods to spelling correction in Tweets. This approach has the advantage of not requiring any kind of lexical model. The paper cites word error rates of the order of 10% for the Latin texts.

4   Data

Trove[3] is the digital document archive of the National Library of Australia (Holley, 2010) and con-

tains a variety of document types such as books, journals and newspapers. The newspaper archive in Trove consists of scanned versions of each page as PDF documents along with a transcription generated by ABBYY FineReader[4], which is is a state-of-the-art commercial optical character recognition (OCR) system. OCR is inherently error-prone and the quality of the transcriptions varies a lot across the archive; in particular, the older samples are of poorer quality due to the degraded nature of the original documents.

To help improve the quality of the OCR transcriptions, Trove provides a web based interface to allow members of the public to correct the transcriptions. This crowd-sourcing approach produces a large number of corrections to newspaper texts and the quality of the collection is constantly improving. As of this writing, the Trove website reports a total of 170 million corrections to newspaper texts[5].

The data for this evaluation was taken from a snapshot of the Trove Newspaper collection given to the Alveo Virtual Laboratory in 2015 (Cassidy, 2016) which consisted of 155 million individual documents. Some of these had already been cor-

[3]http://trove.nla.gov.au/

[4]http://www.abbyy.com
[5]http://trove.nla.gov.au/system/stats

```
OBITUARY MR. J. G. KI.EMM i Mr .lohann Gottfried Klemm. Hi, of Gruenberg.
died on Saturday. He was l$>$orn on .lone $<>$, isa-j, being Tth child
...
```

Figure 2: Sample input provided by Trove.

```
<p><span> OBITUARY</span></p> <p><span> MR.  J.  G.  KLEMM</span></p>
<p><span> Mr  Johann  Gottfried  Klemm,  86,  \ </span><span>
of  Gruenberg.  died  on  Saturday.</span><span>  He  was  born  on
June  6,  1862,  be-</span><span>  ing  7th  child ...
```

Figure 3: Sample target text provided by Trove.

```
OBITUARY MR. J. G. KLEMM Mr Johann Gottfried Klemm, 86, of Gruenberg.
died on Saturday. He was born on June 6, 1862, being 7th child
...
```

Figure 4: Target text after it has been cleaned automatically.

rected and this was recorded in the metadata for each document. For this evaluation, we selected a subset of documents that had no corrections in the 2015 snapshot and for each of these used the Trove API to retrieve the most recent (July 2017) version of the document. Where this newer version contained some manual corrections we included the document pair in the collection.

Figures 2 and 3 show a sample input text and the target text, respectively, as they were provided by Trove. Note the presence of XML markup and the occurrence of words that were split across two spans in the target text. A Python script was used to clean the target text, giving the result of Figure 4 for the example of Figure 3.

Given the nature of the process used to produce the annotations, some errors remained in the final annotations. In particular, not all of the OCR errors of the input text had been corrected by the annotators. In addition, in a number of cases the text provided by Trove included words spanning two lines which were not hyphenated. These words would appear as two separate (incorrect) words in the target text.

The training data contained 6,000 documents. The test data contained 1,941 documents.

5   Evaluation

As in previous ALTA shared tasks, the 2017 shared task was managed and evaluated using Kaggle in Class, with the name "ALTA 2017 Challenge". The Kaggle in Class framework allowed the maintenance of a discussion forum that could be used to communicate among the participants. In addition, thanks to this framework the participants were able to submit runs prior to the submission deadline for immediate feedback.

The test data was partitioned into a public and a private section. Whenever a participating team submitted a run, the evaluation results of the public partition were immediately available to the team, and the best results of each team appeared in a public leaderboard. The evaluation results of the private partition were available to the competition organisers only, and were used for the final ranking after the submission deadline. To split the test data into the public and private partitions, we used the defaults provided by Kaggle in Class. These defaults performed a random partition with 50% of the data falling into the public partition, and the remaining 50% falling into the private partition. The participants were able to see the entire unlabelled evaluation data, but they did knot know what part of the evaluation data belonged to which partition.

Each participating team was allowed to submit up to two (2) runs per day. By limiting the number of runs per day, and by not disclosing the results of the private partition, the risks of overfitting to the private test results were diminished.

The chosen evaluation metric was the mean F1 score. This metric is common in information retrieval tasks, and measures the harmonic mean of recall and precision according to the formula:

$$F1 = 2\frac{p \cdot r}{p + r}$$

Where p is the precision and r is the recall. Recall and precision were computed at the level of bigrams. By operating on bigrams instead of single words, the metric was sensitive to differences of word order.

Furthermore, the participants were asked to remove all bigram duplicates and all bigrams from the solution already occurring in the original text prior to submission. The participants were provided with a Python script that removed such information. By removing all bigrams already occurring in the original text, the evaluation focused on words that were corrected by the systems. This was important, since otherwise a trivial system that did not perform any OCR correction and simply returned the input text unmodified would have achieved an F1 score of 84.6% because many words of the input text do not require correction.

A further constraint on the output was that each word forming a bigram should not contain quotation marks or blank spaces. This constraint was required due to the CSV format used by the files that were processed by the evaluation scripts from Kaggle in Class. The Python script provided to the participants also removed these problematic bigrams.

6 Results

Table 1 shows the results of the public and private partitions for all participating teams. The results in

Table 1: F1 of all participating systems.

System	Category	Public	Private
EOF	Student	0.33497	0.32987
SuperOCR	Student	0.16798	0.16817
Atom	Student	0.14127	0.14654
CTexT	Open	0.08539	0.08625
Natural Language	Student	0.02768	0.02610

the public and private partitions were consistent, and team EOF was a clear winner.

7 Conclusions

The 2017 ALTA Shared Task was the 8th of the series of shared tasks organised by ALTA. This year's shared task focused on OCR correction, and the data was extracted from the Trove database maintained by the National Library of Australia.

The crowdsourcing nature of the annotation process, and the format returned by Trove, caused a number of annotation errors which make this task particularly challenging to the participating teams.

For full details of some of the participating systems, refer to the shared task section of the 2017 ALTA workshop proceedings.

References

H Afli, Z Qiu, A Way, P Sheridan LREC, and 2016. 2016. Using SMT for OCR error correction of historical texts. *computing.dcu.ie* .

Stephen Cassidy. 2016. Publishing the trove newspaper corpus. In *Proceedings of the Tenth International Conference on Language Resources and Evaluation (LREC 2016)*. European Language Resources Association (ELRA).

Steffen Eger, Tim Vor der Brück, and Alexander Mehler. 2016. A comparison of four Character-Level String-to-String translation models for (OCR) spelling error correction. *The Prague Bulletin of Mathematical Linguistics* 105(1):781.

R Holley. 2010. Trove: Innovation in access to information in australia. ariadne, 64. *www.ariadne.ac.uk/issue64/holley* .

OCR P̲ost-Processing T̲ext C̲orrection using Simulated A̲nnealing (OPTeCA)

Gitansh Khirbat
Computing and Information Systems
The University of Melbourne
Australia
`gitansh.khirbat@unimelb.edu.au`

Abstract

This paper describes the system details and results of team "EOF" from the University of Melbourne for the shared task of ALTA 2017, which addresses the problem of text correction for post-processed Optical Character Recognition (OCR) based systems. We developed a two stage system which first detects errors in the given OCR post-processed text with the help of a support vector machine trained using given training dataset, followed by rectifying the errors by employing a confidence-based mechanism using simulated annealing to obtain an optimal correction from a pool of candidate corrections. Our system achieved a F_1-score of 32.98% on the private leaderboard[1], which is the best score among all the participating systems.

1 Introduction

The dawn of digital age on mankind has laid the foundation of connectivity, fostering access and exchange of information practically anywhere in the world. Information can be present in any form, the most common being textual and graphical documents. Capturing and curating documents such as magazines, newspapers, journals and scientific articles is the primary requirement for a digitized, inter-connected society. While most of the textual documents can be stored with a decipherable textual component, the story is not the same for graphical documents which can be a collection of images containing scans of a textual document.

Optical Character Recognition (OCR) is the process of identifying typed, handwritten or printed textual characters within a document containing scanned images or photographs with the help of various image processing and pattern recognition techniques (Tappert et al., 1990), (Gupta et al., 2007). The text obtained by OCR systems often suffers from low accuracy owing to irregularities in images, poor scans or simply the nature of arrangement of letters in a word. For example, reading "lwo" instead of "two", "ia" instead of "is", "m" instead of "rn", to name a few. These erroneous characters severely hamper the quality and readability of a converted document. Identifying and rectifying such erroneous characters in every OCR-processed document manually is a tedious task due to the sheer volume of data. Consequently, a methodology is required to identify such OCR errors and rectify them in order to enforce standards of purity and quality of the archived data. This need has motivated the shared task of ALTA 2017 (Molla and Cassidy, 2017). The task organizers have provided the original outputs of an OCR system together with their corrected version for scanned Australian publications from Trove database[2]. Using this data, the participants are asked to automatically identify and rectify the OCR errors for documents in a separate test dataset.

Considerable research has been conducted previously to automatically correct text obtained by OCR systems using machine learning. (Lund and Ringger, 2009) (Lund et al., 2011) (William B. Lund, 2013) (Lund et al., 2014) introduced various techniques to select the most appropriate correction among a pool of candidates. (Jones and Eisner, 1992), (Kukich, 1992) demonstrated that OCR-generated errors are more diverse than handwriting errors. (Taghva and Stofsky, 2001) used extensive feature engineering to facilitate a robust candidate selection using a probabilistic model. Motivated by (Mei et al., 2016), we adopt a two stage approach to solve this task. First, our system detects errors in the given OCR post-processed

---

[1] https://www.kaggle.com/c/alta-2017-challenge/leaderboard

[2] http://trove.nla.gov.au

Gitansh Khirbat. 2017. OCR Post-Processing Text Correction using Simulated Annealing (OPTeCA). In *Proceedings of Australasian Language Technology Association Workshop*, pages 119–123.

text with the help of a support vector machine (SVM) trained using given training dataset. This is followed by identifying a set of candidate words as corrections for each of the errors guided by allowing a limited number of character modifications. Finally, we rank the candidates by employing a confidence based mechanism using simulated annealing to obtain an optimal correction from the set of candidate corrections.

The rest of the paper is organized as follows. Section 2 describes the methodology in detail. Section 3 describes the experiments and results. Section 4 discusses the error analysis of the obtained results and Section 5 concludes the paper.

2   Methodology

OCR post-processing text correction is a challenging and complex problem. The ever-growing vocabulary constrains it further. In order to solve this problem, we break it down into two sub-problems, namely, identification of erroneous terms from the post-processed OCR text, followed by rectification of the identified erroneous terms. The complete pipeline is shown in Figure 1, with the explanation of each stage as follows.

2.1   Error detection

The first stage of our system is to detect the erroneous terms for a given document. It involves two components as described below.

2.1.1   Pre-processing

The pre-processing module consists of tokenization of a given textual document, i.e. the original output of the OCR. We defined regular expression patterns which split a textual document on delimiters such as full-stop (.), comma (,), semi-colon (;), single quotes (',') or double quotes (","). The tokens are considered for further processing *as-is*, i.e. without undergoing lemmatization. The primary reason to abstain from lemmatization is to preserve the original OCR words in order to rule out the scope of any character-based discrepancy. Additionally, care is taken to preserve the token order. The order is important as it dictates one of the features as defined in Section 2.1.2.

2.1.2   Feature Extraction and Classification

The next step is to classify each token in the document as being erroneous or free of any error. We train a SVM with radial basis function (RBF) kernel and made use of the following features:

- Presence of non alpha-numeric text within a word is one the strongest indicators of an erroneous word. These mainly include special symbols like '$', '#', '%' and punctuation marks like '!', '?', ';', ':', etc. For example, "th?" and "Mr. Pat?rsom" contain a punctuation mark '?'; "***n", "JM**shopB" contain a special symbol '*'. We created a dictionary of such special symbols as observed from the given training data.

- The bigram frequency of a word should be greater than a frequency threshold that varies with different word length. A common word is less likely to be an error word. We adopted this feature from (Mei et al., 2016).

- A word is likely to be correct if this word with its context occurs in other places. We use a sliding window similar to (Mei et al., 2016) to construct n-gram contexts for a word. The frequency of one of the context in n-gram corpus should be greater than a frequency threshold.

Using these features, we train a binary SVM classifier (Pedregosa et al., 2011) which classifies a word being erroneous (1) or not (0). The experimental details are mentioned in Section 3.2.

2.2   Error rectification

The second stage of our system solves the problem of rectifying the erroneous words identified in the first stage. It consists of two major components, namely candidate search and candidate ranking as described below.

2.2.1   Candidate Search

In this module, for each erroneous word, a set of candidate corrections is recommended within a limited number of character modifications based on calculating minimum edit distance between the erroneous word and the candidate correction. We make use of Levenshtein's edit distance (Levenshtein, 1966) to calculate the minimum edit distance consisting of the standard three operations, namely, insertion, deletion or substitution. The threshold is chosen heuristically on the basis of experiments conducted.

2.2.2   Candidate Ranking

This module makes use of the output of previous module, i.e. a set of candidate corrections (w_{ci},

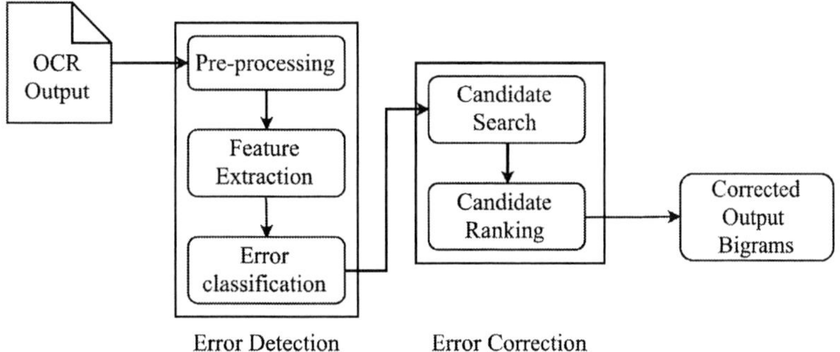

Figure 1: System pipeline

$i \in \mathbb{W}$) for each erroneous term (w_e), to assign a score to each candidate correction using simulated annealing (SA) algorithm (Kirkpatrick et al., 1983). SA requires an aperiodic Markov chain defined on a certain state space, and a cooling schedule to iteratively push the solution towards the optimum. In this module, the state space is set of all candidate corrections. We calculate a similarity score for each of the candidate corrections (w_{ci}) on the basis of the following three factors:

1. Minimum edit distance $d(w_{ci}, w_e)$ as calculated by Levenshtein's edit distance.

2. Normalized longest common subsequence (Allison and Dix, 1986) which takes into account the length of both the shorter and the longer string for normalization.

$$nlcs(w_{ci}, w_e) = \frac{2 * len(lcs(w_{ci}, w_e))^2}{len(w_{ci}) + len(w_e)} \quad (1)$$

3. Normalized maximal consecutive longest common subsequence, which is a modification of aforementioned factor by limiting the common subsequences to be consecutive.

$$nmnlcs(w_{ci}, w_e) = \frac{2 * len(mclcs(w_{ci}, w_e))^2}{len(w_{ci}) + len(w_e)} \quad (2)$$

The final score is calculated as a weighted sum of these three factors:

$$score(w_{ci}, w_e) = \alpha_1 * d(w_{ci}, w_e) + \alpha_2 * nlcs(w_{ci}, w_e) + \alpha_3 * nmnlcs(w_{ci}, w_e)$$

where, α_1, α_2 and α_3 are chosen heuristically. Next, we perturb the given candidate 26 times, i.e.

for all the characters of English alphabet, in order to check which character returns the maximal score. This is followed by validating the presence of that candidate correction by Google Web n-gram corpus[3]. Finally, the candidates are ranked on the basis of this optimized score. The candidate having highest score is returned as the final suggested correction.

3 Experiments and Results

The ALTA shared task is to rectify textual errors in OCR post-processed documents. We first describe the given dataset briefly, followed by experimental setup and results.

3.1 Dataset

The shared task organizers obtained a corpus of approximately 8,000 Australian publications from Trove database. The corpus consists of original output of OCR system for each of the documents, along with their corrected versions. The organizers have provided 6,000 documents and their corrected versions as training dataset. 1,941 documents are provided as the test dataset, for which only the original output of the OCR system is provided. The details of data are given by (Molla and Cassidy, 2017).

3.2 Experimental Setup and Results

Stage 1 of our experiment pertains to error detection which classifies each word of the document to be either erroneous (1) or correct (0). In order to train a binary SVM classifier, we split the given training data into training and development datasets using 5-fold cross validation. The RBF kernel is employed to train the SVM. The test

---

[3]https://catalog.ldc.upenn.edu/LDC2006T13

Features	P	R	F1
Non-alphanumeric character presence	63.2	42.1	50.5
+bigram frequency	67.3	43.9	53.1
+n-gram contexts	69.6	44.2	54.1

Table 1: Stage 1 - Error detection using SVM

Model	$F1_{public}$	$F1_{private}$
Baseline	22.86	23.09
$SA_{0.80}$	25.44	25.83
$SA_{0.85}$	27.52	28.05
$SA_{0.88}$	29.71	30.14
$SA_{0.92}$	**32.98**	**33.48**

Table 2: Stage 2 results - Error rectification

dataset remains unused since the correct labels for erroneous words are unknown. Table 1 reports the intermediate results obtained by adding the features defined in Section 2.1.2 incrementally.

For the stage 2 subproblem of error rectification, first we select the threshold for the Levenshtein's edit distance by measuring the minimum edit distance between the words obtained from corrected and original documents provided in the training dataset. This helps in recommending the candidate corrections by allowing words for which minimum edit distance is less than or equal to the threshold. For candidate ranking, we initialize the score as 0 for each pair of (w_{ci}, w_e) corresponding to an erroneous word. The value of temperature is initialized to 500 and cooling schedule is initialized to 0.8. Table 2 shows the five models that were used to render final results. The baseline model corresponds to ranking of candidate corrections on the basis of total score calculated in Section 2.2.2. $SA_{0.80}$, $SA_{0.85}$, $SA_{0.88}$ and $SA_{0.92}$ correspond to models trained using simulated annealing at the respective cooling schedules.

The trained model is used for predictions corresponding to the public leaderboard which contains 50% of the total data. Finally, at the end of the competition, the predictions are measured against the remaining 50% of data which corresponds to the private leaderboard. The results obtained by using the aforementioned features is shown in Table 2. Standard precision, recall and F1-score metrics are used to report the prediction results.

4 Discussion

Our system performs almost similarly on both public and private leaderboards, which indicates that the model is not overfitting. Table 1 indicates that a collective use of character-level features and contextual features leads to an increase in F1 score, even if it's a marginal increment. The recall of our error detection module is consistently low, which demonstrates the complexity of this sub-problem. Table 2 demonstrates that simulated annealing has proven to show an improvement of about 5% F_1 score over the baseline score-based model.

What worked well: Our system was able to rectify some of the punctuation based errors like "Collision_;" $\rightarrow$ "Collision_<next-word>". We were also able to rectify certain typo-based errors like "ofi" $\rightarrow$ "of".

What did not work: Our system does not always return a correction when text containing a number is identified as an erroneous term. For example, in "October 2fi", the term "2fi" remains undetected.

There are many other features which we could have tried like considering erroneous text location in the document, syntactic structure of sentences within the document and non-English text words, to name a few. However, given the limitation of time, it was not possible to incorporate these features. It would be interesting to expand this system by adding these features in future.

5 Conclusion

OCR post-processed text correction is an important and challenging problem that needs to be addressed to facilitate digitization. In this paper, we describe our participating system, which was based on a supervised classification method to detect erroneous words, followed by suggesting optimal corrections for each erroneous word with a confidence-based mechanism using simulated annealing. Our system was ranked the best with an F1-score of 32.98%.

References

Lloyd Allison and Trevor I Dix. 1986. A bit-string longest-common-subsequence algorithm. *Information Processing Letters*, 23(5):305–310.

Maya R. Gupta, Nathaniel P. Jacobson, and Eric K. Garcia. 2007. Ocr binarization and image preprocessing for searching historical documents. *Pattern Recogn.*, 40(2):389–397, February.

Mark A Jones and Jason M Eisner. 1992. A probabilistic parser and its applications. In *AAAI Workshop on Statistically-Based NLP Techniques*, pages 20–27.

Scott Kirkpatrick, C Daniel Gelatt, Mario P Vecchi, et al. 1983. Optimization by simulated annealing. *science*, 220(4598):671–680.

Karen Kukich. 1992. Techniques for automatically correcting words in text. *ACM Comput. Surv.*, 24(4):377–439, December.

Vladimir I Levenshtein. 1966. Binary codes capable of correcting deletions, insertions, and reversals. In *Soviet physics doklady*, volume 10, pages 707–710.

William B. Lund and Eric K. Ringger. 2009. Improving optical character recognition through efficient multiple system alignment. In *Proceedings of the 9th ACM/IEEE-CS Joint Conference on Digital Libraries*, JCDL '09, pages 231–240, New York, NY, USA. ACM.

W. B. Lund, D. D. Walker, and E. K. Ringger. 2011. Progressive alignment and discriminative error correction for multiple ocr engines. In *2011 International Conference on Document Analysis and Recognition*, pages 764–768, Sept.

William B Lund, Eric K Ringger, and Daniel D Walker. 2014. How well does multiple ocr error correction generalize? Society of Photo-Optical Instrumentation Engineers.

Jie Mei, Aminul Islam, Yajing Wu, Abidalrahman Moh'd, and Evangelos E Milios. 2016. Statistical learning for ocr text correction. *arXiv preprint arXiv:1611.06950*.

Diego Molla and Steve Cassidy. 2017. Overview of the 2017 alta shared task: Correcting ocr errors. In *Proceedings of Australasian Language Technology Association Workshop*, Brisbane, Australia.

F. Pedregosa, G. Varoquaux, A. Gramfort, V. Michel, B. Thirion, O. Grisel, M. Blondel, P. Prettenhofer, R. Weiss, V. Dubourg, J. Vanderplas, A. Passos, D. Cournapeau, M. Brucher, M. Perrot, and E. Duchesnay. 2011. Scikit-learn: Machine learning in Python. *Journal of Machine Learning Research*, 12:2825–2830.

Kazem Taghva and Eric Stofsky. 2001. Ocrspell: an interactive spelling correction system for ocr errors in text. *International Journal on Document Analysis and Recognition*, 3(3):125–137.

C. C. Tappert, C. Y. Suen, and T. Wakahara. 1990. The state of the art in online handwriting recognition. *IEEE Transactions on Pattern Analysis and Machine Intelligence*, 12(8):787–808, Aug.

Eric K. Ringger William B. Lund, Douglas J. Kennard. 2013. Combining multiple thresholding binarization values to improve ocr output.

SuperOCR for ALTA 2017 Shared Task

Yufei Wang
Computer Science and Engineering
UNSW, Sydney, Australia
yufei.wang@student.unsw.edu.au

Abstract

This paper describes the SuperOCR system submitted for the ALTA 2017 shared task, which aims at correcting noisy OCR output for the Trove database. We used heuristic rules and patterns in submitted system and we apply language model to further improve our system. Experiment shows that language model plays an vital role in performance. Surprisingly, a tri-gram language model outperforms LSTM language model in this task.

1 OCR Post-Correction

ALTA 2017 shared task [1] aims at Optical Character Recognition (**OCR**) post-correction for Trove database (Holley, 2010) [2]. OCR extracts text from image, allowing further language analysis. However, OCR is inherently error-prone, in particular for old scanned documents. High quality OCR analysis result benefits downstream NLP task, including named entity recognition (NER) (Mac Kim and Cassidy, 2015) and information extraction (Taghva et al., 2006). In this shared task, given a set of OCR raw-correction pairs, participators are required to build a system to automatically and accurately correct the OCR-ed documents.

Our submitted system achieved averaged F1 score 16.82%, which is 2nd best system. Later, we further improved our submitted system to 20.72% by using context and weighted OCR error information. However, The wining system had achieved averaged F1 score 32.99%, indicating that our system still has large margin to be improved.

Our submitted system mainly targeted in (a) correcting word-level errors, e.g. words with char-

acters being dis-recognized during OCR process, and (b) delete frequent noisy text pattern. For (a), we first filtered out normal words using vocabulary list; then we applied correction to those error-like tokens. For (b), we extracted the frequent corrected patterns from the aligned documents. The experiment result shows that language model and high-quality vocabulary list are vital to boost performance. Surprisingly, a simple tri-gram language model outperforms a state-of-the-art LSTM language model in selecting candidate words for correction.

This paper is organized as follows: Section 2 profiles data set and OCR errors. Section 3 introduces submitted system and improved system. Section 4 shows the experiment result. We summarize our finding in Section 5.

2 OCR Documents and Errors

In this section, we first summarize some basic statistics of the OCR documents from this shared task in Table 1.

#Docs	6000
#avg. Words	571.9
#avg. Errors	39.6
#Error Ratio	6.93%

Table 1: Statistics of Share Task Data

We are also interested in the types of correction made by annotators in this data set. To extract the correction, we first align document pairs and unaligned words in raw documents are the corrections. We characterize them largely based on the vocabulary list used in our final system. We refer words in the list to "in-vocabulary" (**IV**), otherwise "Out-of-Vocabulary" (**OOV**). We categorize these corrections into the following types:

- Single Word Split: Split an IV into two

---

[1] http://www.alta.asn.au/events/sharedtask2017/description.html
[2] http://trove.nla.gov.au/

OOVs. **21.89%**

- Single Word Correction: Change an OOV to an IV. **18.16%**

- Words Deletion: Delete words from OCRed Text. **12.79%**

- Multiple Words Merge: Merge multiple words into a single IV. **8.05%**

- Punctuation Transform: Change a punctuation to another punctuation. **4.52%**

- Known Word Correction: Change an IV to another IV. **4.18%**

- Unknown Word Modify: Change an OOV to another OOV. **3.95%**

- Character Case: Change the character case of a word. **1.44%**

- Other: Other Corrections **25%**

It should be noted that, the correction Single Word Split often splits valid words into two OOVs randomly, for example, randomly modifying "yesterday" to "yes" and "terday"; modifying "Australian" to "Austra" and "lian" etc. We suspect that this is caused by a text processing errors. The correction distribution also shows the difficulties of this shared task as only 6.93% of words are modified while majority of words remain unchanged. Even worse, around 25% of errors are multiple words correction, which cannot be solved by checking single words.

Lastly, we analysis the length of the continuous corrected word sequence in the data set. As shown in Table 2, around 75% errors are length 1. Therefore, most of OCR errors are not continuous and separated by context words.

Len.	1	2	3	4	5+
%	74.9%	13.2%	5.7%	3.9%	2.3%

Table 2: Error Length Distribution

3 System Description

There are two important factors to consider when designing system:

- **Candidate Filtering** In our data, only 6.9% of words are corrected by annotators, which means that we are facing an imbalanced situation. If we apply correction to every word in document, it will generate a lot of false positive examples. Our intuition is that, a valid word is unlikely to be an error in OCRed text.

- **Independent Correction** As shown previously, most of errors are isolated by their unchanged context. Correction using sequence modeling may not be helpful as the dependency between errors are weak. Therefore, we correct words individually in our system.

Therefore, we design our system as shown in Alg 1. The system includes following post-correction components:

- ProcRawText: Correct frequent errors and split text into tokens.

- Word Filtering: Filtering out most of correct words in OCRed text.

- Correction: Correct an OOV word into a non-OOV word.

- ProcessKnownWord: Correct a non-OOV word to another non-OOV word.

Both of our systems follow the above framework and they only differ in strategies used in each component.

Algorithm 1: System Framework

Data: OCRed Text
$WordList$ = ProcRawText(OCR_Text);
Create $CorrectedList$;
foreach $w \in WordList$ **do**
    if w *should be Corrected* **then**
        w = Correction(w);
    else
        w = ProcessKnownWord(w);
    Add w To $CorrectedList$;
return TextJoin($CorrectedList$) ;

3.1 Submitted System

In our submitted system, we mainly used heuristic rules and patterns obtained from training data to correct text.

In $ProcRawText$ part, we used three strategies:

1. Deleting a set of errors patterns with format "-* " and "- * " where "*" stands for one of "$< * > i j : ? ! 1 ; l$". These patterns are the most frequent deleted error sequences in training pairs. Interestingly, these patterns often result in valid words being splitted and their character shapes are similar to each other. So these errors may be caused by similar noise in image input.

2. Splitting text based on white space and removing length one tokens except for "a" and "A". These length one tokens tend to be noise in the data set. Although "I" is indeed a valid word, our experiment result shows that there are much more noisy "I" than the valid one. So, we remove it as well.

3. the leading and following non-alphabet characters are removed from each word except for the following punctuation "." and ",". We skip numbers and punctuation in this step.

In $Word\ Filtering$ part, we constructed a vocabulary list by merging the most frequent 15000 words from corrected OCR documents in training data and most frequent words 10000 from 1 Billion Word Language Model Benchmark [3]. Given the vocabulary list, OOVs or words with most three non-alphabet characters (words with four or more non-alphabet characters are too noisy to be corrected) are selected as correction target. All other words remain unchanged.

In $Correction$ part, we extracted frequent single correction pairs in training data (e.g. "tne" $\Rightarrow$ "the"). If a candidate matched one of the pairs, we would correct it. Otherwise, we exhaustively searched for words in vocabulary list that are k edit distance from the correction target. We refer these two methods as **word-level correction** and **exhaustive correction** respectively. Finally, we will correct the character case based on the original word shape.

We skipped $ProcessKnownWord$ stage in our submitted system.

3.2 Language model enhanced System

This system was submitted after the shared task. Following (Tursun and Cakici, 2017), we used tri-gram KenLM (Heafield et al., 2013) [4] language

model. Experiment result shows that tri-gram language model is sufficient for this task. To train the language model, we used the corrected documents in training data and lower-cased all words before the training. Intuitively, language model would capture the context information and therefore, it is helpful when we rank the correction candidate.

In $ProcRawText$ part, we still used strategy 1 and 2 in submitted system. However, we changed the tokenization method to the one used in the provided evaluation script. This method splits punctuation from words and provides better boundaries between words and punctuation, but, this could potentially lead to inappropriate punctuation split in noisy text. For example, given noisy word "-Mr." whose ground truth of is "Mr.", our method splits it into "-Mr" and ".", making it impossible to merge the punctuation back. To tackle this issue, we collected the frequent cases from training data to correct the errors before tokenization.

In $Word\ Filtering$ part, we constructed the vocabulary list by combining non-singleton words that are no shorter than 5 in training corrected text and words that are no longer than 4 in 1 Billion Language model benchmark.

In $Correction$ part, we additionally applied character error information to suggest correction candidates. We first extracted all Single Word Correction pairs (18.16% of all errors) and then aligned each of them in character level. We refer this as **character-level correction**. Besides, we corrected an OOV by merging or splitting if we can obtain IVs.

To combine both language model and word/char transformation information, we applied "Noisy Channel Model" (Mays et al., 1991) to select optimal candidates. Formally, we tried to find the optimal word c for correction target w such that it maximize $P(c|w)$, as shown in 1:

$$\arg\min_{c} Pr(w|c) * Pr(c) \tag{1}$$

where $Pr(c)$ is the language model score indicating how likely it should be there given the context; while $Pr(w|c)$ is the error model indicating how like w is an error of c. To unify our character-level, word-level and exhaustive correction, we grouped error pairs with same correction target together and normalize their count as weight. We always assigned exhaustive correction a constant weight. Note that, we only applied character transformation once to each word, the combination of trans-

---

[3]http://www.statmt.org/lm-benchmark/
[4]https://github.com/kpu/kenlm

formation have not been considered here.

Given a word, its context window and candidates list, (a) we calculated the language model score for all candidates and original word, with context, which is a window with size of 5, which includes itself and its previous and following two context words. Candidates words that receive higher score than original word are chosen for comparison using above model. If no candidate words get higher score than the original word, we remained original word unchanged.

In $ProcessKnownWord$, our improved model applied known word transformation correction by using the frequent patterns in training data. If a known word was found in the patterns, we used the above Noisy Channel Model to decide if we should make correction.

4   Experiment Result and Discussion

In this section, we show two performance measure, the randomly sampled development set (**Dev.**) and final test set (**Test.**) performance for our systems. During system development, we split provided documents into 5500 documents for training and 500 documents for validation. The performance is shown in Table 3.

System	Dev.	Test.
Sub Sys.	17.72%	16.82%
LM-Imprved Sys.	20.68%	20.72%

Table 3: Performance for both System

Table 3 shows that the language model boosts system performance by around 4%. Additionally, our new system no longer suffered from overfitting as the submitted system did. This indicates that the context information provided by language model surpassed hand-crafted rules in earlier system.

4.1   Ablation Study

To show the effectiveness of each components, an ablation study is conducted for our final system in this section. Note that all reported performance is based on development data set.

Table 4 shows that language model is the most vital component in the system. This shows the importance of context modeling components for spelling correction task. In addition, the contribution of the vocabulary list cannot be neglected. We manually investigated the vocabulary of corrected

System	ave. F1	$\triangle$
Full Sys.	20.68%	-
- LM	9.51%	**-11.17%**
- Vocabulary	15.08%	-5.6%
- Prepossess	18.85%	-1.83%
- Multi Word & Trans.	20.23%	-0.45%
- Wegt. Error	20.53%	-0.15%

Table 4: Ablation Performance. **LM**: Set language model score to be 1.0; **Vocabulary**: Only using words in corrected training data; **Prepossess**: Disable patterns and word cleaning in beginning; **Multi Word & Trans**: No word merge split and known word trans correction; **Wegt. Error**: Removing the Error Model, all weights for correct candidates are 1.0.

OCR text and found that low frequent words tend to be noisy. Many of these low frequent words should have been corrected during the annotation process. This indicates that the quality of training data needs to be improved.

4.2   Optimal Language Model

In our final system, we used a tri-gram traditional language model. Will higher order language model or advanced neural model continuously improve the performance? We conduct an experiment regarding the order of language model in this section.

In this experiment, we applied a language model based on LSTM (Hochreiter and Schmidhuber, 1997). Comparing with transitional language model, LSTM language model can be viewed as ∞-order because LSTM can capture long-range dependent information using the cell and hidden information (Hochreiter and Schmidhuber, 1997). In our experiment, we used the tensorflow implementation [5] of (Kim et al., 2016). We did not change the default parameter setting in the source code as they are optimized based on English Penn Treebank (PTB)(Marcus et al., 1993). We used the corrected documents with the same text prepossess technologies as we train KenLM. We also experimented with uni-, bi-, 4-, 5-, 6-gram KenLM for comparsion. Note that, we used LSTM language model in the same way as we use KenLM.

The performance for different language models

---

[5]https://github.com/dhyeon/character-aware-neural-language-models

are shown in Fig. 4.2. As the result show, bi- and tri-gram language models have already provided satisfying performance. Higher order language model even slightly decrease performance by 0.1%. Surprisingly, the LSTM-based language model dramatically decrease the performance by over 5%. During the LSTM model training, we monitored average perplexity over development set. The final model performance is around 80 perplexity which is a reasonable performance compared with (Kim et al., 2016), showing no overfitting in model training. We argue that two possible reasons could explain this:

1. The training data for neural networks is too noisy. It has been shown that neural networks cannot work well when training on noisy data. (Natarajan et al., 2013)

2. In the task of OCR post-correction, correcting errors only require nearby words, rather than long-dependency information would provide noisy information.

We can conclude that bi- and tri-gram language model are the optimal choice for OCR post-correction task.

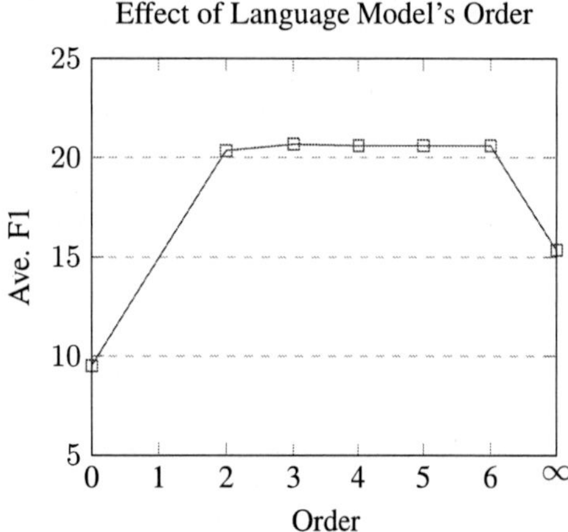

Effect of Language Model's Order

5   Conclusion

We applied heuristic rule and patterns to the task of OCR post-correction. We further apply language model to boost the performance. Our system finally achieve average F1 score 20.68%, a 2_{nd} score in all submitted systems. Experiment result suggest that 3-order language model is more capable in modeling context information than state-of-the-art LSTM-based language model when ranking correction candidates.

Acknowledgments

We would like to thank Prof. Wei Wang for discussion, Dr. Stephen Wan and Dr. Diego Moll-Aliod for their time in proofreading this paper. We would also like to thank the organizers of the shared task for their support.

References

Kenneth Heafield, Ivan Pouzyrevsky, Jonathan H. Clark, and Philipp Koehn. 2013. Scalable modified Kneser-Ney language model estimation. In *Proceedings of the 51st Annual Meeting of the Association for Computational Linguistics*.

Sepp Hochreiter and Jürgen Schmidhuber. 1997. Long short-term memory. *Neural computation* 9(8):1735–1780.

Rose Holley. 2010. Trove: Innovation in access to information in australia. *Ariadne* (64).

Yoon Kim, Yacine Jernite, David Sontag, and Alexander M Rush. 2016. Character-aware neural language models. In *Thirtieth AAAI Conference on Artificial Intelligence*.

Sunghwan Mac Kim and Steve Cassidy. 2015. Finding names in trove: Named entity recognition for australian historical newspapers. In *Proceedings of the Australasian Language Technology Association Workshop 2015*. pages 57–65.

Mitchell P Marcus, Mary Ann Marcinkiewicz, and Beatrice Santorini. 1993. Building a large annotated corpus of english: The penn treebank. *Computational linguistics* 19(2):313–330.

Eric Mays, Fred J Damerau, and Robert L Mercer. 1991. Context based spelling correction. *Information Processing & Management* 27(5):517–522.

Nagarajan Natarajan, Inderjit S Dhillon, Pradeep K Ravikumar, and Ambuj Tewari. 2013. Learning with noisy labels. In *Advances in neural information processing systems*. pages 1196–1204.

Kazem Taghva, Russell Beckley, and Jeffrey Coombs. 2006. The effects of ocr error on the extraction of private information. In *Document Analysis Systems*. Springer, volume 3872, pages 348–357.

Osman Tursun and Ruket Cakici. 2017. Noisy uyghur text normalization. In *Proceedings of the 3rd Workshop on Noisy User-generated Text*. pages 85–93.

Association for Computational Linguistics
209 N. Eighth Street
Stroudsburg, Pennsylvania 18360

ISBN 978-1-5108-5939-5